Focusing on IELTS

Listening and speaking skills

Second edition

Steven Thurlow   Kerry O'Sullivan

First edition published 2002 by the National Centre for English Language Teaching and Research, Macquarie University
(reprinted once)
Second edition published 2011 by
MACMILLAN EDUCATION AUSTRALIA PTY LTD
15–19 Claremont Street, South Yarra 3141

Associated companies and representatives
throughout the world.

Copyright © Steven Thurlow and Kerry O'Sullivan, 2002, 2011
The moral right of the authors has been asserted.

All rights reserved.
Except under the conditions described in the
Copyright Act 1968 of Australia (the Act) and subsequent amendments,
no part of this publication may be reproduced,
stored in a retrieval system, or transmitted in any form or by any means,
electronic, mechanical, photocopying, recording or otherwise,
without the prior written permission of the copyright owner.

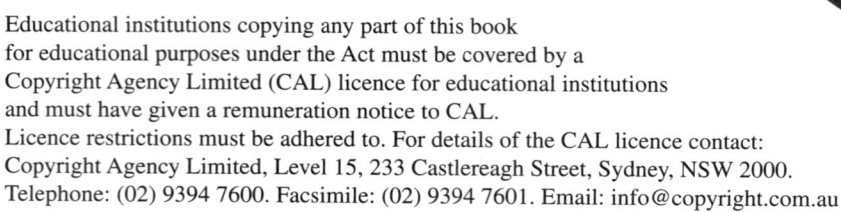

Educational institutions copying any part of this book
for educational purposes under the Act must be covered by a
Copyright Agency Limited (CAL) licence for educational institutions
and must have given a remuneration notice to CAL.
Licence restrictions must be adhered to. For details of the CAL licence contact:
Copyright Agency Limited, Level 15, 233 Castlereagh Street, Sydney, NSW 2000.
Telephone: (02) 9394 7600. Facsimile: (02) 9394 7601. Email: info@copyright.com.au

National Library of Australia
cataloguing in publication data

Author:	Thurlow, Steven, 1963–
Title:	Focusing on IELTS: listening and speaking skills / Steven Thurlow and Kerry O'Sullivan.
Edition:	2nd ed.
ISBN:	9 781 4202 3019 2 (pbk.)
Subjects:	International English Language Testing System.
	English language—Study and teaching—Foreign speakers.
	English language—Examinations.
Other authors/contributors:	O'Sullivan, Kerry, 1952–
Dewey number:	428.0076

Publisher: Vivienne Winter
Project editors: Claire Lavin and Kirstie Innes-Will
Editor: Kirstie Innes-Will
Illustrators: Andy Craig and Nives Porcellato
Cover and text designer: Anne Stanhope
Photo research and permissions clearance: Jes Senbergs
Typeset in 11.5 pt Sabon by Marg Jackson, Emtype Desktop Publishing
Cover image: Jenny Hall

Printed in China

Internet addresses
At the time of printing, the internet addresses appearing in this book were correct. Owing to the dynamic nature of the internet, however, we cannot guarantee that all these addresses will remain correct.

Contents

How to use this book ... v
Acknowledgments ... vii
Listening skills and strategies summary ... viii
Speaking skills and strategies summary ... ix

Unit 1: Listening   1

1.1 What is in the Listening Test? ... 2
1.2 Test-taking tips ... 3
    Be prepared ... 3
    Focus your eyes and ears ... 3
    Guess ... 3
    Manage your time ... 3
    Write accurately ... 4
    Know what to expect ... 4
1.3 Getting to know the test ... 6
    Multiple-choice questions ... 6
    Short-answer questions ... 8
    Sentence completion questions ... 8
    Form/note/summary/flow-chart/table completion questions ... 9
    Labelling a diagram/plan/map ... 10
    Matching questions ... 11
1.4 The listening strategies and skills you need ... 13
    Managing the flow of information ... 13
    Listening for specific information ... 13
    Focusing on more than one question ... 18
    Matching the meaning ... 20
    Understanding what speakers are saying ... 22
    Understanding vocabulary ... 22
    Guessing ... 26
    Recognising meaning through pronunciation ... 28
    Understanding what speakers are doing ... 34
    Anticipating what speakers will do next ... 37
    Giving information: times, dates, numbers and letters ... 38
    Describing procedures and processes ... 40
    Describing objects ... 41
    Explaining cause and effect ... 42
    Making comparisons ... 43
    Classifying ... 43
    Arguing a viewpoint ... 45
    Describing problems and solutions ... 46
    Telling a story ... 47
1.5 Developing an independent study program ... 48
    Identifying your needs ... 48
    Improving your general listening ... 49
    Practising for specific sections ... 50
    Practising specific strategies and skills ... 51
    Exercises for study partners ... 54
1.6 Practice IELTS Listening Test ... 55

Unit 2: Speaking 61

2.1 What is in the Speaking Test? 62
2.2 Test-taking tips 63
    Speak as much as you can 63
    Speak at a reasonable volume and speed 63
    Make a good impression 63
    Know what to expect 63
    Don't panic if asked about an unfamiliar topic 64
    Don't memorise 64
    Try to relax 64
2.3 Getting to know the test 65
    Part 1: Introduction and interview 65
    Part 2: Individual long turn 70
    Part 3: Two-way discussion 74
2.4 The speaking strategies and skills you need 77
    Fluency and coherence 77
    Accuracy and range of vocabulary 89
    Grammatical accuracy and range 99
    Pronunciation 112

2.5 Developing an independent study program 127
    Identifying your needs 127
    Improving your general speaking 128
    Practising for specfic sections 129
    Practising specific strategies and skills 130
2.6 Practice IELTS Speaking Tests 136
    Doing the practice Speaking Tests with a partner 136
    Assessing other candidates doing the practice Speaking Tests 136
    Speaking Test question bank 138

Transcripts 143
Unit 1: Listening 144
Unit 2: Speaking 167

Answer key 185
Unit 1: Listening 186
Unit 2: Speaking 189

How to use this book

You can use this book independently as you prepare for the IELTS test or as a coursebook in an IELTS preparation course with a teacher. All material in the book is suitable for both General Training and Academic candidates.

Throughout this book there are **examples** to follow and **exercises** for you to complete. You can study the book from beginning to end or choose particular sections to study based on your specific needs. To get the most out of this book and achieve your best possible result on the IELTS test make sure you do all the exercises in each unit.

Transcripts of all the recordings, whether for examples, exercises or practice tests, as well as a full answer key, are provided at the back of the book.

Both Unit 1: Listening and Unit 2: Speaking contain the following six sections.

1 What is in the test?

The first section describes the specific IELTS test, with information about its length, how it is conducted and structured, what kinds of questions there are, and how it is assessed. You should read this section in conjunction with the information available on the IELTS website at <www.ielts.org>.

2 Test-taking tips

This section gives you advice about how to manage the test as successfully as possible. These tips will help you to complete the test within the time allowed and get the best mark possible.

3 Getting to know the test

This section tells you what is included in each part or section of the test and how to approach these sections. It includes exercises and examples for familiarising yourself with the requirements of each test section.

4 The strategies and skills you need

This is the main section of each unit because it explains the strategies and skills that you need in order to do well in the Listening and Speaking modules, and it gives you opportunities to practise them. **Strategies** are the practical techniques you can use to meet the specific demands of the test – such as focusing on more than one question in the Listening Test. **Skills** are the abilities needed to perform well in the test – for example, the ability to speak fluently in the Speaking Test. Short exercises are included throughout these sections to help you develop both strategies and skills. You should do these exercises without assistance and try to follow any time limits suggested.

5 Developing an independent study program

This section helps you develop a self-study program. This involves identifying your needs, finding appropriate practice materials and maintaining a regular study schedule. This section includes exercises that are suitable for individual study, and exercises that you can do with a study partner.

6 Practice IELTS tests

The practice tests in these sections simulate real IELTS tests. You can do them before you start studying the other sections of the book to give you an idea of your current abilities, or you can do them after working through the units to consolidate your learning. You should do them without any assistance and follow any time limits given.

Acknowledgments

Author acknowledgments

Steven would like to thank Denise Flipo, Jan Pinder and Susan Shand for their advice and encouragement. He would also like to thank Mary Jane Hogan and Viv Winter for their professional support through the whole project.

Steven Thurlow

Publisher acknowledgments

The author and publisher are grateful to the following for permission to reproduce copyright material:

Photographs

Alamy/Stephen Barnes/Air Travel, **18**, /Trevor Smith, **32**; Dreamstime/Anouaras, **30**, /Gunnar3000, **40**, /Hupeng, **121**, /Gino Santa Maria, **7** (left), /Plumrue, **7** (right), /Vladir09, **27**, /Christoph Weihs, **7** (middle); Getty Images/Emmanuel Faure, **93**, /Mike Powell, **21**; iStockPhoto/Basie B, **38** (top), /Zhang Bo, **54**, /Stuart Burford, **26**, /John Cowie, **78**, /Christopher Futcher, **129**, /Nathan Gleave, **83**, /Mümin Inan, **95**, /David Lentz, **134**, /Matteusus, **84**, /Stephen Morris, **102**, /Narvikk, **52** (bottom), /S. Greg Panosian, **109**, /Alexander Podshivalov, **52** (top), /Chad Reischl, **75**, /Daniel Rodriguez, **14**, /Chris Schmidt, **22**, /Ivan Stevanovic, **100**, /Terraxplorer, **116**, /Frances Twitty, **66**, /Peeter Viisimaa, **118**, /Jeremy Voisey, **72**, /YinYang, **122**; Photolibrary/Kablonk Kablonk, **45**; Shutterstock/Kentoh, **79**, /Grub Lee, **38** (bottom), /My Portfolio, **39**, /Damian Palus, **92** (top), /J.Perez, **76**, /Eduardo Rivero, **17**, **71**, /Orion Trail, **92** (bottom), /Tomasz Trojanowski, **80**.

While every care has been taken to trace and acknowledge copyright, the publishers tender their apologies for any accidental infringement where copyright has proved untraceable. They would be pleased to come to a suitable arrangement with the rightful owner in each case.

Listening skills and strategies summary

This table indicates which exercises provide practice at different question types, skills and strategies for the IELTS Listening Test.

		Exercise number

Category	Skill/Strategy	1	2	3	4	5	6	7	8	9	10	11	12	13	14	15	16	17	18	19	20	21	22	23	24	25	26	27	28	29	30	31	32	33	34	35	36	37	38	39
Type of question	Multiple-choice questions	✓													✓																									
	Short-answer questions		✓																																					
	Sentence completion questions			✓								✓																			✓									
	Form/note/summary/flow-chart/table completion questions				✓				✓																								✓							
	Labelling a diagram/plan/map					✓								✓																										
	Matching questions						✓	✓								✓																		✓		✓				
Managing the flow of information	Listening for specific information								✓	✓	✓	✓																												
	Focusing on more than one question												✓	✓																										
	Matching the meaning														✓	✓																								
Understanding what speakers are saying	Understanding vocabulary																✓	✓																						
	Guessing																		✓	✓																				
	Recognising meaning through pronunciation																				✓	✓	✓	✓	✓															
Understanding what speakers are doing	Guessing what speakers are doing																									✓	✓													
	Anticipating what speakers will do next																											✓	✓											
	Listening for times, dates, numbers and letters																													✓	✓									
	Listening for procedures and processes																															✓								
	Listening for descriptions of objects																																✓							
	Listening for explanations of cause and effect																																	✓						
	Listening for comparisons																																		✓	✓				
	Listening for classifications																																			✓				
	Listening for arguments																																				✓	✓		
	Listening for descriptions of problems and solutions																																						✓	
	Listening for stories																																							✓

Speaking skills and strategies summary

This table indicates which exercises provide practice at the different parts of, and skills and strategies required for the IELTS Speaking Test.

Parts of Test / Skill	Sub-skill	Exercise numbers (ticked)
Parts of Test	Part 1: Introduction and interview	1 ✓, 2 ✓, 3 ✓
	Part 2: Individual long turn	4 ✓, 5 ✓, 6 ✓
	Part 3: Two-way discussion	7 ✓, 8 ✓, 9 ✓
Fluency and coherence	Speaking fluently	10 ✓, 11 ✓, 12 ✓, 16 ✓
	Speaking coherently	13 ✓, 14 ✓, 15 ✓, 16 ✓, 17 ✓
	Using discourse markers and other cohesive features	6 ✓, 7 ✓, 14 ✓
Accuracy and range of vocabulary	Using accurate vocabulary	19 ✓, 25 ✓
	Using a range of vocabulary	21 ✓, 22 ✓, 23 ✓, 26 ✓
	Paraphrasing	23 ✓, 24 ✓
Grammatical range and accuracy	Speaking with accurate grammar	26 ✓, 27 ✓, 28 ✓, 29 ✓, 30 ✓, 32 ✓, 33 ✓
	Speaking with a range of grammar	31 ✓, 32 ✓, 33 ✓
Pronunciation	Individual sounds	34 ✓, 35 ✓, 36 ✓, 40 ✓
	Word and sentence stress	37 ✓, 38 ✓, 39 ✓, 40 ✓
	Rhythm	41 ✓, 42 ✓, 43 ✓, 44 ✓, 47 ✓
	Intonation and pitch	41 ✓, 42 ✓, 45 ✓, 46 ✓, 47 ✓

Unit 1
Listening

1.1 What is in the Listening Test?

The IELTS Listening Test is the same for both Academic and General Training candidates.

Time allowed	Approximately 30 minutes, plus 10 minutes to transfer answers
Procedure	The Listening Test is the first IELTS test you will sit. It is held in an examination room. You are given a question booklet. As you listen to the recording, you write your answers in the question booklet. The recording is played only once, and pauses are included to allow you time to read the questions and check your answers. When the recording ends, you are given 10 minutes to transfer your answers to a separate answer sheet.
Number of questions	A total of 40 questions in four sections (usually 10 questions per section)
Types of questions	Multiple-choice Short answer Sentence completion Form/note/summary/flow-chart/table completion Labelling a diagram/plan/map Matching
Structure	**Section 1:** A conversation between two speakers about a social (non-academic) topic **Section 2:** A monologue (i.e. spoken by one speaker) about a social (non-academic) topic **Section 3:** A conversation between two to four speakers about an academic topic **Section 4:** A university-style presentation by one speaker about an academic topic Note: The level of complexity increases throughout the test, i.e. Section 4 is the most difficult section of the test.
Skills focus	**Sections 1 and 2:** Listening for and noting specific factual information **Section 3:** Listening for specific information, attitudes and speakers' opinions in a conversation **Section 4:** Listening for main ideas, specific information, attitudes and speakers' opinions in an academic presentation
Scoring	You will receive a band score between 0 and 9 depending on how many questions you answer correctly. Scores can be reported in whole or half band scores, e.g. 8.0 or 7.5.

1.2 Test-taking tips

What should you do when you take the IELTS Listening Test? Here are some suggestions about how to manage the test as successfully as possible.

Be prepared

Make sure you arrive at the examination centre early so that you are relaxed and calm when the test begins. Dress comfortably. Bring at least two pens and two pencils. Answers in the Listening Test must be written in *pencil*.

Remember: the Listening Test comes first.

Focus your eyes and ears

One of the main challenges of the Listening Test is that you must do three things, more or less at the same time:

- listen
- read
- write.

To achieve this, you need to concentrate. Throughout the test, keep your eyes on the question paper (so that you can read the questions and write your answers) and keep your ears focused on the recording (so that you can hear what the speakers are saying). There is no point in looking up – it will reduce your ability to concentrate on reading the questions and writing the answers.

You should practise listening to people *without seeing them*. When listening to recorded voices, try to visualise the people who are speaking. Also, it is useful to practise this type of highly focused listening while there are some distractions (for example, people coughing or moving their chairs, or with some noises from outside the room).

Guess

Try to answer all the questions. If you miss a question completely, *guess* the answer. There are no penalties for wrong answers. Finalise all your answers at the end of each section – don't wait until the end of the test, as it will be more difficult to select or guess answers then.

Manage your time

The Listening Test requires careful time management and self-discipline.

You will hear the recording once only. There may be a pause for reading ahead during Sections 1, 2 and 3, but not in Section 4.

You are usually given 30 seconds to read each set of questions before the recording is played. A set of questions is usually around five questions. Use this time to predict what kind of information is needed to answer each question in the set.

You are also given half a minute to review each set of answers. Use this time fully and don't be tempted to look ahead at the next section.

If you cannot answer a question don't become 'stuck' on it. Guess the answer, then move on when the spoken instructions tell you to.

Throughout the test don't waste time by erasing; just draw a line through the word you want to change and keep going.

Write accurately

Although this is a listening test, your ability to *write* accurate answers is also relevant. Incorrect grammar or spelling in your answers will be penalised. At the end of the test you are given 10 minutes to transfer your answers from the question paper to the answer sheet. Make sure you transfer all your answers completely and accurately. As you transfer, check whether your grammar is correct (for example, think: should this noun be singular or plural?). Also check your spelling. You can cross out and change your answers – untidiness is not penalised, as long as your writing can be clearly understood.

Know what to expect

It is important to know what to expect in the Listening Test. Make sure that you are thoroughly familiar with both the content and the structure of the test.

Remember that the topics used for the test are non-technical and should be reasonably familiar to all candidates doing the test, no matter what their background. There are a mixture of English accents and dialects used in the recording. For example, you could be listening to Canadian English or Scottish English – so it's a good idea to become familiar with the different varieties of international English. See Exercise 20 on page 29 for more practice in this area.

Ensure you know how the test is organised. For example, remember that the test becomes more difficult as you move from Section 1 to Section 4. Expect this and stay calm.

It is also important to know how the recording will instruct you during the test.

> At the beginning of each section of the Listening Test, the speaker on the recording gives a brief introduction to the situation. Remember: you hear this, but you do not see it on the question paper.
>
> The speaker then gives instructions:
>
> > Read questions 1 to 5. As you listen to the recording, write the correct answer in the spaces provided.
>
> The speaker then tells you to look at the questions:
>
> > First you have some time to look at questions 1 to 5.
>
> Then the recording is silent for 30 seconds to give you time to carefully read the questions. After 30 seconds, the speaker then repeats which questions you have to answer:
>
> > Now listen and answer questions 1 to 5.
>
> Finally, the section will be played.

To become familiar with how instructions are given in the Listening Test, you should do several practice tests, starting with the practice test provided in 1.6.

Also make sure that you familiarise yourself with the different question types in the Listening Test. The following section (1.3) gives information on how to handle different types of questions.

1.3 Getting to know the test

The IELTS Listening Test features a number of question types, spread randomly throughout the test. The following types of questions are used.

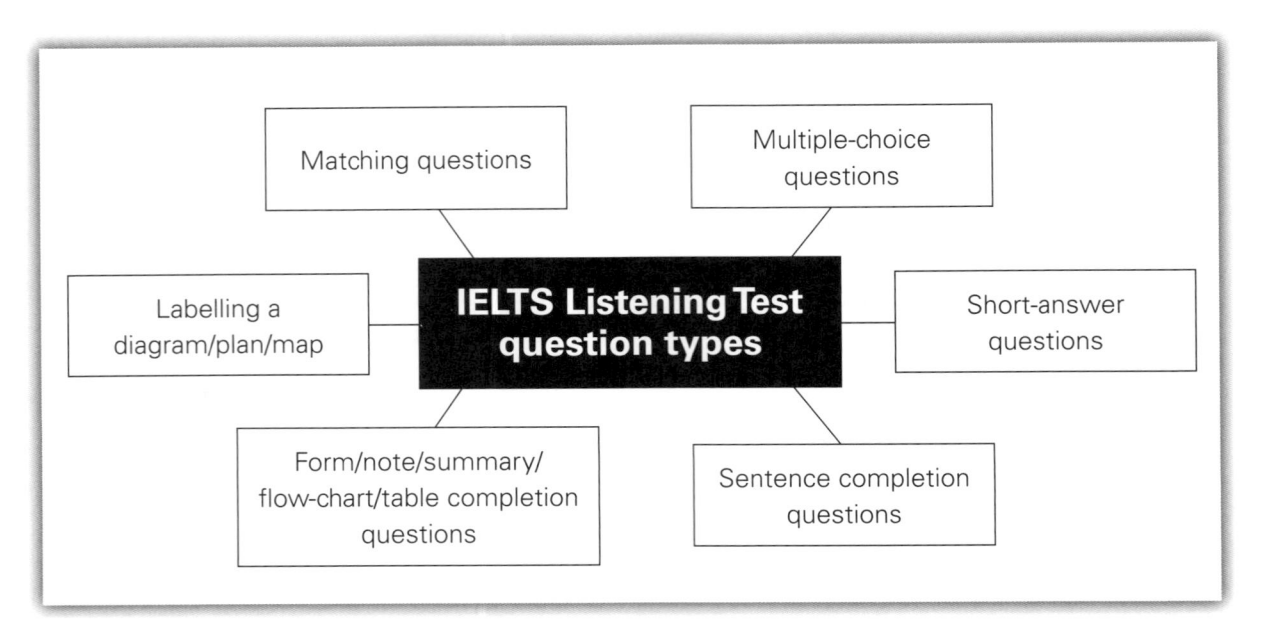

```
                Matching questions          Multiple-choice questions

Labelling a                 IELTS Listening Test                Short-answer
diagram/plan/map            question types                      questions

         Form/note/summary/              Sentence completion
         flow-chart/table completion     questions
         questions
```

Knowing how best to handle these different kinds of questions is essential to performing well in the test. Exercises 1 to 7 on the following pages, will show you how to complete each different question type. For each of these exercises, listen to part of a conversation, which takes place in a computer shop, and then complete the questions.

Multiple-choice questions

What do I have to do?

With multiple-choice questions you are given a question followed by three possible answers and you need to choose the correct answer. Sometimes, you will have a question that asks you to choose two answers. If this is the case, you will be given a longer list of possible answers.

In some multiple-choice questions you are given part of a sentence – a sentence 'stem' – and you have to choose the best *sentence ending* from three choices.

Exercise 1 gives you practice at answering different types of multiple-choice questions.

Exercise 1 Multiple-choice questions

Listen to the recording and answer questions 1 and 2.

Questions 1–2

Circle the correct letter, A, B or C.

1   Which type of shop is Martina in?
    A   computer rentals
    B   new computers
    C   secondhand computers

2   Martina wants to get a
    A   laptop computer.   B   desktop computer.   C   mini-notebook computer.

How do I approach multiple-choice questions?

Multiple-choice questions are written so that every response has the appearance of being correct. The correct answer can only be selected through carefully listening for the information indicated in the stem.

After listening to the recording, if it is not immediately clear which is the correct answer, use a **process of elimination** to answer the question.

▼ Eliminate any obviously incorrect answers.

▼ Underline any answers with vocabulary that you believe should be in the answer.

▼ Check each of these possible answers for words that qualify or change the meaning of nouns or verbs (for example, *all*, *never*, *some*, etc) and also for logical connectors (for example, *and*, *or*, *not*, etc) that also change the meaning.

▼ Select the best answer or, if you are still unsure, guess the answer.

▼ Don't answer the question based on your own personal opinions or knowledge.

▼ Don't choose an answer just because you hear a word or phrase from it in the recording.

▼ Keep listening even after you think you've heard the answer – speakers may change their minds or add other information.

Unit 1: Listening

Short-answer questions

What do I have to do?

With short-answer questions you are given a question that asks you to write a short answer using information you have heard in the recording. These questions always specify how many words or numbers you need to write. A common word limit is three words. You are not required to write contractions and, as a general rule, hyphenated words count as single words (i.e. *single-handed* would count as one word). Spelling is particularly important with these questions.

Exercise 2 gives you practice at answering short-answer questions.

Exercise 2   Short-answer questions

Listen to the recording and answer questions 3 and 4.

Questions 3–4

Write **NO MORE THAN THREE WORDS** *for each answer.*

3   What type of computer does the shop sell most of? *laptops*

4   What will Martina mainly use the computer for? *word processing*

How do I approach short-answer questions?

- Predict the type of information that might be required to answer the question.
- Underline or highlight the key word(s) in the question before you listen.
- As you listen, note word(s) or expressions with a similar meaning in the recording.
- Don't write a complete sentence as your answer.
- Don't write more than the specified number of words (or numbers).
- Check your spelling when you write your answers on the answer sheet.

Sentence completion questions

What do I have to do?

Also known as 'fill in the blank' or 'gap-fill' questions, sentence completion questions require you to complete a sentence with a suitable word or words from the recording. The incomplete sentence may gather together several pieces of information from one part of the Listening Test. You need to write the missing word(s) in the gap on the question paper for later transferral to the answer sheet.

Exercise 3 gives you practice at answering sentence completion questions.

Exercise 3 — Sentence completion questions

Listen to the recording and answer questions 5 and 6.

Questions 5–6

Write NO MORE THAN THREE WORDS *for each answer.*

Light laptops are usually **5** ...*more expensive*... than heavy laptops.

The Apex is the most expensive because it is the **6** ...*lightest*... .

How do I approach sentence completion questions?

- ▼ Before listening, check how many words you need to write and think about what type of word (i.e. noun, verb, adjective, etc) might fit into the gap.
- ▼ Use nearby words and/or headings to predict words that may be suitable.
- ▼ Guess the missing word(s) if you miss the answer – you still have a good chance of being correct.
- ▼ Don't get stuck on one particular gap and miss the answers to the following questions.
- ▼ Don't write more than the specified number of words (or numbers).
- ▼ When the recording finishes, check that the whole sentence makes sense grammatically and that your spelling is correct.

Form/note/summary/flow-chart/table completion questions

What do I have to do?

When answering form/note/summary/flow-chart/table completion questions, you have to complete gaps in a representation based on the main ideas from a recording. This representation could be a form or a set of notes, a summary, a flow-chart (diagram) or a table. You may be able to choose suitable words from a list or you may have to supply a word or words from the recording. Except when completing a summary, complete sentences are not required when filling in the gaps.

Exercise 4 gives you practice at answering form/note/summary/flow-chart/table completion questions.

Exercise 4 — Form/note/summary/flow-chart/table completion questions

Listen to the recording and answer questions 7 and 8.

Questions 7–8

Complete the notes.

Apex	Sunray	Nu-tech
1.7 kg	**7** ...*2.4 kg*...	3.1 kg
most convenient	**8** ...*most powerful*...	cheapest

Unit 1: Listening

How do I approach form/note/summary/flow-chart/table completion questions?

▼ Before you listen, examine the whole representation to gain an overall sense of what it is and what its aim or purpose might be.

▼ Pay attention to any headings or words in bold.

▼ Predict what type of information may be required to complete the gaps.

▼ If there is a process or sequence involved, check that your additions make logical sense.

▼ Don't write more than the specified number of words (or numbers).

▼ When the recording finishes, check that the whole sentence makes sense grammatically and that your spelling is correct.

Labelling a diagram/plan/map

What do I have to do?

With this type of question, you have to complete the labels on some type of visual. This visual may be in the form of a line drawing, a plan, a map, or one or more pictures. The answers can sometimes be selected from a list on the question paper. You need to supply the missing word(s).

Exercise 5 gives you practice at labelling a diagram/plan/map.

Exercise 5 — Labelling a diagram/plan/map

Listen to the recording and answer questions 9 and 10.

Questions 9–10

Complete the diagram.

Write **NO MORE THAN THREE WORDS** for each answer.

9. CD/DVD drive
10. Microphone

How do I approach labelling a diagram/plan/map?

- ▼ Look at the title and try to understand the visual before you hear the recording.
- ▼ Predict what type of information and what type of word (that is, noun, verb, adjective, etc) you might need to complete the gaps. Pencil any guesses you have onto the visual.
- ▼ Note the number order of the gaps – this is the order you will hear the answers. Sometimes this ordering system will be 'non-standard' – that is, the numbers will be scattered around the page.
- ▼ Pay particular attention to prepositions of place (*next to*, *behind*, etc). These will tell you how the different features in the visual relate to each other.
- ▼ Don't forget that you will hear some 'warm-up' language before the visual is discussed (for example, *In the diagram you can see ...*).
- ▼ Don't panic if you can't recognise, at first, what the visual is representing – some diagrams can be quite technical, but you do not require special knowledge to complete the task of labelling.
- ▼ Before doing the Listening Test, practise reading maps, plans and diagrams, and extracting information from them.

Matching questions

What do I have to do?

With matching questions, you have to match a numbered list of specific items to a set of options. The options could be a set of acronyms, *→abbreviation / contraction* a list of descriptive words or phrases, a set of criteria, or something similar. This question type tests your ability to distinguish between *factual details*.

Matching questions can take several different forms. Exercises 6 and 7 give you practice at two of the most common types of matching questions found in the Listening Test.

Exercise 6 — Matching questions

Listen to the recording and answer questions 11 to 13.

Questions 11–13

Complete the table showing the types of pointing devices used by different computers.

- **TCM** = Traditional Corded Mouse
- **CLM** = Cordless Laser Mouse
- **OWM** = Optical Wireless Mouse

	Sunray laptop	Apex laptop	Nu-tech laptop
Type of pointing device	11 *OWM*	12 *CLM*	13 *TCM*

Unit 1: Listening 11

Exercise 7 — Matching

Listen to the recording and answer questions 14 to 16.

Questions 14–16

Match the computers in questions 14 to 16 with the appropriate labels, A, B or C.

14 Apex ......C......
15 Sunray ......A......
16 Nu-tech ......B......

A	B	C
12 MONTHS PARTS ONLY — 12 MONTHS GUARANTEE	6 MONTHS PARTS ONLY GUARANTEE	12 MONTHS PARTS AND LABOUR — 12 GUARANTEE

How do I approach matching questions?

- Analyse all the information you have been given. If you have a graph or table, look at the labels across the top or down the left-hand side.
- Study the information given in each list/set. Try to think of synonyms for these words or pictures before the recording starts.
- Work out key differences in the options you have been given and underline these differences before the recording starts.
- Be ready for repetition of key words.
- Be flexible. You may have more questions than there are options to match them with. In this case, you will need to use one or more options more than once. In some tests, one option may not be used at all.
- Spell the words from the key correctly in your answer.
- Remember to guess the answer if you are not sure – you will still have a good chance of being correct.

Focusing on IELTS Listening and Speaking Skills

1.4 The listening strategies and skills you need

Managing the flow of information

The IELTS Listening Test sends an intense flow of spoken information to your brain for processing. It is essential to manage this torrent of words while you are doing the test and not let it wash over you. The strategies and skills in this section will help you to approach the Listening Test in the most effective way. Specifically, this section will help teach you how to:

- listen for the specific information you need to answer the questions
- focus on more than one question at a time while you are listening
- match what you read on the question paper with what you hear on the recording.

Listening for specific information

It is not necessary to comprehend every word in every section of the Listening Test. Of course, you will listen *to* every word in the recording, but you don't need to listen *for* every word.

What is the difference between 'listening *to*' something and 'listening *for*' something?

Listening to	You hear the words. You listen carefully to everything that is being said. This is **passive listening**.
Listening for	You are *waiting* to hear something. You are ready to catch a specific piece of information. This is **active listening**.

In the Listening Test you only need to listen for the *specific information that answers the question*. The strategy of listening for specific information is similar to 'scanning' when you are reading (see *Focusing on IELTS: Reading and Writing Skills*, page 32). As with scanning, you focus on catching one piece of information, not all of the information.

Predicting

The key to listening for specific information is predicting the type of information that you need to listen for. Through predicting you can activate your broad background knowledge about a topic. Then listening to an extended recording about this topic will become much easier. This is a useful strategy for all question types in the Listening Test.

For example, you read the following question on the question paper:

Why did Martin leave work early?

Unit 1: Listening

Before you hear the recording you can predict that there might be a reason given, using words like *because* or *so*, and perhaps information given about being ill, having an appointment or being tired.

It is important to make good use of the 30 seconds of silence the recording gives you for each set of questions. The recording will say something like: 'First you have some time to look at questions x to y.' As quickly as possible, read the questions and decide what kind of information you will listen for.

For example, with multiple-choice questions you could identify the differences in the different answers and then decide what to listen for.

Example

How many Canadian speakers will attend the conference?
- **A** 20
- **B** 30
- **C** 25

For this question you know you need to be ready to listen for just one piece of information: a *number*. When the recording starts, you expect to hear something like: 'There will be (*number*) Canadian speakers at the conference.'

Sometimes you need to listen for two pieces of information.

Example

What type of accommodation does he want to rent?
- **A** a two-bedroom house
- **B** a one-bedroom apartment
- **C** a three-bedroom apartment

You can see that the answers in this question differ in two ways. You have to listen for two pieces of information:

1 Does he want a house or an apartment?
2 How many bedrooms does he want?

Exercise 8 Listening for specific information

What would you listen for if you saw the following questions? In the middle column, predict the type of information needed. The first one has been done for you as an example.

continued ▶

	Information needed	Answer
1 When is Bill going to finish his assignment?	A time/a day	tomorrow
2 Why did he enjoy his assignment?	An excuse	intrested
3 What proportion of university students are female?	a number	50%
4 How many women Vice-Chancellors are there?	a number	three
5 What part of his assignment remains unfinished?	a thing / part	references

Now listen to the recording and write your answers in the final column.

Identifying key words

One practical way to help you predict what information to listen for is to underline or highlight key parts of the question. When you read the questions, underline or highlight the words that ask for the information. These could include question words (usually *wh-* words, such as *what*) and nouns. Words that join pieces of information together, such as *and*, *of*, *the* and *so*, are not usually question words. Verbs such as forms of the verbs *to be* (for example, *is* and *was*) or *to do* (*do*, *did*, etc) are not usually key words.

Examples

Where is the computer?

What is the advantage of using solar power?

What are the two main causes of an ageing population?

When will the conference begin?

Exercise 9 Identifying key words

Take 30 seconds to look at the questions, underline or highlight the key words and get ready to listen to the recording.

Now listen to the recording and answer the questions.

Write NO MORE THAN THREE WORDS for each answer.

1 At what time did the robbery take place? 9 o'clock
2 What is the name of the robbed bank? Central Bank
3 How many customers were in the bank at the time of the robbery? none
4 How many people were involved in robbing the bank? 3
5 What telephone number should people call to give information? 935 7799

Unit 1: Listening

Changing pictures into words

Sometimes you need to decide what to listen for when you have a question that contains diagrams or pictures. During the 30 seconds you have to study the questions, try to turn these images into words. Quickly identify different details and express them in words in your mind. Then you can listen for those words when the recording is played.

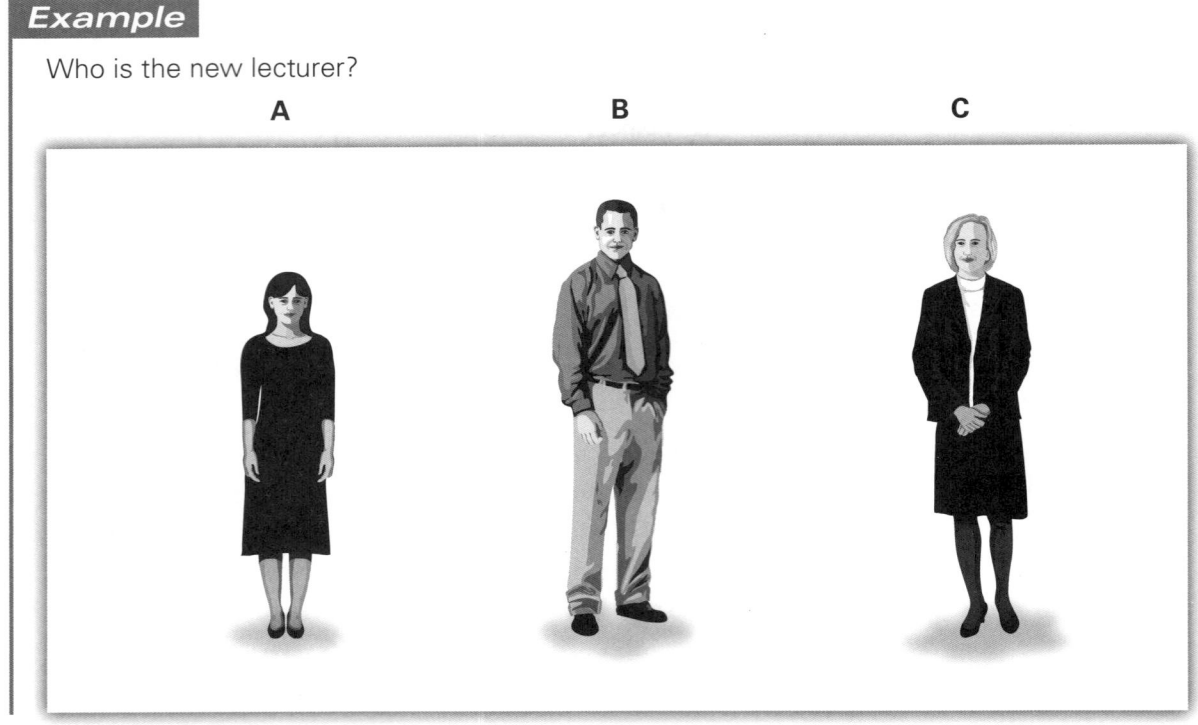

Example

Who is the new lecturer?

        A   **B**   **C**

For this question, you are ready to listen for two details:

1. Is the person a man or woman?
2. Is the person short or tall?

Then, when you listen to the recording and hear 'her', 'she' and 'tall', you know that the correct answer is C.

Let's do some more practice. In the next section, you will hear a conversation about finding a rare book. The question is:

Which copy of the book will the library user take?

From this, you know what you will be listening *for*: information about a copy of a particular book. If you hear other information about books, you know it is not relevant, so you can ignore it. During the Listening Test, it is common to have to ignore large sections of irrelevant information. Stay calm and keep waiting. *Keep listening for the information you need.*

Exercise 10 Listening for specific information

Which copy of the book will the library user take?
Listen to the recording and circle the correct answer.

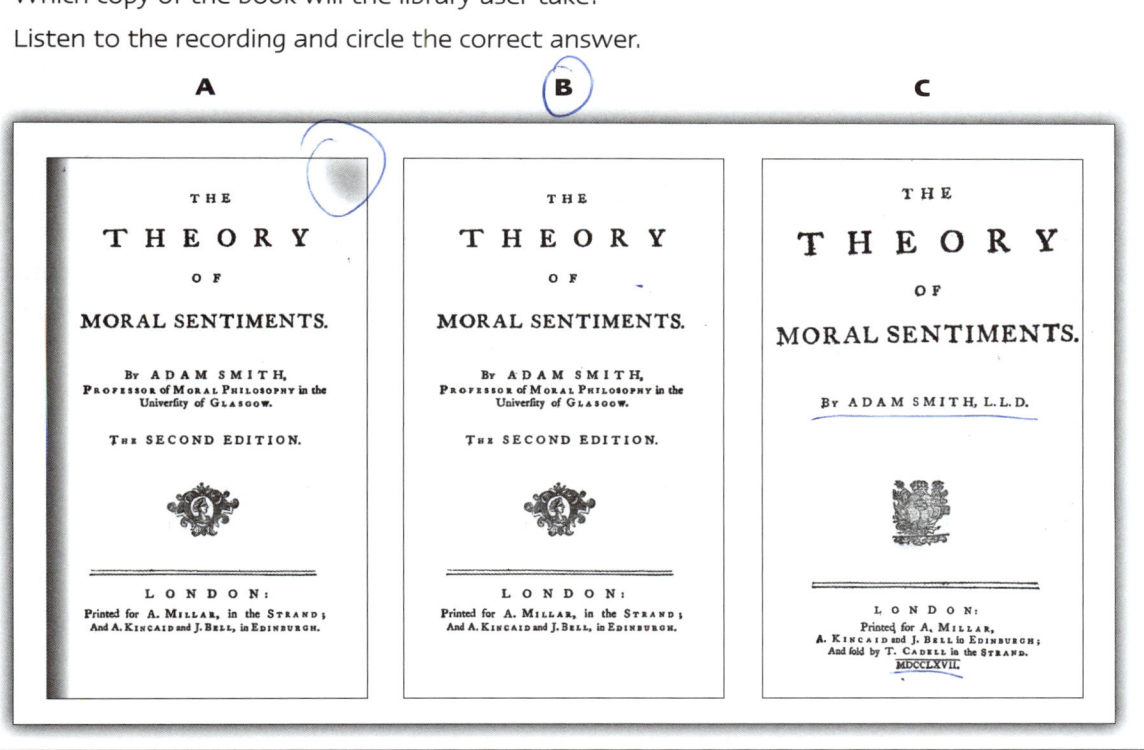

A **B** (circled) **C**

The strategy of predicting what information you need to listen for in order to answer questions and then actively listening for that specific information applies to all sections of the Listening Test and all types of questions. Exercise 11 allows you to practise this strategy while doing a note completion question.

Exercise 11 Listening for specific information

Complete the notes to the right. Write NO MORE THAN THREE WORDS for each answer.

Look at the notes and quickly decide what you will need to listen for in order to complete them.

Now listen to the recording and complete the notes.

ESSAY

Topic: Attitudes towards public transport
Length: 1 *10 pages*
2 *Methodology* open (e.g. telephone survey, face-to-face interviews or case study)
Due date: 3 *11th September*
Requirements: word processed
A 4 *Title page*
description of methodology

Unit 1: Listening 17

Focusing on more than one question

Focusing on more than one question is an extension of the previous strategy (listening for specific information). It is necessary because although the recording tells you when to move on to the next section, it does not tell you when to move on to the next question *within* each section.

For example, if you are doing a short-answer task, the recording does not tell you that you have already heard the information for Question 3 and should now move on to Question 4 – you need to decide this for yourself. If you focus only on Question 3, you may miss the information that will help you to answer the next question. You may lose your place entirely and panic. To avoid this, you need to focus on more than one question at all times. That is, you need to listen for information to answer at least two questions *at the same time*.

Example

On your question paper you'll see the following:

Flight number	1	....
Departure time:	2	....
Cost of ticket:	3	....
Cost of departure tax:	4	....

As you listen to the recording for these questions, you need to focus on at least two questions at a time. You may talk to yourself like this:

1 I'm listening for a flight number and a time.
2 (after you catch and fill in answer **1**): I'm listening for a time and a cost.
3 (after you catch the time and fill in answer **2**): I'm listening for the cost of the ticket and the cost of the tax. And so on.

Sometimes it is possible to group the questions by topic, for example: **3** and **4** – I'm listening for two costs. Underlining the key words during the reading time will help you as you listen for several answers at once.

Exercise 12 Focusing on more than one question

CD 1 • Track 13

Mia is telephoning an airline company.
Listen to the conversation and answer the questions.
Write NO MORE THAN THREE WORDS for each answer.

1 What is Mia's flight number? ......SA 233..........
2 For what date is Mia's original flight reservation?
......January 21st..........

continued ▶

3	How many times per week does Sky Air fly direct to Honolulu?	*3*
4	Where does Mia want to sit?	*window seat*
5	How many kilograms of luggage is Mia allowed to take on the flight?	*22 kilos*
6	What will Mia have to do if her luggage is too heavy?	*pay extra*
7	Did Mia achieve the main things she wanted to in her telephone call?	*yes*

> **The sequence of information on the recording always follows the same sequence as the questions. This helps you to follow (and answer) the questions in the right order.**

Sometimes the information you need to answer a question is presented more than once by the speaker or by another speaker. This gives you a chance to select the correct answer and then confirm your selection. For example, in Exercise 12 the information you need to answer Question 1 (the flight number) is given twice in the dialogue. When the information is repeated later you can go back to Question 1 and confirm your selection.

Some questions require you to listen for information that is presented over a large section of speech. For example, in Exercise 12 the information you need to answer Question 7 is spread throughout the dialogue. You need to consider most of the dialogue in order to answer the question. Although Exercise 12 is an example of a Section 1 task, the strategy of focusing on more than one question at a time is necessary in *all* sections of the Listening Test.

Exercise 13 gives you practice at this strategy while labelling a diagram.

Exercise 13 Focusing on more than one question

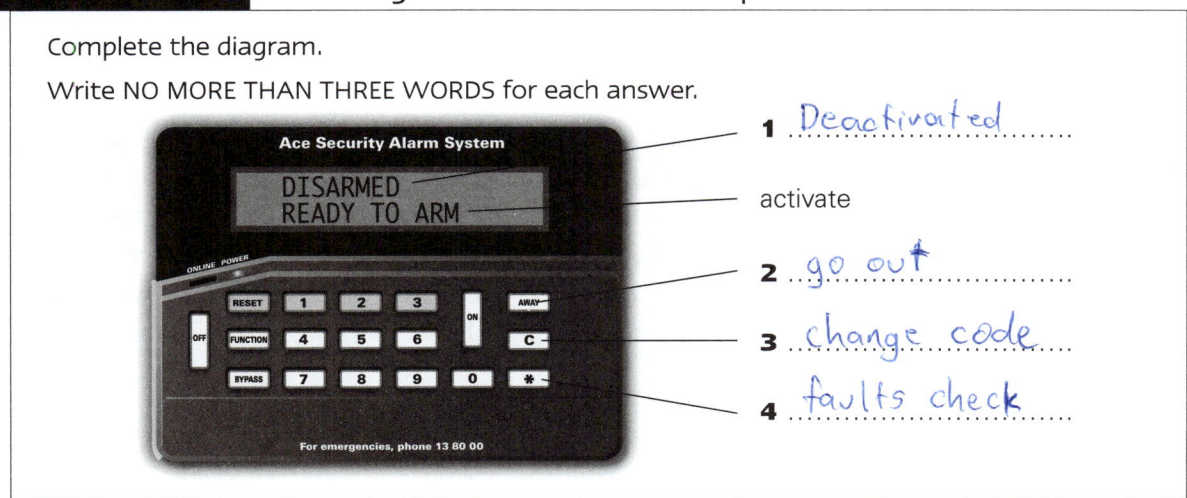

CD 1 • Track 14

Complete the diagram.
Write NO MORE THAN THREE WORDS for each answer.

1 *Deactivated*

activate

2 *go out*

3 *change code*

4 *faults check*

For more practice in using this strategy, see 1.5, page 52.

Unit 1: Listening   19

Matching the meaning

In the Listening Test, you must often match what you see on the question paper with what you hear on the recording. Sometimes, it is easy to make this match because you hear exactly the same words as you see.

For example, you see this question on the question paper.

Example

Why didn't he go back to university?
- **A** he wanted to get a better job
- **B** he didn't have enough money
- **C** he had already earned enough money

You hear this sentence on the recording:

I didn't have enough money.

The answer is clearly **B** because the words match exactly. Often, however, you will not hear the exact words; instead you will hear words that share the same *meaning*.

For example, you see this question on the question paper.

Example

Why didn't he go back to university?
- **A** he wanted to get a job
- **B** he couldn't afford it
- **C** he had already earned enough money

You hear this sentence on the recording.

I didn't have enough money.

Again, answer **B** is correct. Although it uses words that are different from the recording, it has the same meaning. For this question, you need to match not only words but also meanings. Knowing *synonyms* (words with the same meaning, such as *help* and *assist*, *enough* and *sufficient*, *finish* and *complete*, *can't afford* and *don't have enough money*) will help you to match the meaning. Learning synonyms is an important part of vocabulary learning – especially at more advanced levels of English (see 1.4, pages 23–25).

Exercise 14   Matching the meaning

Circle the correct letter, **A**, **B** or **C**.

1   Swimmers wear full-length swimsuits because
    A   they like the way the swimsuits look.
    B   this is required in competitive swimming.
    C   they enhance swimmers' performance.
2   The experiments in 1990 showed that shaving body hair
    A   helps swimmers to swim faster.
    B   lowers swimmers' consumption of oxygen.
    C   reduces drag by around 10%.
3   The new-style swimsuits
    A   resemble shark skin.
    B   are made of shark skin.
    C   are covered with shark skin.
4   Sharks are able to swim so fast because their skin
    A   is very smooth.
    B   has very small ridges.
    C   has survived for a long time.

Exercise 14 shows you the type of questions in Section 4. However, the strategy of matching meaning is necessary in all sections of the test and with all question types.

Note that matching meanings can be *indirect*. In fact, the answer you need to give may be an *inference*: that is, a conclusion based on the evidence available. In the following exercise, for example, you need to draw conclusions about the speakers' views. Although the speakers do not necessarily express their views directly (avoiding such phrases as 'I support this idea' or 'I am in favour of that proposal'), it is possible to draw inferences about their views. The evidence includes both the intonation they use (for example, very enthusiastic or very dismissive) and their word usage (for example, 'I think that's ridiculous').

Unit 1: Listening

Exercise 15 — Matching the meaning

Match the students' names with their views about politicians. Write the correct letter in the table below. Note that there could be more than one answer for some questions. Answer **2** has been given as an example.

Anna = A **Mark** = M
John = J **Sally** = S

View	Student
Supports the idea that politicians need to have a university qualification	1 ...... M ......
Supports the idea that politicians should have good ethical standards	2 ...... S ......
Supports the idea that politicians need to be able to see the difference between opinions and facts	3 ...... J & S ......
Supports the idea that younger people should be encouraged to become politicians	4 ...... S ......
Supports the idea that there needs to be a minimum age requirement for political candidates	5 ...... J ......

For more practice in matching the meaning, see 1.5, page 52.

Understanding what speakers are saying

Effective listeners are able to understand what they hear. Specifically, they are able to:
- understand the vocabulary they hear
- guess the meaning of any unfamiliar words using the context
- recognise the pronunciation of words and phrases.

Understanding vocabulary

To do well in the Listening Test, you need to understand the words that the speakers use. This means two things: you need to *know* as many words as possible and you need to be able to *guess* the meaning of the words that you don't know.

Learning useful words

There are a lot of words in English. There is little agreement about exactly how many words there are in the English language but most standard 'desk' dictionaries have over 100,000 words. Specialist dictionaries can have over 600,000. When you take into account geographical, zoological, botanical and other scientific words, present-day English could have over a million words.

Because of this huge number of words, it isn't possible to learn every new word you encounter. Even native English speakers do not know every word in English. You should only try to learn (memorise) *useful* words. For IELTS candidates there are two types of useful vocabulary: **versatile** and **specific** words.

Versatile words

Versatile words are words that can be used in many different situations and with a variety of topics. They are also high-frequency words, which means that they often occur in everyday speech. Here are some examples.

Versatile words	Example sentences
Complex (adj.), aspect (n.)	Conservation is a complex subject which has many different aspects.
Excessive (adj.)	Excessive eating is not good for your health.
Plunge (v.)	The dollar plunged when the news broke.

Specific words

For IELTS candidates, specific words are those commonly used when talking about topics that occur frequently in the Listening Test. They are useful to learn in preparing for the IELTS test, as you can use this vocabulary not only in the Listening Test but also in the Speaking and Writing Tests.

Common topic areas in IELTS include:

- university/college study
- accommodation
- transport
- travel
- social services, such as banking
- recreation.

Note: This is not a complete list of topics that could occur in the IELTS test.

Here are some examples of specific words.

Specific words	Example sentences
semester (n.)	This semester is only 12 weeks long.
well-maintained (adj.)	This small, well-maintained apartment is on the ground floor.
route (n.)	The number six tram offers the quickest route.
frequent (adj.)	The frequent train service makes the journey much easier.
deposit (n., v.)	She deposited half her salary into his account.
leisurely (adv.)	I had a long, leisurely walk on Sunday.

Now practise identifying which words might be useful to learn for the IELTS test.

Exercise 16   Learning useful words

Listen to the recording as you read the following paragraph. Do you recognise all the vocabulary that has been used in it? If not, decide which words you would consider learning and underline them.

He currently works as a tutor in molecular science at one of the local colleges. Apparently he earns around 50% more than he used to. The workload is oppressively heavy, but he has a reasonable amount of annual vacation. By and large, he's satisfied with his new position and responsibilities.

Check the answer key for suggested lists of versatile and specific words to learn, and words probably *not* worth learning.

Learning new words is a large, ongoing task. It requires steady attention, like practising a sport. For each new word that you decide you want to learn, first check that you understand:

▼ its meaning(s)
▼ what part of speech it is (for example, adjective, verb or noun)
▼ how to use it in a sentence
▼ its level of formality (is it slang or formal?)
▼ other words it commonly collocates (is used) with
▼ how the word sounds when it is spoken (including stress).

The last point is particularly important. In the Listening Test, it is useless to know all the other information about a word if you cannot recognise the word when it is spoken.

After finding out about a new word, it is important to *memorise* the word. This will stop words 'flying in one ear and out of another'. Here are some memorisation techniques you can try:

▼ Say new words aloud many times (checking their pronunciation before you start).

▼ Write new words many times.

▼ Write new words on pieces of paper and put them in places where you will often see them.

▼ Turn an exercise book into your personal dictionary, dividing it into categories (for example: university, feelings, food, phrasal verbs, etc) and adding a few new words every day. Make sure you include as much information about the word as you can.

▼ Create a simple example sentence to help you remember a new word. For example, if you want to remember the word 'workload', create a sentence such as: *Doctors usually have heavy workloads*.

Synonyms

It is also useful to learn **synonyms**, that is, words which have the same (or very similar) meanings. As we saw in 1.3 (page 12), successful matching may involve recognising synonyms. A dictionary of synonyms (called a thesaurus) can help expand your knowledge of synonyms.

Exercise 17   Synonyms

Provide at least three synonyms for each of the following words. Where possible, find out the differences between the synonyms. The first one has been done for you as an example.

Word	Synonym 1	Synonym 2	Synonym 3
1 friend (n.)	*pal* (colloquial)	*mate* (colloquial)	*confidant* (very close friend)
2 man (n.)			
3 good (adj.)	nice	fine	
4 bad (adj.)			
5 big (adj.)			
6 to reduce (v.)			

Sample answers are provided in the answer key.

Unit 1: Listening

Guessing

Despite learning a lot of words, you will still encounter some that you do not know. Even in your first language you may not always know the meaning of every word that you hear and need to guess. This skill of guessing is even more necessary when you are listening to a foreign or second language (and while doing the Listening Test).

There are two main ways we can make this process of guessing the meaning of unfamiliar words easier:

1 analysing how the word is written by **decoding** information from different parts of the word
2 examining the **context** (surrounding words/ideas) to figure out what the word might mean.

Decoding words

When you are confronted by unknown words, it is sometimes possible to guess their meaning by examining how the word has been put together. First, we need to decide which part of speech the word is: that is, whether the word is a noun, verb, adjective, adverb, etc. Then, by analysing the letters at the beginning or end of the word, we can make an educated guess what the word might mean.

Let's look at an example:

agronomy

We can work out that this is probably a noun, as the *-omy* ending is similar to other nouns, such as *economy* or *taxonomy*. The first three letters, *agr-*, are also a clue. We might guess that this word is related to *agr*iculture. So, our educated guess is that this noun is something to do with growing or raising farm products. Indeed, the Macquarie Dictionary defines agronomy as follows:

> (noun) the applied aspects of both soil science and the several plant sciences, often limited to applied plant sciences dealing with crops.

Many words in English share common stems of words (called prefixes) or word endings (called suffixes) that help us decode meaning. For example, the prefix *pre-* is used with nouns, verbs and adjectives, and means 'before'. It is found with words like *precaution* and *preliminary*.

Exercise 18 gives you practice at decoding the meaning of common prefixes.

Exercise 18   Decoding prefixes

Match the prefix to its meaning. The first answer has been given as an example.

Note: You can use one letter twice.

1 pre- = ...*E*.... (e.g. prewar)
2 co-   = ...   (e.g. cooperate)
3 dis- = ...   (e.g. disbelief)
4 in-   = ...   (e.g. inexpensive)
5 inter- = ... (e.g. intermarry)
6 mis- = ...   (e.g. misprint)
7 re-   = ...   (e.g. rebook)
8 un-   = ...   (e.g. unmake)

Meaning / How it is used	Parts of speech it is applied to
A bad, mistaken, wrong, or negative meaning	nouns and verbs
B association, jointly, together	adjectives, adverbs, nouns and verbs
C repetition, withdrawal or backward motion	nouns and verbs
D among, between, mutually, together	nouns, verbs and adjectives
E before, early, prior to, in advance of, in front of	nouns, verbs and adjectives
F not – reverses or removes some action or state	used before adjectives, adverbs, nouns and verbs
G gives the negative, opposite or reverse meaning	used before adjectives, adverbs, nouns and verbs

Guessing meaning from context

Another way to guess the meaning of an unknown word is to look at the context of the word. This means analysing the surrounding words or ideas, and using logic and common knowledge to figure out what the word may mean.

Example

I bought an old radio made out of bakelite.

Poor listeners may hear the word *bakelite* and say to themselves 'I don't know what that word means', panic, and stop listening. More effective listeners hear the word, quickly judge the context, say to themselves 'I guess it means some kind of material', and calmly keep listening.

Unit 1: Listening

Exercise 19 Guessing meaning from context

Below are some words that may be new for you. Listen to the recording and guess the meaning of each word based on what you hear. Then check a dictionary or the answer key to see if your guesses were (approximately) correct. The first one has been done for you as an example.

CD 1 • Track 18

Word	Predicted meaning
1 bakelite	a kind of material, maybe a hard material like metal or plastic
2 pediatrician	a person who treats sick kids
3 jingles	an ads with music
4 embezzlement	stealing the bank
5 allamanda	a type of plant which grows on walls
6 hardy	

Recognising meaning through pronunciation

In order to understand what people are saying in the Listening Test, you need to be able to comprehend the way that speakers pronounce things in English. This includes the ability to:

- recognise individual words
- recognise content words
- catch the sentence focus
- understand the status of information.

We will look at these areas one by one. However, first it's important to note the following information regarding speed of delivery and the range of different accents used in the Listening Test.

Speed

In the Listening Test, you will hear clear speech delivered at a speed that is *slightly slower than normal*. However, if you are not used to listening to English, the speed of speaking may seem very fast. The speakers on the recording accompanying this book speak with a similar speed to those in the Listening Test.

28 Focusing on IELTS Listening and Speaking Skills

Accent

A speaker's accent greatly affects their pronunciation. Accent is the way or manner in which you speak a language, and it usually results from where and how you learnt that language. The speakers in the Listening Test generally have standard British, Australian or North American accents, although other accents like Irish, New Zealand or South African English can occasionally be heard.

Understanding different accents is particularly challenging for people who have learnt English mostly through reading. If you have limited experience in listening to different accents, then you may need to do some wider listening practice (see 1.5, pages 49–50).

Recognising words

Sometimes you may fail to recognise familiar words when spoken by English speakers. Exercise 20 will show you how difficult it can be to pick up every word when listening to spoken English.

Exercise 20   Recognising words (dictation)

CD 1 · Track 19

Listen to a short passage as it is read at normal speed three times. The first time it is read simply listen. The second and third times copy down as many words as you can.

As the train *slows to enter the station on this clear friday morning I suddenly aware certain clear on the huge central Bank building it is*

Now compare your version with the one in the answer key. Did you manage to pick up all 36 words from the dictation? Think about the words you heard clearly. What sort of words were they? What about the words you missed? Were they important in your final understanding of the passage? Why did you miss some words?

There are a number of possible reasons why listeners might miss words:

▼ English speakers do not pronounce all of the syllables of words equally clearly and strongly. They give **main** (**primary**) **stress** to only one of the syllables in each word. For example, the main stress in 'international' is on the third of its five syllables: *in-ter-NA-tion-al*.

▼ Speakers of English often **contract** (shorten) words when they speak. For example, they may contract *it will stop* to *it'll stop* and *did not go* to *didn't go*. In informal speech, contraction is common and sometimes a word almost disappears completely (for example, in *Have you seen it?* the beginning of *have* may disappear, and the *v* may join the *you* so that it sounds like *Vyou seen it?*).

▼ English speakers often **reduce** unstressed or weak syllables to a very short sound that is commonly called the schwa. This sound /ə/ is found in the first syllable of words such as *ago* and *o'clock* and the last syllable of *teacher* and *centre*. The schwa is the most common sound in English.

▼ When some sounds occur side by side, they may change. For example, in *Did you go?* the second *d* joins the *y* to create a new *j* sound resulting in *Di-jou go?*

There is more information on word stress in 2.4 (page 115) in the context of the IELTS Speaking Test.

Recognising content words

English speakers stress some words in sentences when they speak and leave others unstressed. They strongly stress **content words** – that is, words that give new information to the listener – and leave other words, such as those that join the content words together, unstressed or weak.

Example

The crisis in handwriting began with the first computer.

The four most important words that communicate meaning in this sentence are all stressed.

Exercise 21 Recognising content words

Listen to the following talk on the decline of handwriting. Underline the words you predict the speaker will probably stress to communicate the main information. Then listen to the recording to check whether your predictions were correct. The first sentence has been done for you as an example.

The <u>way</u> a person <u>writes</u> displays individual <u>style</u> and <u>personality</u>. In previous <u>centuries</u>, children were taught <u>techniques</u> to write properly and letter-writing became an <u>art form</u>. However, with the emergence of <u>computers</u> and <u>mobile phones</u>, many children are <u>no longer capable</u> of producing good handwriting. This is a great <u>pity</u> for several reasons. Firstly, a piece of well-ordered script written with flow <u>and flair</u> is pleasing to the <u>eye</u> – kind of like a firm <u>handshake</u> or a <u>nice smile</u> when you meet <u>someone new</u>. Mastery of <u>handwriting</u> also assists young people to control their hand and promotes hand–eye coordination. Finally, it teaches them to <u>slow</u> their <u>thinking</u> and reflect before writing.

Focusing on IELTS Listening and Speaking Skills

Catching the focus

English speakers frequently use very strong **focus stress** to show what part of their message they want their listeners to focus on.

Example

A Professor, can I talk to you about my research project?

B Let's talk about your <u>essay</u> first.

Sometimes English speakers give a word focus stress in order to correct their listener's comprehension mistakes, or to contrast information.

No, I didn't go to <u>Liverpool</u>. I went to <u>Newcastle</u>.

In the Listening Test, focus stress can help you to predict where the answers might be, as key information to answer questions may be presented with strong focus stress.

Exercise 22 Catching the focus

Now, listen to the final part of the talk on the decline of handwriting. Underline the words the speaker wants the listener to focus on. Why does she particularly stress these words?

Devices such as notebooks, interactive whiteboards and e-book readers have all found a place in our schools and universities. Texting and social networking sites like Facebook completely dominate our lives outside of work. But as we continue to embrace new technology, what role do we leave for traditional forms of text construction, such as handwriting? Are we disadvantaging our young people with this blind acceptance of digital technologies? Indeed, many young people struggle to form words by hand and can't even spell. This has already become a significant problem both in school and tertiary education, as handwritten exams still form the main method of assessment.

Now check the answer key and read the comments on the use of focus stress in this passage.

There is more information on focus stress in 2.4 (pages 117–18) in the context of the IELTS Speaking Test.

Unit 1: Listening

Understanding the status of information

Listening to a person's **intonation** (the way their voice goes up and down) can help you understand the **status**, or role, of the information that the speaker is giving. If the information they are giving is main information, a rising or high tone is used (↗). If the information is additional or is a comment on the main information, a falling or low tone is used (↘). In the Listening Test, paying attention to intonation patterns can help you predict where the answers might be found.

Example

This year I'm studying chemistry ↗↘ – in fact I've just bought the main textbook – and physics. ↗↘

Exercise 23 — Understanding the status of information

Listen to part of a lecture on educational multimedia. As you listen, pay particular attention to the intonation the speaker is using and indicate *important* or *main information* by adding directional arrows above the relevant parts of the sentence. The first few sentences have been done for you as an example.

Good morning, class. Today, I'd like to talk about ↗

producing educational multimedia. This particular

type of multimedia ↘ – as distinct from entertainment

multimedia ↗ – is an area of interest for educators

everywhere. I'd particularly like to discuss the process of producing this type of

multimedia. Your first consideration, apart from deciding what medium you're

going to deliver your product through, is your audience. Who they are, what they

expect and, most importantly, what they need. After you have determined this

basic information about your users, then you can go on to the all important area

of content.

Attention to intonation can help you to predict what is coming next in a long talk. This is particularly relevant in Section 4 of the Listening Test, where you need to listen to part of an academic lecture. Specifically, it can help you determine what is **finished** and **unfinished information**. If a speaker is about to finish giving information, their intonation will rise and then fall sharply, but if the information is unfinished, with more to come, the intonation will be steady with a low rise.

In the following sentence, the speaker uses intonation to indicate she has *finished* her list.

Example

I think we're ready. We've got pens, pencils, erasers and a stapler.

Exercise 24   Understanding the status of information

Listen to the intonation in the following sentences and determine whether the information is complete or not. As you listen, write **C** for 'complete' or **I** for 'incomplete' next to the sentences. The first sentence has been done for you as an example.

1 Cacti are part of a group of plants called succulents.   *I*
2 I'd like you to meet my friend, Vanessa.   ....
3 We have a wide variety of language courses, including Arabic, Tagalog, Thai.   ....
4 Educational multimedia can be delivered via CD-ROM or over the Internet.   ....
5 Flight number 823 from Kuala Lumpur is delayed.   ....
6 I'd like to speak to the Managing Director, please.   ....

Exercises 44 to 46 on pages 123–5 give you a chance to practise intonation in the context of the IELTS Speaking Test.

Unit 1: Listening

Understanding what speakers are doing

As well as understanding what speakers are saying, effective listeners understand what speakers are doing. They understand the **purpose** of speech.

People always have a reason for speaking, that is, they are trying to *do* things when they speak. For example, they may want to explain, thank, apologise, invite, complain or persuade. If you can determine what speakers are *doing*, it will be easier to understand what they are *saying*.

You are able to work out what people are doing when they speak because you:

▼ are familiar with some of the standard ways of doing these things. For example, you know that when people make a request they often use words like *would you mind* or *could you* or *please*, and the way they speak sounds like a question

▼ can see the 'big picture' or context. For example, if the speakers are at an airline check-in desk you can guess that they are probably doing things like requesting, asking for information, explaining and/or thanking.

In the Listening Test speakers have conversations and present monologues.

CONVERSATIONS (Two or more people talking to each other)		MONOLOGUES (One person talking)	
Section 1	**Section 3**	**Section 2**	**Section 4**
A conversation between two people	A conversation between two to four speakers	A speaker making an announcement or presenting some information to an audience	A speaker presenting a talk to an audience
Speakers do things like greeting, giving and asking for information about things and about themselves, telling stories, requesting, explaining, giving and asking for opinions, or talking about events, plans and preferences.		A single speaker does things like giving information, explaining, advising, warning, arguing, describing, comparing, classifying, or describing processes or problems and solutions.	

It is not possible to predict exactly what type of conversations or monologues will occur in the Listening Test. The best way to prepare for the test is to have extensive practice in listening to a *very wide range* of conversations and monologues. See the suggestions about how to extend your practice in 1.5 (pages 48–54).

In Sections 1 and 3 of the Listening Test, it is important to be able to work out what speakers are doing in conversations or monologues of different lengths. Exercise 25 gives you practice in understanding what speakers are doing in short extracts of conversations, while Exercise 26 features longer conversations.

Exercise 25 Guessing what speakers are doing

Listen to the recording and decide what the speakers are doing. Select from the possible answers below. There is one more answer than you need. The first answer has been given as an example.

asking for information	reassuring	requesting	arguing
giving advice	inviting	declining	insisting
asking for advice	~~greeting~~	describing	

1 ....*greeting*..
2 ....
3 ....
4 ....
5 ....
6 ....
7 ....
8 ....
9 ....
10 ....

When you listen to longer conversations or monologues, you would normally use three types of information together to work out what a speaker is doing:

1 your knowledge of vocabulary: What key words are the speakers using?
2 the context (situation): Who are the speakers and where are they?
3 your judgment about the speakers' attitudes: How do the speakers sound (angry, happy, confused, etc)?

Listen to the woman on the recording. Three questions will help you decide what she is doing.

Example

1 How does she sound? *She sounds angry/upset.*
2 What is the context? *She is in a supermarket (speaking to the manager).*
3 What are some of the key words she uses? *really unhappy, disgusting*

When you consider these three things together, you can see that she is: *complaining*.

Unit 1: Listening

Exercise 26 Guessing what speakers are doing

LISTENING
CD 1 · Track 30

Listen to the five situations. For each situation, decide what the woman (the first speaker) is doing. The first one has been done for you as an example. You may need to listen to each situation twice before deciding.

1 a	How does she sound?	happy, warm, positive
b	What is the context?	a university (because of 'pass', 'distinction', 'student union')
c	What are some of the key words she uses?	good news, wonderful, well done, happy for you
d	What is she doing?	She is congratulating (the other person).
2 a	How does she sound?	
b	What is the context?	
c	What are some of the key words she uses?	
d	What is she doing?	
3 a	How does she sound?	
b	What is the context?	
c	What are some of the key words she uses?	
d	What is she doing?	
4 a	How does she sound?	
b	What is the context?	
c	What are some of the key words she uses?	
d	What is she doing?	
5 a	How does she sound?	
b	What is the context?	
c	What are some of the key words she uses?	
d	What is she doing?	

Sample answers are provided in the answer key.

Focusing on IELTS Listening and Speaking Skills

Anticipating what speakers will do next

When people speak they use words that help their listener work out the direction of a conversation or monologue. Examples include words such as *however*, *although*, *because*, *that*, *but* and *on the other hand*. When we hear these words, we can anticipate the type of information that will be given next. For example:

The food at that restaurant was fantastic *but* the service ...

Because you know that *but* introduces a **contrast**, you can anticipate that the next statement will be negative (maybe something like: *but the service was terrible*).

We can call these words **link words** because they link two different pieces of information (for example, 'food fantastic'/'service terrible') or **signpost words** because they show you what direction the speaker is going to take next. Effective listeners catch these signpost words and use them to anticipate what the speaker is going to do next (explain further, compare, etc). This helps them follow conversations and monologues more successfully.

Exercise 27   Anticipating what speakers will do next

The following sentences contain a number of incomplete statements, each including a common signpost word (in *italics*). What do these signpost words tell you about what is coming next? Select your answers from the boxed options and write the appropriate letter beside the statement. The first one has been done for you as an example.

A	describe a cause	**D**	express a contrast
B	give an example or illustration	**E**	make a comparison
C	describe a possibility	**F**	provide further information

1 He was hoping that the weather would be fine *but* ...   *E*
2 Three students will have to repeat the assignment, *namely* Mark, ...
3 There are so many ways to improve your fitness, *for instance* ...   .
4 Women tend to express their feelings more openly, *while* men ...   .
5 The outdoor concert had to be cancelled *due to* ...   .
6 People living in rural areas tend to be *more* conservative *than* ...   .
7 To everyone's surprise he was given a promotion at work *despite* ...   .
8 *Although* she was very nervous in the interview, she ...   .
9 You can get calcium in many foods, *such as* ...   .
10 This photocopier is *not as* clear *as* ...   .
11 He thought the boss would change his mind. *However*, ...
12 *If* she passes the test, she will ...   .

Unit 1: Listening

Exercise 28 provides practice in anticipating what might be coming next in a short talk. This is particularly useful for Section 4 of the Listening Test.

Exercise 28 Anticipating what speakers will do next

You are going to listen to a short presentation about gardens. Throughout the presentation there are brief pauses. Each time you hear a pause, anticipate:

▼ what the speaker is going to do next (for example, give a reason, express a contrast, etc)

and/or

▼ what words the speaker might say next.

As the speaker continues, note whether you have anticipated correctly. Finally, check the transcript for the complete talk.

Giving information: times, dates, numbers and letters

One very common thing that people do in conversations and monologues is to **give information**. This information may include times, dates, numbers and letters. For the Listening Test, especially Section 1, you may have to understand times, dates, numbers and letters as spoken by native speakers. Listen to the following examples.

Examples

Category	Examples
times	a quarter past four, ten to nine, half past twelve
dates	the 5th of March, the 21st of November, the 13th of February
numbers	three point five, seventeen, seventy, fifth, three quarters, eight and a half million
letters	UN, USA, S-t-e-v-e-n, IBM, c-a-t-e-g-o-r-y, M-a-r-i-a, c-l-i-c-k

In the Listening Test, it is also important to be able to *record this information on the answer sheet correctly* because incorrectly spelt responses could be marked as wrong. Dates and numbers are particularly challenging to spell. Do you know how to spell the days of the week and the months in English? For numbers, it is usually acceptable to write either numerals (for example, 5.6, 7000) or words (five point six, seven thousand) in your answer. Large and decimal numbers (for example, 1,200,000, 6.2) need correct punctuation, and ordinal numbers and fractions (for example, fourth or 4th, two-thirds or 2/3) need to be written or spelt correctly.

Exercise 29 — Giving information: times, dates, numbers and letters

Complete these lists of the days of the week and the months.

Days of the week	Months
Monday	January
1	**4**
2	March
Thursday	April
Friday	May
3	**5**
Sunday	July
	August
	September
	6
	November
	7

Fill in the missing information in the following table by giving the corresponding numeral or number written out in words.

Numerals	Number in words
250,000	**8**
9	Fiftieth
6.4	**10**
11	Four million, six-hundred thousand
2/5	**12**
13	Nine thousand and seventy-six

Unit 1: Listening   39

Exercise 30 — Listening for times, dates, numbers and letters

Answer the questions below.
Write NO MORE THAN THREE WORDS OR NUMBERS for each answer.

1 What is the caller's membership number? ....
2 What is the surname currently written on her library card? ....
3 What is the correct spelling of her family name? ....
4 What is her first name? ....
5 What is her full address? .... Clapham
6 When was her book due to be returned? ....
7 What is the new due date for returning her book? ....
8 What is her mother's hobby? ....
9 Who wrote the book she is looking for? ....
10 When does she think the book was published? ....
11 When is she going to collect the book? ....
12 What time does the library open during the week? ....
13 What time does the library close during the week? ....
14 What time does the library close on a Sunday? ....
15 What is the librarian's name? ....

Describing procedures and processes

Speakers sometimes describe procedures (what you should do) and processes (how things are done). For example:

> Fill in this form, attach a photo and submit it to the visa section. Your application will then be considered and you will be notified by mail.

Typical features of processes and procedures include:

- sequencing or ordering language, such as *first*, *then*, *after that*, *finally*
- instructions or imperatives, such as '*lift* the lid', '*switch on* the power', '*click on* start', or words such as *should* or *need to*
- descriptions of steps in the process using passive verb forms, such as 'the water *is heated*', 'the impurities *are removed*', 'the water *is bottled*'.

Focusing on IELTS Listening and Speaking Skills

Exercise 31 — Listening for processes

Listen to the recording and complete questions 1 to 5 in the table below.
Write NO MORE THAN THREE WORDS for each answer.

Flour milling

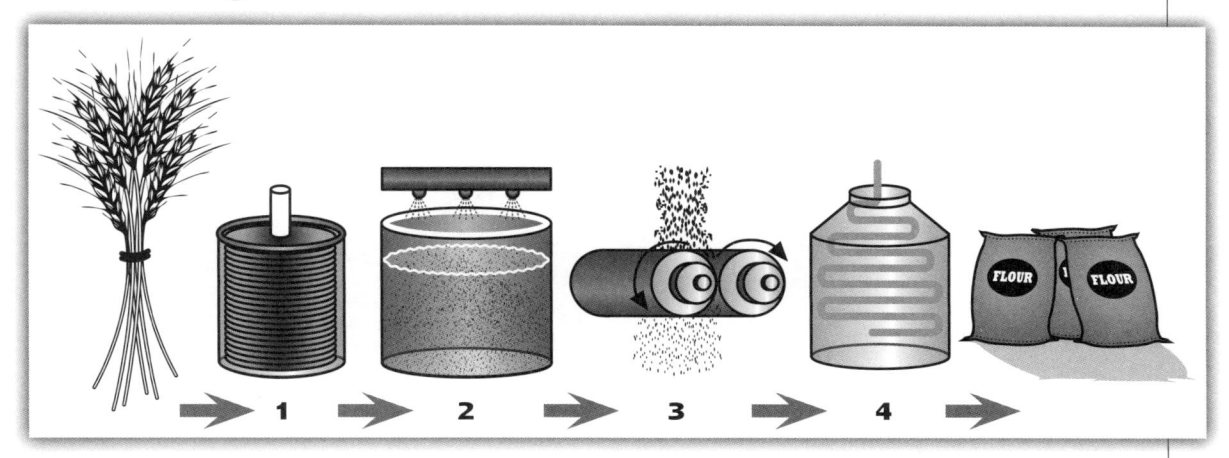

Stage	cleaning	1	2	bleaching	5 ....
Equipment	bins	sprinklers	3	vats	sacks
Result	removes dirt/debris	makes the kernels soft	splits the kernels	makes the flour 4	packs the flour

Describing objects

Speakers occasionally describe objects. For example:

This is a gas heater. Here are the controls: the on–off button is here on the left, and this is the temperature control.

Typical features of descriptions of objects are:

▼ descriptions of location, using such prepositions of place as *in*, *behind*, *in front of*, *below*, *to the left of*

▼ descriptions of the object's component parts, including *consists of*, *comprise*, *made of*

▼ descriptions of the object's operation, using verbs such as *moves*, *slides*, *grinds*, *chops*, *removes*, *filters*, *measures*.

Unit 1: Listening

Exercise 32 — Listening for descriptions of objects

Listen to the recording and label the diagram of the barometer.
Write NO MORE THAN THREE WORDS for each answer.

1 .... barometer means non- 2 ....

needle

vacuum chamber

3 ....
4 ....
5 ....
6 ....

Explaining cause and effect

Speakers sometimes explain cause and effect. For example:

Children nowadays are more violent because of the television they watch and the computer games they play.

Here the cause is television and computer games, and the effect (or result) is violence among children.

Cause and effect statements typically include words that link causes to effects: for example, *because*, *be due to*, *can be attributed to*, *result from*, *cause*, *lead to*.

Exercise 33 — Listening for explanations of cause and effect

Listen to the recording. As you listen, decide if each of the items in the list below is a cause (**C**) or an effect (**E**). One answer has been given for you as an example.

1. his flight was delayed .... C ....
2. driver fatigue ....
3. five-per-cent fall in the New York stock exchange ....
4. greater numbers of native birds in garden ....
5. more loose sea ice ....
6. endless delays ....
7. she didn't pass the medical ....
8. massive increase in flooding ....

Making comparisons

Speakers often compare things. For example:

National phone calls after 8 pm are usually much cheaper than calls during the day.

Typical features of comparisons are:

▼ words that link the things being compared, such as *whereas, on the other hand, but, although, while, than, not as ... as*

▼ words that describe the comparison, such as *same, similar, different, older, oldest, (much) more beautiful, most beautiful, less, the least.*

Exercise 34 Listening for comparisons

Listen to the recording and complete the table below.

	Trinidad	Tobago
Area	4,828 km²	300 km²
Shape	1	2 ....
Elevation	3 .... m	4 .... m
Percentage of population	5 .... %	6 .... %
Year colonised by Britain	7	8 ....

When you finish, check the answer key and then read the transcript and identify the speaker's signpost words (for example 'whereas') and comparison words (for example, 'larger').

Classifying

Speakers occasionally classify (categorise). For example:

There are three kinds of bus ticket available: daily, weekly or monthly.

Words that typically introduce classification (categorisation) include *there are, kinds, types, sorts, ways, can be divided into.*

Unit 1: Listening

Exercise 35 Listening for classifications

Listen to the recording and complete the classification diagrams below. The first one has been done for you as an example.

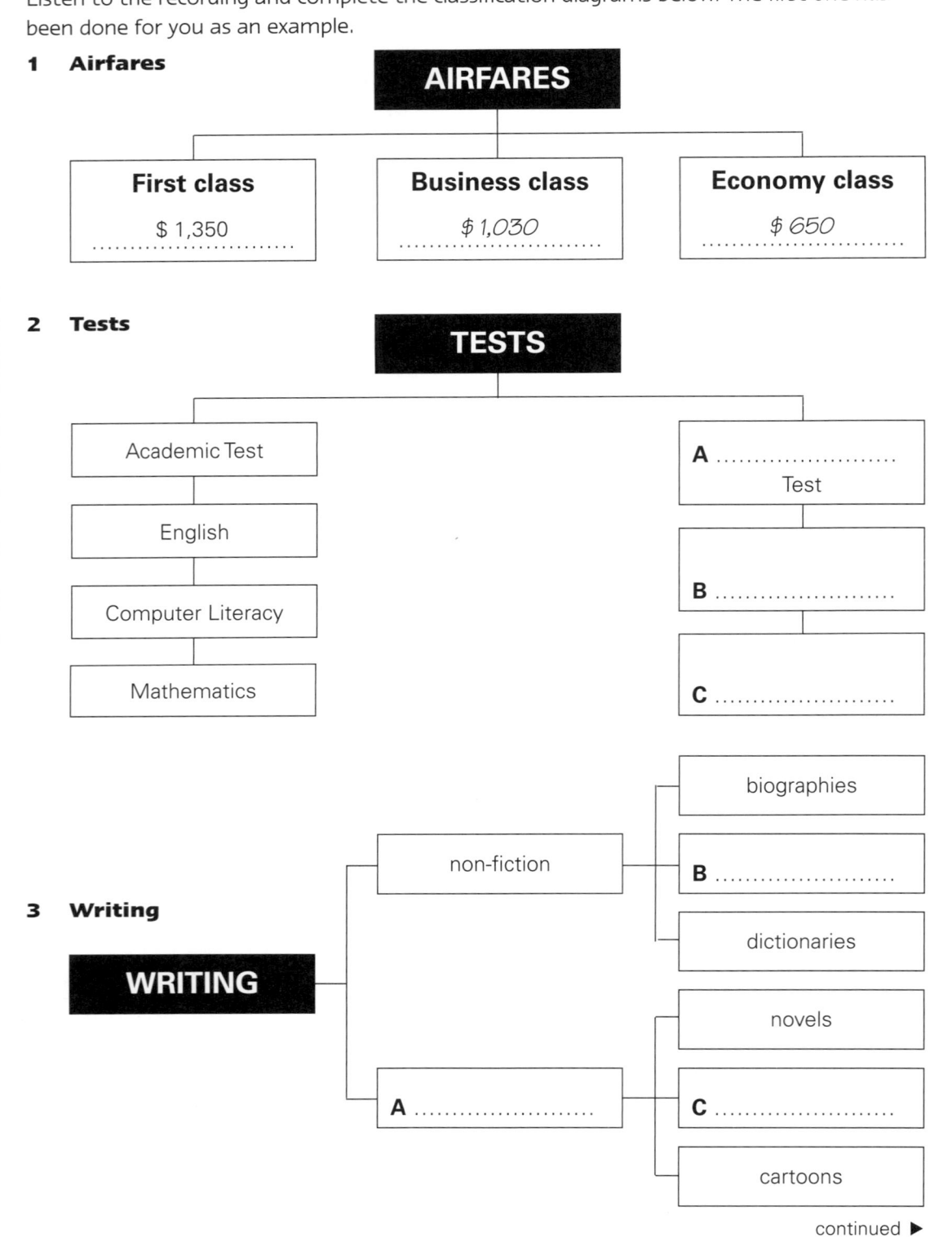

1 Airfares

```
                    AIRFARES
       ┌───────────────┼───────────────┐
  First class     Business class   Economy class
   $ 1,350          $ 1,030           $ 650
```

2 Tests

```
                    TESTS
       ┌───────────────────────────────┐
  Academic Test                  A ............ Test
       │
    English                      B ............
       │
  Computer Literacy
       │
   Mathematics                   C ............
```

3 Writing

```
                            ┌──── biographies
              ┌─ non-fiction ─┼──── B ............
              │               └──── dictionaries
   WRITING ───┤
              │               ┌──── novels
              └─ A ........... ┼──── C ............
                              └──── cartoons
```

continued ▶

44 Focusing on IELTS Listening and Speaking Skills

4 Languages

A ....   B ....   C ....

5 Australian flightless birds

Name of bird	A	
B	Western	Eastern
C	darker colour	lighter colour
	develops white collar around neck when breeding	does not change colour when breeding

Arguing a viewpoint

Speakers sometimes argue (present and strongly support their opinions). For example:

I believe the other candidate holds an outdated idea about this issue and needs to update their knowledge in this area.

In a typical argument, the speaker presents a position, opinion or viewpoint. For example: *I think/believe we should/ought to adopt this method*. To support this, the speaker may present:

▼ evidence: for example, *in the research study, injuries fell by 20%*

▼ comparisons: for example, *this method is safer*

▼ reasons: for example, *because it will reduce accidents*

▼ examples: for example, *for instance, in factories ...*

Exercise 36 Listening for arguments

Listen to the speakers and answer the questions.
Write the first letter of the name below

T = **T**om   D = **D**iane
M = **M**rs Blake   J = **J**ulie

1 Who is in favour of continuous assessment?

   ....

2 Who is in favour of formal examinations?

   ....

When you finish, check your answers. Then look at the transcript and underline the reasons which people give to support their opinions.

Unit 1: Listening

Exercise 37   Listening for arguments

Listen to speakers 1 to 5. As you listen, decide whether the speaker agrees or disagrees with the statements listed below. Write 'Agree' or 'Disagree' next to the statement

1   We should use more solar power.   ....
2   Anti-drug television commercials can be very effective.   ....
3   Distance study has many advantages.   ....
4   Marine pollution is not as serious as we first thought.   ....
5   Boxing should be banned.   ....

Describing problems and solutions

Speakers occasionally describe problems and present solutions. For example:

The city has an unsustainably high level of consumption of state-supplied water. However, the problem could be solved if gray water was recycled and citizens were encouraged to save and use their own water rather than rely on the government.

Typical features of describing problems and solutions are:

▼ The speaker gives information about a problem and then gives a range of possible solutions.

▼ To present the problem, the speaker uses a range of structures to indicate the extent of the problem: for example, 'The water shortage has been particularly severe since 2008'. They may also focus on the causes of or reasons for the problem: for example, 'There are several reasons why the city faces an acute water issue'.

▼ When offering solutions, the speaker uses ordering (sequencing) language: for example, 'One possible solution' or 'Another way to fix the problem'.

Exercise 38   Listening for descriptions of problems and solutions

Listen to the short talk and complete the summary below using ONE WORD only.

Effective group work in higher education can help produce graduates who hold well-developed **1** .... and negotiation skills. To encourage this, careful attention to group composition is very important. The **2** .... way to organise groups is to allow group members to self-select who they will work with. However, **3** .... groups often produce much better results. To ensure the group runs smoothly, you need to check members **4** .... with each other and have the same **5** .... regarding quality of work and grades.

Telling a story

Speakers often narrate or tell a story. For example:

A strange thing happened to me in the office today. It was just after lunch and I was going through my emails, when …

Typical features of story-telling are:

▼ Speakers make extended use of the first person (*I*, *me*, *my*) and other personal pronouns, such as *him/her*, *they*, etc.

▼ Speakers may use ordering language: for example, *first*, *after that*.

▼ In common with most spoken language, the speaker may use long, rambling clauses connected with simple clause connectors (such as *and*, *so* and *but*) and vague, idiomatic or slang language.

▼ Reporting verbs are used to describe actions in the past: for example, 'she *told* me', 'they *asked* me'.

Exercise 39 Listening for stories

Label the map. Choose your answers from the box below. Write the appropriate letters, **B** to **E**, on the map below.

A registration
B conference hub
C poster hall
D cafeteria
E main presentation hall

1 ....
4 ....
3 ....
2 ....

Unit 1: Listening

1.5 Developing an independent study program

To prepare for the IELTS Listening Test you need to devise a study program that will help you develop your listening strategies and skills independently. The first step is to identify your needs.

Identifying your needs

Think about what you need to work on in your study program and tick those items in the checklist below.

Listening checklist ✓

1 **Do you need to improve your general listening? Which areas need particular attention?**
   - [ ] Understanding vocabulary
   - [ ] Guessing the meaning of unknown words
   - [ ] Recognising meaning through pronunciation

2 **Which aspects of the Listening Test do you need to find out more about and practise?**
   - [ ] The format of the test (number of sections, types of questions, etc)
   - [ ] Section 1: A conversation between two speakers about a social (non-academic) topic
   - [ ] Section 2: A monologue about a social (non-academic) topic
   - [ ] Section 3: A conversation between two to four speakers about an academic topic
   - [ ] Section 4: A university-style presentation by one speaker about an academic topic

3 **Which specific strategies and skills do you need to improve for the Listening Test?**
   - [ ] Listening for specific information
   - [ ] Focusing on more than one question
   - [ ] Matching the meaning
   - [ ] Anticipating what speakers will do next
   - [ ] Listening for times, dates, numbers and letters
   - [ ] Listening for procedures and processes
   - [ ] Listening for descriptions of objects
   - [ ] Listening for explanations of cause and effect
   - [ ] Listening for comparisons
   - [ ] Listening for classifications
   - [ ] Listening for arguments
   - [ ] Listening for descriptions of problems and solutions
   - [ ] Listening for stories

When you have completed the checklist, note the section(s) where you have the most ticks and read the relevant section below to discover how you can develop an effective and relevant program of independent study. You can also check the Listening skills and strategies summary on page viii to make sure you've completed the relevant exercises.

Improving your general listening

If you need to learn more new vocabulary, guess the meaning of unknown words more efficiently or understand spoken pronunciation better, the suggestions below will help you. It is important to immerse yourself in spoken English to improve your general listening skills. Listen to one or more of the following sources *daily*.

Radio

Find local and national English-language radio stations that feature interviews or talkback (where listeners telephone the station to give their views on current issues). International English-language radio stations, such as the BBC World Service, Voice of America, the Canadian Broadcasting Corporation or Radio Australia, provide live streaming and podcasts through their websites.

Television

Watch English-language television as much as possible. Look for material that features conversations (for example, soap operas, talk shows) and announcements or presentations (for example, news or current affairs programs, documentaries). Record these programs to watch again so you can analyse the language the presenters use.

DVDs/Videos

Use DVDs or videos (for example, films, documentaries) to practise listening to extended examples of spoken English. Try to get material with a variety of accents – not just Hollywood movies in American English. Display the subtitles if you are having trouble understanding what you hear, but don't leave the subtitles on for extended periods (you will be doing more reading than listening). Stop and replay scenes to catch what you missed the first time around.

Websites

Search for relevant websites on the Internet. A useful starting point is the official IELTS site: <www.ielts.org>. Use a reliable search engine like Google, <www.google.com>, to find web-based IELTS practice resources. Search for 'IELTS listening practice online' or 'IELTS listening practice material' to bring up hundreds of sites. New websites are being created all the time (and existing websites change), so be prepared to search often and extensively.

ESL listening resources

English as a Second Language (ESL) listening resources are usually the best source of material for structured listening practice. Check public libraries, specialist ESL bookshops or online bookshops, such as Amazon.com, for specific IELTS listening materials – usually a book and CD(s) that you buy together as a package. Look for resources that contain conversations, announcements and short presentations or lectures at an upper-intermediate or advanced level. Try to find listening material that presents both male and female speakers using a range of accents and featuring both individual and multiple speakers. It is useful if the package includes transcripts of the recordings to use for follow-up or when listening for a second time.

Listening preparation materials for other exams, such as the Test of English as a Foreign Language (TOEFL) and the Cambridge Certificate in Advanced English (CAE), can also be useful for IELTS if used selectively.

Practising for specific sections

Your first resource for finding out more about the Listening Test is the recording accompanying this book. If you haven't already done so, make sure you do all the exercises in the unit.

You can also find out more about the demands of the test by interviewing people who have already successfully completed IELTS. Ask them what they did to prepare for the Listening Test and ask for their advice. If possible, record what they have to say.

Practice Listening Tests

If you are still not confident about the format of the Listening Test after studying Unit 1 of this book, it may be useful to complete a number of practice tests. By doing these, you can familiarise yourself with the layout and appearance of the IELTS test and practise transferring your answers to the answer sheet. You can also get used to the flow of the test as it progresses from Section 1 to Section 4. There is a practice test in 1.6, pages 55–60 of this book.

> It is not useful to do large numbers of practice tests – one or two per week in the month leading up to the real exam is a good amount to aim for. It is also not at all useful to memorise practice test material, nor to do a practice test more than once.

Practice for Sections 1 and 2

In Sections 1 and 2, the focus is on listening for and noting specific factual information while listening to speaker(s) in an informal context. If you live in an English-speaking country, you can easily practise this type of listening in almost any informal social situation. Listen to people's conversations in shops, on public transport, or at cafes or restaurants. Eavesdrop on people and listen to the way they use and pronounce words. Note how people stress words and listen to their intonation. If you don't live in an English-speaking country, you can do the same thing but you will need to access non-live listening material from multimedia resources, such as the Internet or commercial listening resources.

Practice for Section 3

In Section 3, the focus is on listening for specific information, attitudes and speakers' opinions in a conversation in an academic context. This means you need to practise listening to more complex conversations, often involving three or four people discussing something to do with their studies at college or university. This is difficult to do in real life unless you are going to college or university in an English-speaking country. However, try to access other material where you can listen to people clearly expressing their opinions or attitudes in discussions. For example, many English-language television dramas or soap operas include such conversations.

Practice for Section 4

In Section 4, the focus is on listening for main ideas, specific information, attitudes and speakers' opinions in a short academic presentation. A good way to practise is to listen to authentic academic lectures on a variety of topics. You may be able to access these from individual university websites, although they are usually provided without written transcripts. Commercially produced listening resources for English for Academic Purposes (EAP) are a good source of mini-lectures about different topics.

Practising specific strategies and skills

If you need to practise the different strategies and skills required for the Listening Test, covered in 1.4, the following suggestions will help you organise your study.

Listen for specific information

When using commercially produced ESL textbooks to practise listening, look at the questions carefully first and decide what specific information you need to listen for in order to answer the questions (review Exercises 8 to 11 on pages 14–17 as a reminder of this strategy). Practise the strategy when you do any listening exercises and when you do the practice test in 1.6.

You can also make up your own **focus questions** when you listen to other material. For example, before you watch the television news, set yourself some simple questions to focus your listening, such as:

- What is the first news item about today?
- How many stories mention England?
- List all of the countries mentioned today.
- How many positive or happy stories are there today?
- How many news stories today will mention the words *injury* or *injured*?

Focus on more than one question

When doing the Listening Test, you will need to focus on more than one question at a time so that you do not miss an answer and fall behind. Exercises 12 and 13 on pages 18 and 19 provide specific practice at this, and you can also practise this strategy when you do other exercises (for example, Exercises 14, 30 to 32, and 34) and apply it when you do the practice test.

To practise this strategy by yourself, have **sets of questions** ready before listening. One easy set of questions to use is the *wh-* set – *who, what, when, what time, where, why* – and maybe *how*. You could choose three of these and when listening to the radio or television news, or the practice exercises on the recording, you can be ready to answer these questions. For example: *Who* is this about? *What* happened? *Where* did it happen? In this way, you are focusing on three questions at the same time, as you will need to do in the Listening Test. As you become more confident, you can add more *wh-* questions to your set. As you listen, you can make notes to help answer the questions.

Match the meaning

When matching what you see in the question paper with what you hear on the recording, you are trying to find the same *meaning*, not just the same words. You can practise matching the meaning when you do multiple-choice questions (for example, Exercise 10, page 17). Look at the answers offered and think of other ways of saying them. Then listen to the recording and match.

If you have access to English-language newspapers, television or radio, you can do a **multimedia match**. For example, first read the headlines of three stories on the front page of the newspaper. Then think of other ways of expressing the same meaning as the headlines; for example, what synonyms could be used? Then listen to the news on the television or

52 **Focusing on IELTS** Listening and Speaking Skills

radio and note what words have been used to convey the same meaning. If possible, record the broadcast so that you can compare the different versions more closely. Learn any useful synonyms you find.

Listen to people's pronunciation

To catch what people are saying in the Listening Test, you must be able to understand their pronunciation. To practise listening to people, it is best to record them. In this way you can pause and repeat as many times as you need.

If you have recordings of native speakers, **transcribe** what you hear and ask a suitable person to correct your transcription. If there are errors, see how these errors might relate to difficulties you have in listening to English native-speaker pronunciation.

A useful independent study exercise is to listen to a **short talk** in English – it's also useful to have a transcript of the talk so you can check it later. Any topic is suitable, as long as it is not too technical. As you play the recording, listen to how the speaker pronounces words. You may need to listen several times. As a follow-up exercise, you could listen again and count the number of words in particular sentences or transcribe a paragraph. It is likely that you will underestimate the number of words that you hear. This is because many words are contracted or unstressed in spoken English.

To learn how **stress** and **intonation** are used in English, listen to a conversation, short talk or lecture in English for which you have a transcript (or write one yourself). Mark on the transcript the words that are strongly stressed. This will show you how speakers use stress to highlight information. Think about why certain words are stressed. Is it to give opposite or contrasting information? Is it to add information?

Listen to people's vocabulary

Try to catch **new words** when listening to a news story on the radio or television (key words are often repeated several times in a story). Then search for the same story in a newspaper to see if the same new words are used. Then cross-check for these words in a dictionary and thesaurus. Take note of any useful new words you find and write them in your personal dictionary. Keep expanding your vocabulary – try to learn at least *three* new words a day.

Listen to what people are doing

You need to be able to follow what people are doing when they speak, whether they are, for example, apologising, describing, comparing or complaining. Exercises 25 and 26 on pages 35 and 36 provide practice at working out what speakers are doing.

For further practice, each time you listen to something, ask yourself: what am I listening to? Is it a conversation or a monologue (an announcement, presentation or lecture)? More specifically, ask yourself what the speaker is doing: for example, comparing, greeting, explaining, apologising or describing a process. You can also do this in **real-life listening**. For example, what are the people in the seat in the front of you in the train doing? Are they chatting about the weather, discussing their plans, teasing each other or complaining about their boss?

Another important skill to practise is **anticipating**, or knowing what the speaker is going to say or do *next*. Exercises 27 and 28 on pages 37 and 38 provide practice at this. To practise this, use any recording in this book. Stop the recording at different points and see if you can anticipate what the speaker is going to say or do next. Then continue listening and see how accurately you have anticipated.

You can also practise this strategy when you are **watching television**. For example, you could record an English-language TV drama and then play it back, pausing the action in a dramatic scene and anticipating what your favourite character is going to say next. Start the recording again and check whether your prediction was right. You can also practise this (in your mind) when you are listening to live speakers.

Exercises for study partners

If possible, choose a partner of the same English language level – maybe someone from your class who wants to do the IELTS test at the same time as you. It would be best if this person spoke a different first language from you, so you can work solely in English. Having a study partner to practise listening with can be enjoyable and motivating.

Write short-answer questions

Choose a listening passage with a transcript. Write a series of *wh-* questions based on information in the passage. Exercise 9 on page 15 shows examples of the kinds of question you could write. Give the questions to your partner and allow him or her 30 seconds to read the questions. Then read the passage aloud once without pausing, while your partner answers the questions.

Listen and compare

You and your study partner could watch English-language movies on television, DVD or online together. After key scenes, stop the film and discuss what you have heard. Working together, try to summarise how the scene develops the narrative (story) of the film and anticipate what will come next. You could even try to remember the dialogue of a particular scene and act it out with your partner, noting key vocabulary and copying pronunciation patterns from what you have heard.

1.6 Practice IELTS Listening Test

This practice IELTS Listening Test has been written to simulate the real IELTS Listening Test in style, format and length. You should simulate the conditions of the IELTS Listening Test by doing the test by yourself, sitting at a distance from the recording and playing it once only, without pausing or stopping. When you finish the test, check your answers using the answer key.

Practice IELTS Listening Test

TIME ALLOWED: APPROXIMATELY 30 MINUTES, PLUS 10 MINUTES TO TRANSFER ANSWERS

NUMBER OF QUESTIONS: 40

Instructions

You will hear four different recordings and you will have to answer questions on what you hear.

There will be time for you to read the instructions and questions before the recording is played. You will also have the opportunity to check your answers.

The recordings will be played ONCE only.

The test is in four sections. Write your answers on the question sheet as you listen. At the end of Section 4, you have ten minutes to transfer your answers onto the answer sheet, which is on page 60. When you finish, check the answers at the back of the book.

SECTION 1

Questions 1–10

Questions 1–5

Complete the notes below.

Write NO MORE THAN TWO WORDS AND/OR A NUMBER for each answer.

Real estate agent: Jill Brown

Suburb suggested: 1 ....

Facilities: The **2** .... in this suburb is very good.

Transport and Location:

- Can take the **3** .... to work.
- **4** .... km from the city centre.
- Best to catch the **5** .... to the city.

Questions 6–10

Choose the correct letter, A, B or C.

6   What does the real estate agent say about the first flat?
    A   it has two small bedrooms
    B   it has two bedrooms plus an office
    C   it has one big and one small bedroom

7   Michael likes the second flat because it is
    A   away from street noise.
    B   on a higher floor.
    C   in a better building.

8   Which room in the second flat has been recently decorated?
    A   the bathroom
    B   the kitchen
    C   the living area

9   How much is the rent on the second flat?
    A $325 per week
    B $350 per week
    C $375 per week

10   What day will Michael and his wife visit the flat?
    A   Tuesday
    B   Wednesday
    C   Thursday

SECTION 2

Questions 11–20

Questions 11–15

Why should the employees see the following staff members?

Choose your answers from the box and write the correct letters, A–G, next to questions 11–15.

A to get material photocopied	E to get help with sales
B to arrange a meeting with the boss	F to get a new computer
C to deal with money problems	G to get telephone messages
D to send out an order	

11 Mark Rogers   ....
12 Lucy Scott   ....
13 Janet Bowden   ....
14 James Ferguson   ....
15 Peter Harding   ....

Questions 16–20

Complete the sentences below.

Write NO MORE THAN TWO WORDS for each answer.

16 Visitors need to get a .... to enter the building.

17 The new staff are all being given a set of ....

18 The staff are encouraged to take an exercise break of .... at regular intervals.

19 The staff are told about new products on ....

20 The staff send their completed order forms to the correct department by ....

Unit 1: Listening   57

SECTION 3

QUESTIONS 21–30

Questions 21–26

Label the diagram below.

Choose your answers from the box and write the correct letters, **A–I**, next to questions **21–26**.

A carbon	D chocolate	G ozone
B carrots	E nuts	H plastic bottles
C cast iron	F oxygen	I potatoes

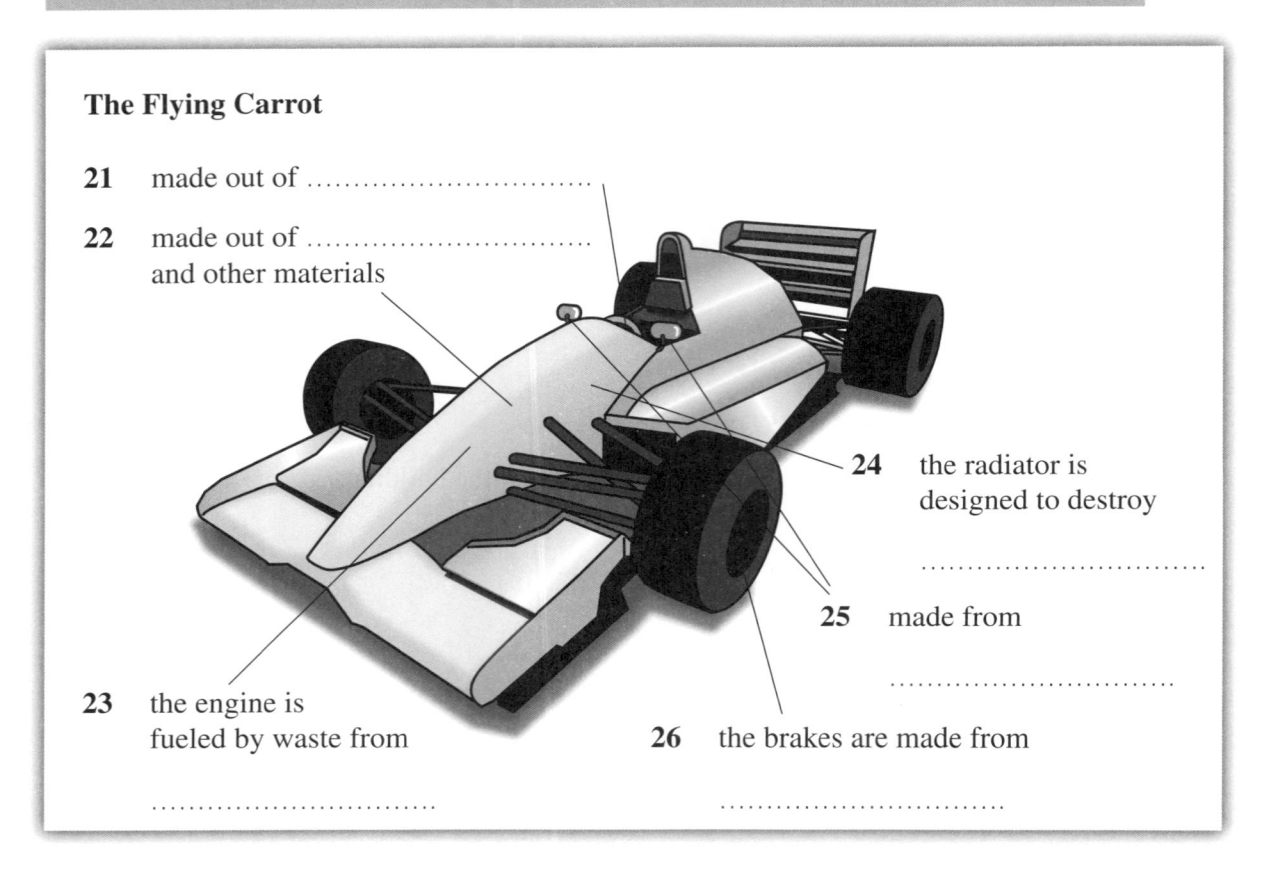

The Flying Carrot

21 made out of ....

22 made out of .... and other materials

23 the engine is fueled by waste from ....

24 the radiator is designed to destroy ....

25 made from ....

26 the brakes are made from ....

Questions 27–30

Choose the correct letter **A**, **B** or **C**.

27 Why did the design team make the car?

   A   to highlight the use of recycled materials
   B   to persuade car manufacturers to use plant-based materials
   C   to enter a design competition for environmentally friendly cars

28 Why did the design team choose a racing car?

    A   because it would attract more publicity

    B   because of recent problems in that industry

    C   because no one else has done it before

29 What do the design team plan to work on next?

    A   making the car more comfortable

    B   ensuring the car is safer to drive

    C   increasing the maximum speed of the car

30 What do the design team hope to use the car for?

    A   to promote their engineering course

    B   to take part in Formula 1 races

    C   to make people aware of the environment

SECTION 4   Questions 31–40

Questions 31–40

Complete the notes below.

*Write **NO MORE THAN TWO WORDS AND/OR A NUMBER** for each answer.*

Evolutionary biology

Definition:

▼   The study of how plants and animals evolve

Recent study:

Purpose: to find out why leaves change colour in autumn

Theory:

▼   Bright colours serve as a **31** .... (for example, to indicate there is a harmful **32** .... in the leaves or they are not nutritious).

Testing the theory:

▼   Bright colours should disappear over time in **33** .... areas.

▼   Managed to establish this in a shorter period by studying **34** ....

▼   Tests carried out in **35** .... showed trees there had the least tendency to change colour.

▼   A further test suggested that **36** .... or .... leaves were the most harmful.

Other possible theories:

i   The colours protect the leaves from **37** ....

ii   The colours help keep the trees **38** .... for longer.

iii   The colours help trees store **39** .... for winter.

iv   The colours reduce the number of **40** .... by making them easy to see.

LISTENING ANSWER SHEET

Pencil must be used to complete this sheet.

#		#	
1		21	
2		22	
3		23	
4		24	
5		25	
6		26	
7		27	
8		28	
9		29	
10		30	
11		31	
12		32	
13		33	
14		34	
15		35	
16		36	
17		37	
18		38	
19		39	
20		40	
		Total	

Unit 2
Speaking

2.1 What is in the Speaking Test?

The IELTS Speaking Test is the same for both Academic and General Training candidates.

Time allowed	11 to 14 minutes
Procedure	The Speaking Test is the last IELTS test you will sit. An examiner calls or brings you into an examination room from a waiting area. You and the examiner are alone in the examination room, sitting facing each other, with a desk between you. The examiner switches on a recorder at the beginning of the test. The purpose of this recording is to ensure that the examiner has conducted the test correctly.
Structure of test	The test consists of three parts, each with a different format. **Part 1:** Introduction and interview (4 to 5 minutes) You come into the examination room and are invited to sit down. You and the examiner exchange greetings and the examiner confirms your identity. The examiner asks a few initial questions to help you relax and then goes on to ask questions about your life, your interests and other familiar topic areas. **Part 2:** Individual long turn (3 to 4 minutes, including 1 minute to think and prepare) The examiner gives you a card with a topic written on it. You have 1 minute to think about this topic and prepare what you are going to say. Then you must speak about the topic for 1 to 2 minutes. After you finish talking, the examiner may ask one or two follow-up questions. **Part 3:** Two-way discussion (4 to 5 minutes) The examiner engages you in a discussion about topics that have the same general theme as Part 2. While some questions are reasonably straightforward, others are more complex. Note: The level of complexity increases throughout the test, i.e. Part 3 is the most difficult section of the test.
Scoring	Marks are awarded in four areas: fluency and coherence, lexical resource (vocabulary), grammatical range and accuracy, and pronunciation. You will receive a band score between 0 and 9 depending on your performance. Scores can be reported in whole or half band scores, e.g. 7.0 or 7.5.

2.2 Test-taking tips

What should you do when you take the IELTS Speaking Test? Here are some suggestions about how to manage the test as successfully as possible.

Speak as much as you can

The most important thing to do in the Speaking Test is to speak as much as possible. You should speak far more than the examiner, who should mainly be listening to what you are saying. If the examiner has to speak more than you do, then you won't do well in the test. Especially in Parts 2 and 3 of the test, give as much information as possible to answers, and don't ever give one-word answers.

Speak at a reasonable volume and speed

Speak at an appropriate volume for the examiner to hear you comfortably. Don't whisper and don't shout. Direct your voice at the examiner and not at the recorder on the desk. Remember that if you speak too softly, the examiner may ask you to speak more loudly, and you may appear less fluent. Also, be aware that when you are nervous you will tend to speak more quickly. This may make it more difficult for the examiner to understand you, particularly if you have pronunciation problems. So slow down to make what you are saying clearer.

Make a good impression

The examiner does not evaluate how you look during the test (for example, how you dress, how you sit, how confident you look, and so on), but these things may have an unconscious impact on the examiner's perception of you. As with a job interview, it is important to make a good visual impression.

- ▼ Wear neat, casual clothes. Dress comfortably, so that you feel as relaxed as possible.

- ▼ Manage your posture (the way you walk into the room, the way you hold your body while you sit). Walk into the examination room confidently. During the test, sit in a way that shows you are ready to actively participate, for example, sitting up straight with your body inclined slightly forward. Don't fold your arms across your chest or clasp your hands on your head.

- ▼ Manage your non-verbal behaviour. Look directly at the examiner when you first meet and maintain consistent eye contact with him or her throughout the test. Remember that Western cultures generally use more sustained eye contact than non-Western cultures. Your facial expression should show that you are listening. It is not necessary to smile all the time. Try to reduce any nervous gestures or expressions that you may have, such as giggling (laughing) or fidgeting (moving too much).

Know what to expect

Know what to expect in the test. Make sure that you are thoroughly familiar with the structure of the test and that you know what you have to do in each part. You don't have to worry about time management – the examiner will tell you when your time in each part of the test is finished. Like the IELTS Listening Test, the Speaking Test becomes progressively more difficult. For example, you may find that Part 1 is quite easy, but that in Part 3 you have trouble expressing your ideas. Expect this and be prepared.

Remember that the structure of the test is standardised. The examiner must follow standard procedures and questions in conducting each test so that it is fair for every candidate. This is why the examiner will record your test. If necessary, the Test Administrator can check that the examiner has conducted the test in an appropriate way.

You also should follow standard procedures. Do not ask the examiner:
- personal questions
- your result or score at the end of the test
- to evaluate your performance or to give you feedback at the end of the test.

Don't panic if asked about an unfamiliar topic

In Part 3 of the test there is a possibility that you will be asked to speak about an unfamiliar topic. If you are asked about a subject you know nothing about, you should state that you are not familiar with the area and then go on to tell the examiner anything you do know about the topic. These may be things directly or indirectly connected to the topic. To speak about related topic areas is better than no response at all. Always remember that you are being tested on your ability to communicate and *not* your general knowledge.

While thinking about your response, you should use a variety of thinking time techniques (see 'Fillers' and Exercise 11 in 2.4 on page 79).

Don't memorise

It is important to know what to expect in the Speaking Test. However, this does not mean, that you should memorise what you are going to say. If you do, the examiner will quickly see that you are saying something you have prepared, and will change the topic. It is useful to anticipate the kinds of topics and questions you may encounter in the test (see 2.3, pages 65–76), but this does not mean that you should prepare a fixed speech in advance. There are many activities in this unit that will give you ideas for good quality responses.

Try to relax

It is natural to be nervous in the Speaking Test. Examiners expect this, so there is no point in saying something like 'I am very nervous'. To manage your nervousness, try to find relaxation techniques that you can do before the test. For example, while you are waiting for the test to begin, prepare yourself for the stress of the test with slow, deep breathing; visualising relaxing images and saying positive, calming things to yourself. Also, improve your performance during the test itself by giving yourself a few moments to breathe deeply before replying to a difficult question.

2.3 Getting to know the test

The aim of this section is to familiarise you with the structure of the three parts of the IELTS Speaking Test:

- **Part 1:** Introduction and interview (4 to 5 minutes)
- **Part 2:** Individual long turn (3 to 4 minutes)
- **Part 3:** Two-way discussion (4 to 5 minutes).

It also introduces a range of topics that may occur during your interview and provides help in answering questions about these topics.

Part 1: Introduction and interview (4 to 5 minutes)

In this part of the Speaking Test you will be asked to identify yourself and to discuss familiar topics related to your personal background.

The first stage of Part 1 is concerned with recording administrative detail. After greeting you and bringing you into the room, the examiner will start the recorder and record some basic information about the interview, such as date and place, and information about the candidate and examiner.

After this, you will be asked for proof of identity. This is commonly a passport or an identity card. The examiner will also ask about your preferred 'friendly name' or 'nickname' by saying something like 'What should I call you?' Simply say the name you would like the examiner to use. There is no need to explain why you use this particular name or what your name means.

You will be asked to talk about **two or three specific topics** in Part 1. These are given by the examiner in the form of short, direct questions so you need to keep your answers brief and relevant to the topic you have been asked about – no mini-speeches required! In this part of the test, you could be using language to describe, express preferences, give opinions and reasons, explain, suggest, compare and contrast.

In the first section of Part 1, you could be asked to discuss at least *one* of the following topics. Please note that this is *not* a complete list of topics that could occur in this part of the Speaking Test.

Unit 2: Speaking

Part 1: possible initial topics

Your home

Your family home and surroundings: appearance, location, size, etc

Your home town: physical appearance, notable features, population/size, historical background, etc

Your job or studies

Job: main responsibilities, things you like or dislike about it, how long you have been doing it, etc

Studies: subjects studied, why you're studying, things you like or dislike about your course, how long you will study, what qualification you will gain, etc

You should be ready to discuss all aspects of your home, home town, job or studies in this part of the interview.

Examples

Question: How many rooms does your current accommodation have?
Response: It's only got four – a bedroom, living room, a kitchen and a bathroom.
Question: What course are you studying?
Response: I'm just finishing my last semester of a Master of Forensic Science at Monash University.

Exercise 1 — Part 1 topics – asking/answering home, job or study questions

Use information from the box 'Part 1: possible initial topics' to make questions on the topics of home and job or studies. Ask a partner your questions and note the responses. The first one has been done for you as an example to follow.

Questions about home	Responses
How long have you lived in your home town?	My family moved there from a small village in the country when I was four.

Questions about job or studies	Responses

When you have finished, check the answer key for other possible questions and responses about these topics.

After speaking about your home and job or studies, you could be asked to talk about at least *one* and possibly *two* general topics that are related to you and/or your personal background. These could include the following.

Part 1: possible general topics

1. Your family
2. Your daily routine
3. Your leisure or free-time activities
4. Your local area
5. Learning English or other languages
6. Food and drink
7. Your country and culture

Again, please note that this is *not* a complete list of topics that could occur in this section of the Speaking Test.

Unit 2: Speaking

Exercise 2 — Part 1 – asking/answering questions about general topics

Study the list of general topics in the box 'Part 1: possible general topics'. Expand on each subject area by making at least two possible questions and two possible responses for each. Then ask a partner your questions. Some examples have been given for you to follow.

General topic	Possible questions	Possible responses
1 Your family	*Do you have a large family?*	*Yes, I come from a big family.* *No, my family is quite small.*
	How many brothers and sisters do you have?	*I have one brother and one sister.* *I'm the middle child.* *I'm the only child in my family.*
	Do you still live with your family?	*No, I moved out to live by myself last year.*
2 Your daily routine	*What do you do on Monday nights?*	*I usually …*
3 Your leisure or free-time activities		*I really enjoy ………… ing …*
4 Your local area	*Is there much open space near where you live?*	
5 Learning English or other languages		
6 Food and drink		
7 Your country and culture		

When you have finished, check the answer key for other possible questions and responses about these topics.

68 **Focusing on IELTS** Listening and Speaking Skills

Exercise 3 — Listening to Part 1

Listen to Part 1 of a sample interview three times. In the first column of the table below write down the general subject areas of the questions. Then listen again and write the exact questions the examiner asked. On your final listening, concentrate on the answers given by the candidate and decide whether the answers were clear and related to the question or not. The first one has been done for you as an example.

General subject area	Exact question asked by examiner	Is the answer clear and related to the question?
1 Job/study	Are you currently studying or do you work?	Yes
2 Study	And why …	
3		
4		
5		
6		
7		
8		
9		
10		
11		

Unit 2: Speaking

Part 2: Individual long turn (3 to 4 minutes)

In Part 2 of the Speaking Test, you are given a topic and then have one minute to prepare a short presentation – this is called the individual long turn. You are asked to speak on this topic for one to two minutes. The examiner will stop you after two minutes.

In this section of the interview, you are encouraged to extend your discourse; that is, to develop one idea thoroughly by using more varied sentence structures and linking words. In Part 2 you could be using language to describe, explain, give or justify your opinion, tell a story, summarise and suggest.

The topics that you are asked to talk about in Part 2 should be familiar to you. They cover a range of subjects that are related to your normal everyday life. Note that the examiner will usually select a Part 2 topic before meeting you and it is *not* possible to request to change your topic for a different one during the interview.

A particular focus of this section is organising your ideas into a *cohesive presentation* within a time limit and making your listener understand what you are saying. You could use a mixture of formal and informal language in your talk, but overall the register (style) of your presentation should be more formal than informal.

Preparing your presentation

You have one minute to prepare what you are going to say. It is important to use *all* this time effectively. The first thing to do is to make sure you have understood what you need to talk about. If you are not entirely clear about the topic you have been given, it is perfectly OK to check your understanding with the examiner.

After you have read and understood the topic, you should think about **possible ideas** and make some **written notes** about what you are going to say. The examiner will encourage this by giving you some paper and a pencil to note down ideas. To ensure your talk is organised and follows a clear structure, these notes should relate to the points, or 'prompts', listed on the topic card. When your preparation time is finished, the examiner will tell you that you should start speaking. You are allowed to keep the topic card during your one- to two-minute talk.

The following is an example of a topic card from Part 2 of the Speaking Test.

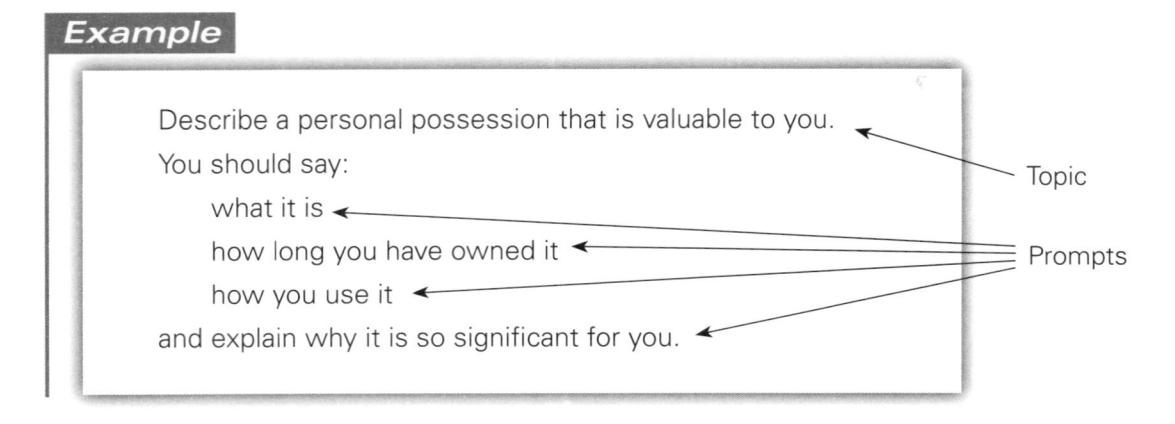

Example

Describe a personal possession that is valuable to you. — Topic
You should say:
- what it is
- how long you have owned it
- how you use it
- and explain why it is so significant for you.

— Prompts

In the example opposite, the central idea involves something you *possess* (own). Therefore, you cannot talk about a person, such as your mother or a friend; it needs to be something you have in your possession. You will notice that the central topic has already been broken down for you into a series of suggested prompts. Use these points or your own ideas (or a combination of both) in answering this question. Below is an example of one student's notes on this topic.

Example

My gold wedding ring

Since marriage fourteen years ago

Ring finger on my left hand

Symbolises continuing love and respect for each other.

Exercise 4   Practising Part 2

Consider the topic: *Describe a personal possession that is valuable to you.* In one minute, write some notes about how you would respond to this prompt.

Topic card	Your notes
Describe a personal possession that is valuable to you. You should say: 　　what it is 　　how long you have owned it 　　how you use it and explain why it is so significant for you.	

Other ideas

When you have finished, deliver your Part 2 presentation to a partner. Make sure your talk is *no longer than two minutes*.

Unit 2: Speaking

Linking your ideas

A particular focus of the long turn is the ability to extend your answers by using **compound** or **complex sentences**. There are many **linking words** in English that are used to expand ideas and present more complex information. These can be simple conjunctions, such as *and*, *but* or *so*, or more complex conjunctions, such as *although* or *because*. An important point to remember is that you should only use connecting words that sound natural when you are using them. For example, you should generally avoid formal conjunctive adverbs like *moreover* and *thus*, which are mainly used in written English.

Example

I'm going to talk about my wedding ring **and** what it means to me. I've worn it on this finger **since** we got married fourteen years ago. **However**, last year I had to have it resized as it was getting too tight for my finger.

   complex conjunction   simple conjunction   complex conjunction

Exercise 5 — Linking ideas in Part 2

1. Listen to part of a long turn about a valuable possession. Circle the conjunctions that the speaker uses to link her ideas.

   and but for or so because since

2. Listen to another long turn on the same topic. Write any linking words you hear below.

   because, ... , ... , ... , ...

   Now check your answers and read the comments on the two candidates' use of conjunctions.

In the long turn of the Speaking Test, you should use a variety of linking words to extend your ideas. For more information about and practice in using linking words, see 'Coherence' (2.4, pages 80–7) and 'Grammatical range' (2.4, pages 105–11).

Exercise 6 — Linking your ideas in Part 2

Work with a partner. Choose one of the topics below. Your partner will give you one minute to prepare notes. Then give a two-minute presentation to your partner.

A sample answer for the first topic is provided, with the linking words underlined, in the answer key. You can also listen to it on CD.

continued ▶

72   **Focusing on IELTS**   Listening and Speaking Skills

1 **Topic:** A city you would like to visit. Say:
what city it is
Rome
....
why you would like to go there
Architecture
....
how long you would stay
At least a month
....
and explain why it is such a special city for you.
Most historic and romantic city in Europe
....

2 **Topic:** A book/movie that I have recently enjoyed. Say:
what book/movie it was

....
who the main characters were

....
how it differed to similar books/movies

....
and explain why it was such a special experience for you.

....

3 **Topic:** A leader who has greatly influenced me. Say:
who he or she is or was

....
what he or she did that was so significant

....
what other people think about this person

....
and explain how he or she personally influenced your life.

....

4 **Topic:** An unforgettable event in your life. Say:
what the event was

....
why it was so significant

....
who else it was unforgettable for

....
and explain how it changed your life.

....

Unit 2: Speaking

Part 3: Two-way discussion (4 to 5 minutes)

The final part of the Speaking Test is a two-way discussion, in which you participate in a more abstract discussion. The subject is always related to the topic you have spoken about in Part 2. The focus of this section is on developing or expanding an idea into a free-flowing discussion with the examiner. For example, if the topic of the presentation in Part 2 was schools or schooling, the topic under discussion in Part 3 could be one of the following:

1 differences between national educational systems
2 recent developments in education or educational technology and how they have influenced teaching
3 different styles or methods of teaching and learning between different cultures.

Recognising what you are being asked to do

In this section you could be using language to describe, speculate, evaluate, suggest, identify, assess, explain, consider, predict, exemplify (give examples), compare or contrast. Because of the complexity and interactive nature of this section, you may also be using language to clarify meaning and repair communication breakdowns if they occur.

Exercise 7 — Recognising what you are being asked to do

Look at the following list of language functions that you may be required to use in Part 3 of the Speaking Test. Check to make sure you know what they mean. Listed below them are a number of the sort of questions that may appear in Part 3. Match a question to a function and write the appropriate letter in the space provided. Use each function once only. The first one has been done for you as an example to follow.

Functions

A Explain	C Contrast	E Identify	G Suggest
B Evaluate	D Speculate	F Describe	H Predict

1 What will be some major technological trends in the next 50 years? ......H......
2 What are some differences in the use of technology between developed and developing countries? ....
3 How can we make the best use of technology in education? ....
4 How can we account for the recent explosive growth in online education? ....
5 Are the effects of technological change in the field of education always positive? ....
6 In your opinion, which school subjects could be taught more effectively with computers? ....
7 Will technology ever reach a stage where it is considered perfect, or will it always be changing and evolving? ....
8 What are some qualities that make a good teacher? ....

Expanding your answers

Part 1 and Part 3 of the Speaking Test are similar in some ways. However, the main difference is that in Part 1 you are simply required to answer the question, while in Part 3 you are expected to give an answer that *extends* and *expands* the topic under discussion. In particular, the examiner is looking for an answer that uses complex sentences and a wide range of vocabulary and grammatical structures.

Example

Question: Where do you think technology will take us in the next 20 years?

Response: Well, I think that technology will take us in many new directions, but I think one of the most dynamic areas will be in the area of teaching and learning. For example, in many countries, online courses will replace some classroom-based courses, and students will interact with their teachers in a totally different way.

Exercise 8 Expanding your answers

Study the questions below. First think of some ideas and then deliver answers to your partner in an *extended* and *well-linked* way. The first one has been done for you as an example to follow.

1 How has technology changed methods of food production in your country in the last 50 years?

Ideas

Before: heavy labour for men and women, agricultural machinery unavailable, limited range of crops planted, all crops sold locally

Now: reduced labour, agricultural machinery available and used on most farms, many different crops planted, sold nationally and internationally

Possible response

Technology has radically changed food production methods in my country since the 1960s. Fifty years ago, any agricultural work involved heavy manual work for both men and women because of the lack of machinery. Also, back then, the harvested crop was mostly rice, which was sold locally. Now farms produce a range of crops and some of it is even sold on the international market.

2 Are changes to food production methods that increase the quantity of food produced always positive?

Ideas

Lack of taste of mass-produced food, increased amount of chemicals used

....

....

continued ▶

Unit 2: Speaking

3 Compare the types of food consumed in your grandparents' time to the types of food you consume now.
Ideas

....

....

4 How will shopping for food change or evolve in the next few decades?
Ideas

....

....

Sample answers to these questions are provided in the answer key.

Exercise 9 Further practice for Part 3

With a partner, give extended answers to the questions below on education. Make sure that you use complex sentences and a variety of vocabulary in your answers.

1 Do you think computers will replace the majority of classroom teachers in the future?
2 Has the standard of education changed for the better or worse in the past decade in your country?
3 In your experience, do government schools or private schools prepare their students better for successful adult lives?
4 What are the reasons behind the worldwide trend in most countries for students to continue into higher education after finishing school?
5 Who do you think is primarily responsible for the development of children and teenagers into responsible adults?

Ideas in Part 3

There are no 'right' or 'wrong' answers in Part 3. The examiner is not looking for you to provide the correct answer in the Speaking Test – in fact, there are no 'correct' answers for the types of questions you may be asked. Instead, the examiner is assessing the *way* you present your information: your ability to present any information you may know on the topic in a clear and confident way.

See 2.5, pages 128–35, for more information on how to come up with suitable ideas to use in the Speaking Test.

2.4 The speaking strategies and skills you need

In assessing your performance on the IELTS Speaking Test, the examiner considers your spoken ability in four skill areas: fluency and coherence, lexical resource, grammatical accuracy and range, and pronunciation.

Skill areas

Fluency and coherence

Fluency means talking at normal speed without stopping too frequently. Coherence is organising and linking your speech in a logical way. This also involves using cohesive devices such as discourse markers.

Lexical resource (Accuracy and range of vocabulary)

Lexical resource means the range of vocabulary you use and how effectively you use it. This involves using a range of vocabulary to clearly express your meaning and choosing words accurately.

Grammatical accuracy and range

Here, accuracy means using grammar and sentence structure correctly. Range refers to using different kinds of grammatical structures that are appropriate to the topic and discussion. This involves, for instance, the appropriate use of tenses and agreement, and also avoiding any errors that interfere with communication.

Pronunciation

Pronunciation means speaking clearly. This includes how natural and understandable your speech sounds in terms of stress, rhythm, intonation and pitch. Also assessed are any possible pronunciation problems caused by the influence of your first language.

The examiner awards a band score from 1 to 9 in each of these four areas and then the four scores are averaged to give you your result for the Speaking Test.

In this section we will look at each of the four skills in turn. We will also look at some specific strategies to improve your overall performance in the test. In each of the sections there are exercises that give you opportunities to:

▼ practise speaking strategies and skills

▼ complete tasks similar to parts of the Speaking Test

▼ assess your own ability.

Fluency and coherence

The examiner awards a score from 1 to 9 for your fluency and coherence.

Fluency

Fluency means being able to speak *smoothly* and *continuously*. Of course, it is normal and natural to pause sometimes when you speak, in order to think about what you are saying or are going to say next. If, however, you have frequent and lengthy silences, or if you keep repeating yourself and cannot continue speaking, then clearly you are having difficulty knowing what to say next, or how to say it. This will lower your score.

Speaking fluently does *not* mean speaking *quickly*. It is not realistic or necessary to try to speak as quickly in English as in your first language. Rather, aim to speak continuously and at a relaxed pace. The delivery should be smooth, not 'stop–start'. Speaking too fast or too slowly can also affect your rhythm in English. See 2.4, page 121, for more on this.

Sometimes candidates hesitate too long because they don't know what to say next or can't remember the English word(s) they want to express their meaning. This happens especially when they are translating in their minds from their first language. For example, a candidate may say:

My country has very high … [*silence*] … I don't know how to say.

In this example, the candidate does not speak fluently. He cannot think of the English word 'inflation'. Instead of hesitating and staying silent, the candidate should quickly avoid the problem and use words which he does know, and which give more or less the same meaning.

My country has very high … the price of everything in my country goes up very quickly.

Here the candidate has repaired the problem by avoiding it. Familiar words are used with confidence and the same meaning is achieved.

Successful communicators are good at using what they know and avoiding what they don't know. They also use other words to express their meaning. See 'Accuracy and range of vocabulary' (2.4, pages 89–99) for more information on this skill.

Exercise 10 Assessing fluency

Listen to two candidates from the practice Speaking Tests and decide which one is speaking more fluently. In making your assessment, consider these issues:

▼ Do they speak smoothly and continuously?
▼ Do they speak at a reasonable pace?
▼ Are there many significant pauses?
▼ Are they able to fill the pauses?

1 Listen and complete the sentence below.
   I think Candidate ……… is more fluent.

2 Listen again. This time read the transcript while you listen and underline examples in the transcript which support your assessment. When you have finished, read the assessment provided in the answer key.

Fillers

Wherever possible, you should *avoid silence* in the Speaking Test. English-speaking cultures generally expect 'noisy' conversations where there is little 'dead' (silent) time, and this is reflected in the Speaking Test.

When faced with a difficult question or when you are searching for something to say, you can use a filler; that is, a piece of language that tells your listener you are organising a suitable answer. Fillers will give you the time to think and help you to keep going.

Examples of fillers include:

Let me see …

That's a difficult/interesting/complex question.

Well, in my opinion …

I guess I would have to say …

It is also acceptable to rephrase the question as a filler.

What do I usually do on the weekend? Well, that depends on the weather …

A less effective but common type of filler, is a sound filler such as *um*, *ah* and *er*.

Exercise 11   Listening for fillers

Listen to two examples of Part 3 of the Speaking Test. In the table below, note what fillers were used by the two candidates. Were they successful or not?

Candidate	Fillers used	Successful?
Candidate 1	Recent development? Let me see. OK.	Partially successful
Candidate 2		

Check the answer key to see if your evaluation was correct.

Unit 2:   Speaking

Exercise 12 — Giving fluent answers

Give extended answers to the following questions. If possible, work with a partner.

1 Do you come from a large or small family?
2 What did you enjoy most about your school days?
3 How would you describe your parents' attitudes towards your education?
4 What are the main differences between education today and in your parents' time?
5 How do you think schools will change in the future?

When answering, try to speak as fluently as possible:

- Speak at a reasonable pace.
- Speak smoothly and continuously.
- Speak without too many (long) pauses.
- If you have pauses, try to fill them with words or sounds.
- If you have any difficulty finding the word you want, use other similar words to express your meaning.

Speak for one to two minutes. Record your presentation and assess your fluency or ask a partner to comment on your fluency.

Coherence

When you speak coherently, you make your meaning clear; that is, you present your ideas or information in a *clear and logical sequence* in a way that your listener can easily understand.

Example

Examiner: Do you think boys are naturally better at mathematics than girls?
Candidate: Mathematics difficult girls clever boys good I think.

In this conversation, the candidate has not spoken coherently. The meaning is *unclear*.

Example

Examiner: Where do you come from?
Candidate: I really like music.

In this conversation, the candidate has spoken accurately (for example, the grammar is correct), but has not spoken coherently. This answer does not make sense because it does not relate to the question. The answer is *incoherent*.

In the following example from a practice Speaking Test, the candidate's answer is reasonably accurate but it is not coherent. It does not relate to the examiner's question.

Example

Examiner: In what way does a good system of public transportation affect the quality of life for city dwellers?

Candidate: Yeah. Public. Mm, public transportation? For the, ah, public buses I, ah, sometimes very confused to, how to use the buses and … which bus is going which, ah, which place, you know. And, ah, so, how to pay a fee is different from the each cities. It's very confusing.

Coherent speech is achieved through using cohesive devices, such as discourse markers, and tying your answer to the question through the use of pronouns and other parts of speech, to ensure a logical ordering of ideas. Using this type of organisational language will make what you say more coherent.

Discourse markers

In spoken English, discourse markers are the words that let our listeners know that we are structuring ('packaging') information in a certain way. They help us make our ideas more coherent by connecting the ideas in different sentences together. For this reason they are usually used at the beginnings of sentences. For example, in Part 2, you may use time-based discourse markers such as *first*, *next* and *finally* to describe an event that happened to you in the past.

Discourse markers are usually connected to a particular *function*. Some common functions of discourse markers include:

- indicating order of importance
- indicating a time sequence
- giving examples
- giving extra information
- giving a cause or reason
- giving an effect or result
- introducing an opposite idea
- intensifying (make stronger)
- comparing
- contrasting.

Exercise 13 — Discourse markers

Put the discourse markers below into the correct part of the table. For each function find *two* discourse markers associated with it. One discourse marker can be used twice.

also	after that	as a result	as a result of
besides	due to	indeed	for example
for instance	however	in contrast	in fact
instead	similarly	~~more importantly~~	most importantly
nevertheless	~~since then~~	therefore	

Function	Discourse markers
Indicate order of importance	*more importantly*
Indicate a time sequence	*since then*
Give examples	
Give extra information	
Give a cause or reason	
Give an effect or result	
Introduce an opposite idea	
Compare	
Contrast	

Tying your answer to the question

Candidates who speak coherently relate what they say to what the examiner says. It is a good idea to show this relationship explicitly by using pronouns and other parts of speech. When answering questions in Part 1, for example, you should link your answers very directly to the examiner's questions.

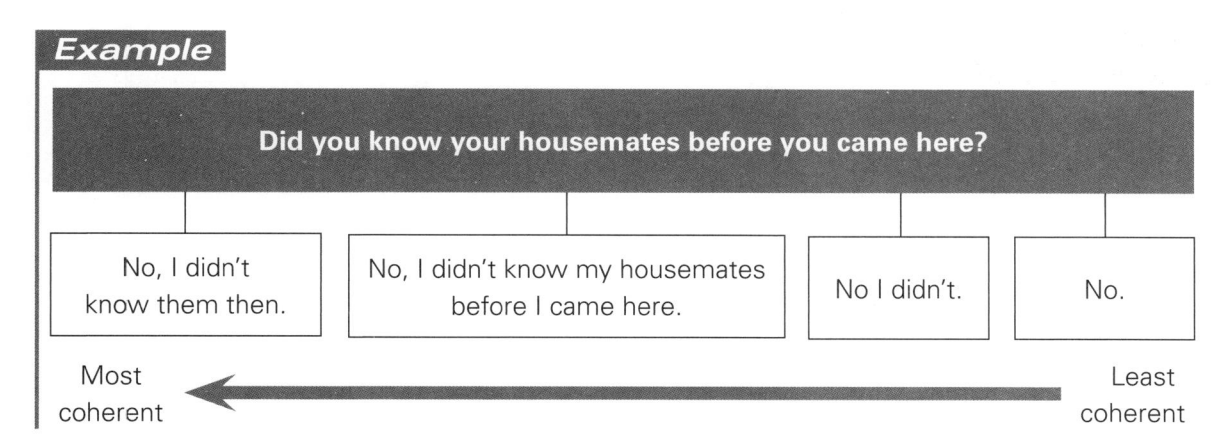

Example

Did you know your housemates before you came here?

| No, I didn't know them then. | No, I didn't know my housemates before I came here. | No I didn't. | No. |

Most coherent ←——————————————————————→ Least coherent

In the example above, the answer 'No' has the least connection to the question.

The answer 'No, I didn't' is more coherent because it connects more directly to the question and correctly follows the past tense used in the question.

The answer 'No, I didn't know my housemates before I came here' is even more coherent because it repeats or 'echoes' the question.

'No, I didn't know them then' is a **highly coherent** answer. It uses the pronoun *them* to refer to the noun *housemates* and uses the adverb *then* to refer to the adverbial clause *before I came here*.

Highly coherent communication uses such ways of referring to previous ideas. Rather than just repeating the question, it rephrases it (says it in a different way).

Here's another example from a practice Speaking Test.

Example

Examiner: Why do you think some people are better at learning languages than other people?

Candidate: Ah, I think that some people do better in some languages because if the languages that they are studying has got, like, ah, the same, um, language structure, will be much more easier for them to, to, um, handle with the language.

This answer is coherent. The candidate echoes the question and thus ties the answer very directly to it. In repeating, she changes the verb, but this works. She then uses the link word 'because' to connect to a reason. She also uses the pronoun 'them' to connect with 'some people' in the question.

Now practise making *your* answers as coherent as possible when responding to Part 1 questions, by doing Exercise 14.

Unit 2: Speaking

Exercise 14   Coherence in Part 1

Respond to the following questions, making sure that you connect your answers very directly to the questions. The first one has been done for you as an example to follow.

1   Do you like your housemates?
    Yes, I do. I like them very much.

2   What's the climate like in your country?

3   Do you regularly read the newspaper?

4   What do you do in your spare time?

5   Have you ever visited a European country?

6   Do you have trams in your home town?

7   Are there private (non-government) schools in your country?

8   Is there much crime in your home town?

Sample answers are provided in the answer key.

In the long turn in Part 2, you have a minute to organise what you are going to say. As well as thinking about *ideas* for your talk, you also need to consider how to make it *coherent*. Your examiner will be assessing your ability to present information and ideas in a clear and logical sequence in which all the main points are well linked.

Exercise 15   Coherence in Part 2

Read this extract from Part 2 of a Speaking Test. Circle any cohesive devices the speaker has used to make their presentation more coherent. The first one has been done for you as an example.

continued ▶

> **Examiner:** I'd like you to describe somewhere you have enjoyed living.
>
> **Candidate:** Yes. Ah, the place that I, ah, I have enjoyed living is, um, Kyoto City. I grew up and, ah, I, so, ah. I went to the university in Kyoto and (it) was very fine. Ah, Kyoto is a very popular city for foreigners but I think Kyoto is a, has another as … aspect, so it is a city of students. Kyoto has many school, high school and especially universities, so I was attending one of these universities. And Kyoto has a lot of, um, entertaining place and the cheap restaurants, as well as the very traditional temples or shrines. So I didn't go any, any of these temples or shrines though, but I enjoyed living there.
>
> **Examiner:** Do you think it's, um, still much the same place now or has it changed?
>
> **Candidate:** Mm, I, I don't think, ah, it's changed. It's always a city for stu… many students.
>
> Read the comments on this response in the answer key.

It is important to learn some of the standard ways of connecting answers to questions. For example, you should know how to respond when the examiner asks your opinion. This is particularly important in Part 3 of the test, in which you will often be asked for your opinion.

Example

> **Examiner:** Do you think coordinated action on climate change will succeed?
>
> **Candidate:** Yes, I think so. I believe …
>
> No, I don't think it will. I'm afraid …
>
> I hope so, for the sake of …
>
> I don't know if it will or not. It's difficult to …

Exercise 16 Coherence in Part 3

For each question below, give two answers: a short answer, and a longer answer that connects very directly to the question. The first one has been done for you as an example.

1. Do you think smoking should be banned in all restaurants?
   No, I don't think so. (short answer)
   No, I don't think it should because … (longer answer)

2. Are there any benefits of living in a globalised world?
   ....
   ....

3. Do you think there is any danger in children watching action movies?
   ....
   ....

continued ▶

4 Does the quality of teachers affect the education students receive?

....

....

5 Do you think political leaders should be required to be university graduates?

....

....

6 Do you believe that one day everyone will communicate in English?

....

....

7 Do you think school children should have drug education at school?

....

....

8 Do you think robots will replace pets in the future?

....

....

Sample answers are provided in the answer key.

Degree questions

Sometimes the examiner will ask your opinion using *how* followed by an adjective or adverb. For example:

How important is good health in your opinion?

How difficult is it to find rental accommodation in your home town?

How strongly do people feel about protecting the environment in your country?

In order to give a coherent response to this question, you need to specify a *degree* in your answer. For example:

I think it is extremely important / quite important / very important / rather unimportant.

I don't think it's important at all.

Another point to remember is that a negative opinion may be structured differently in English to your first language. In English, the standard structure for a negative opinion includes the helping verb *to do*. For example: *I **don't** think he will come*. Whereas in some languages the structure is: *I think he will not come*. Make sure that you know how to express negative opinions correctly in English.

Exercise 17 Answering degree questions

For each question below, give a highly coherent answer by clearly specifying a degree. Then practise adding an extension to this statement (for example, a positive or a negative opinion). The first two have been done for you as examples to follow.

1. How important is good health?
   It's extremely important. I don't think other things have any value without good health.

2. How difficult is it to get in contact with your teachers at university?
   It's not difficult at all. I don't think I've ever had any problems accessing them.

3. How widespread is the use of the Internet in your community?

4. How hard should it be to get a driver's licence?

5. How large a role does television play in your society?

6. How important do you think it is to educate young children about environmental issues?

7. How important is it to have success in your career?

8. To what extent should governments censor the media?

Sample answers are provided in the answer key.

Exercise 18 — Self-assessment of fluency and coherence

Answer the questions below by giving reasonably detailed answers – simply answering 'yes' or 'no' is not enough. Record your answers.

Part 1 questions

1. What is the climate like in your country?
2. What do you like to do in your spare time?
3. Which television programs do you regularly watch?
4. How well can you cook?
5. What are the private (non-government) schools like in your country?

Part 3 questions

6. Do you think anti-drug commercials on television help reduce the drug problem?
7. How important is it to have success in your career?
8. How difficult should it be to get a university degree?
9. Do you think most teaching will be done online in the future?
10. How essential are computers in education nowadays?

Listen to your recordings and assess them for fluency and coherence using the questions below. Tick the box that applies to you.

Questions about your performance	Yes	No	Sometimes	Not sure
Do you speak at a reasonable pace?				
Do you keep pauses relatively brief (and fill them appropriately)?				
Does your manner of speaking sound smooth?				
If you have difficulty finding the right words, do you use other words to express your meaning?				
Are your answers totally relevant to the question?				
Do your answers refer back very directly to the questions (for example, through reference pronouns)?				
Do your answers clearly show that you have understood the questions (by echoing or rephrasing them)?				

If you answered 'not sure' to any of these questions, it might be useful to ask other people (study partners, teachers, etc) to assess your fluency and coherence.

Accuracy and range of vocabulary

The examiner awards a score from 1 to 9 for your lexical resource. Lexical resource refers to your ability to use vocabulary effectively. You should:

▼ use a wide range of appropriate and accurate words when you speak

▼ use other words to express your meaning successfully when you lack some of the vocabulary usually used to convey that meaning.

Accuracy

The accuracy of your vocabulary refers to choosing *the right words for the context*. For example, the vocabulary in the following sentence contains inaccurate vocabulary.

I opened the television and listened to the news.

Accurate words to use in this sentence would be *turned on* or *switched on*, not *opened*.

As well as confusing different words, poor choice of **word form** can affect accuracy. Many words in English share the same word root (or base) but the form of the word can differ according to its function in a sentence.

> *Example*
>
> *economy (noun)*: There are significant problems with the **economy**.
> *economic (adjective)*: The country is suffering from severe **economic** problems.
> *economically (adverb)*: The country is doing well **economically**.
> *economist (noun)*: **Economists** predict that taxes will rise.

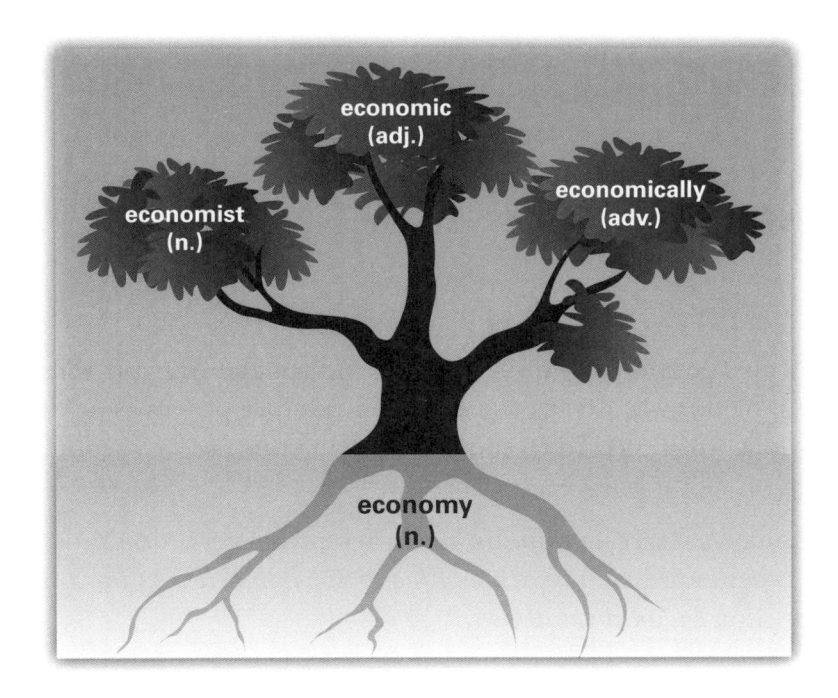

Unit 2:   Speaking

Exercise 19 — Accuracy of vocabulary

Circle the appropriate form of the word to complete each sentence. Note the part of speech of your chosen word. The first one has been done for you as an example to follow.

1 We won't notice the **effect** / effective of the new curriculum until next year. ...*noun*...

2 After the 2004 election, successive / successful governments attempted to reduce foreign debt. ....

3 Her paper's theme / thematic relates to her work in the area of tropical medicine. ....

4 For workers in the field, the significant / significance of their study is obvious. ....

5 The coincide / coincidence of two sets showing exactly the same results is too important to ignore. ....

6 As the results showed some promise original / originally, more funding became available. ....

7 Work on the establish / establishment of a research centre is proceeding far too slowly. ....

8 The influence / influential nature of her new book cannot be highlighted too strongly. ....

The vocabulary you use in the test should also be *appropriate*. That is, you should use appropriate words for the situation: in this case, a formal interview with an examiner. For instance, answering a question with 'yeah' or 'yep' (informal versions of 'yes') is not appropriate in a formal interview.

The best way to learn more about the appropriateness of vocabulary is to read and listen to as much English as possible. Good dictionaries will also give you information about style and usage for individual words. See 2.5, pages 131–2, for more information on this skill.

Range

The examiner will also consider the range of your vocabulary. Are you able to use a variety of different words, or do you always use a limited number of words again and again? In the Speaking Test you are expected to show variety in your use of vocabulary.

For example:

▼ when the examiner asks your **opinion** on different matters, don't always begin with *I think* ... Try other expressions, such as *I feel/believe that* ..., *As far as I can see/tell* ..., *In my opinion* ... or *I would say that* ...

- when describing **quantity**, don't always use the same word, for example, *many*. Try other expressions, such as *quite a lot of, a lot of, lots of, a large/huge/enormous amount/number of, the majority of …*
- when describing what you **like**, don't always use *I like …* Try other expressions, such as *I really enjoy …, I'm really keen on …, I'm fond of …, My favourite …*
- when describing the **degree of something**, don't always use *very* or *some*. Try other expressions, such as *extremely, somewhat, rather, quite* or *really*.

Of course, these various alternatives do not have exactly the same meaning. You need to check the differences in their meaning and usage, and then use them appropriately.

Exercise 20   Using a range of vocabulary

For each of the questions below, think of how to say the given answers in different ways. Try to come up with at least two different ways. The first one has been done for you as an example to follow.

1 Do you think schools should teach physical education?
   No, I don't.
   No, I certainly don't.
   No, I'm definitely not in favour of that.
   No, I'm completely opposed to that idea.

2 Do you think sport should be compulsory at school?
   Yes, I do.

3 Do you have a lot of crime in your country?
   Yes, it's very bad.

4 What is your apartment like.
   It's very big and very nice.

5 How do you feel about smoking in restaurants?
   I think it should be banned.

Sample answers are provided in the answer key.

Unit 2: Speaking

A wide range of vocabulary includes a command of common **idioms**. An idiom can occur when two (or more) words are used together to form a new meaning.

> **Example**
>
> **Idiom:** hidden agenda
>
> **Example sentence:** It seems to me that newspapers sometimes have a *hidden agenda*.

In this case, it is reasonably easy to understand that the newspaper's agenda (its list of things to be discussed) is not fully revealed; it is hidden from its readers.

However, in other cases, it is often very difficult to guess what an idiom means from looking at its different parts and how it is constructed grammatically. Let's look at a more challenging example.

> **Example**
>
> **Idiom:** over the top
>
> **Example sentence:** The trouble is that the response from the government is completely *over the top*.

In this example, the idiom involves two seemingly unrelated words – 'over' and 'top' – joined by the article 'the'. It is an old military expression which means to charge the enemy by going over a defensive position. Because a connection between the words is not immediately clear, the idiom could be difficult to understand and use.

Other idioms involve similes. A simile involves saying that something is similar to something else. They are often used to give the listener an instant mental picture and avoid the use of a lot of words.

> **Example**
>
> **Simile:** to sleep like a log
>
> **Example sentence:** My bed was so comfortable that I *slept like a log*.

In this sentence, the speaker is saying that they had a very sound sleep, implying that their sleep was so deep that their body was like a piece of wood in the bed.

Idioms are frequently used in spoken English but are far less frequent in written English. English speakers will use idioms in conversations or other less formal situations to make their language more interesting and/or to build a bond with their listener(s).

People learning English often avoid idioms, as they think they are very difficult to get right and also think they can sound rather odd and old-fashioned when spoken aloud.

However, if you are aiming for a high score for vocabulary in the Speaking Test, you should use a few idioms during your interview.

While expanding the range of your vocabulary, it is useful to note the relationship between the words you are learning and other words they usually combine or **collocate** with. For example:

I now have a *key role* in the new organisation.

In this sentence, the noun *role* collocates with the adjective *key*. It is possible to put other adjectives (such as *decisive*, *pivotal*, etc) before *role*, but in spoken English, *key role* is a common choice.

It is not just nouns and adjectives that collocate: it is also common for verbs to collocate with certain nouns, adverbs and prepositions. For example:

Please don't *spoil* my *fun* during the movie by talking loudly.

In this sentence, the verb *spoil* is found close to the noun *fun*. The verb *spoil* often collocates with nouns such as *fun* or *enjoyment*, so it is useful to learn these words together as a phrase.

The combination of a verb and a preposition – called a phrasal verb – is very common in spoken English. There are thousands of phrasal verbs, such as *come in*, *turn up*, *bring on*, *take out*, etc. However, they can sometimes be difficult to use – especially those that have more than one meaning. For example, *work out* can have several meanings:

1 to succeed: *I started a new business, but it didn't **work out**.*
2 to exercise: *This morning, I **worked out** at the gym.*
3 to discover something: *It's quite simple for most students to **work out** the meaning.*

Exercise 21 gives you some practice at recognising phrasal verbs.

Exercise 21 Range of vocabulary – matching parts of phrasal verbs

Match the verb with the preposition that it is commonly found with. You can use some prepositions more than once. The first one has been done for you as an example

as   ~~from~~   into   of   between   in   to   on   for

1 benefit ......*from*......
2 compensate ....
3 concentrate ....
4 convert ....
5 dispose ....
6 exclude ....
7 identify ....
8 participate ....
9 remove ....
10 respond ....
11 vary ....

Wide reading and using a **good dictionary** effectively will give you information about collocated words. Make sure that you record information about words that collocate in a way that will make it easy for you to recall them when you speak. See 2.5, pages 131–2, for more information on how to develop your knowledge of collocations, idioms and other types of vocabulary. Exercise 22 gives you more practice in using a range of vocabulary.

Exercise 22   Using a range of vocabulary

Below are some extracts from Part 1 and Part 3 of practice Speaking Tests. In each extract, respond to the examiner's two questions, making sure that your second response uses different vocabulary from your first response. The first two have been done for you as examples to follow.

1   **Examiner:** Do you think voting should be compulsory?
    Candidate: *Yes, I do. I feel that it's our obligation to vote.*
    Examiner: So do you think people should be fined if they don't vote?
    Candidate: *Yes, definitely. I really believe that the government should force people to vote.*

2   **Examiner:** How does this city compare to your home town?
    Candidate: *Well, it's much bigger and more expensive.*
    Examiner: Are there any other differences?
    Candidate: *Yes, there certainly are. My home town is far more beautiful.*

3   **Examiner:** Are there many cinemas in your home town?
    Candidate: *Oh, yes, there are a lot. People really enjoy going to the cinema.*
    Examiner: And what about restaurants?
    Candidate: ....

4   **Examiner:** Do you think computers will replace traditional schools in the future?
    Candidate: ....
    Examiner: So will children study at home in future, do you think?
    Candidate: ....

5   **Examiner:** Is studying at university harder than studying at high school?
    Candidate: ....
    Examiner: Is it more enjoyable?
    Candidate: ....

6   **Examiner:** Are adults better at learning foreign languages than children?
    Candidate: ....
    Examiner: And are women better than men at learning foreign languages?
    Candidate: ....

continued ▶

7	**Examiner:**	What's it like in the southern part of your country?
	Candidate:	....
	Examiner:	And what's the northern part like?
	Candidate:	....
8	**Examiner:**	Do you think primary school children should wear uniforms to school?
	Candidate:	....
	Examiner:	What about high school? Should high school students wear uniforms?
	Candidate:	....

Sample answers are provided in the answer key.

Paraphrasing

In assessing your use of vocabulary, the examiner will judge your ability to **paraphrase**. Paraphrasing is the ability to express your meaning successfully, even when you lack some of the vocabulary normally used to convey that meaning. It also involves the ability to talk at length on a topic without using the same words and/or phrases. This is an important skill. If you can paraphrase, it will help your fluency.

Let's look at some successful and not so successful paraphrasing by test candidates.

Example

Candidate: Um, I think security probably the major reason. Ah, so if people uh ... who choose to live in the gated community, they plobably, plobably (oh, sorry, I have the problem with that word). Um, they perhaps, ah, the reason for them to choose is for the concern of security, as I just say earlier.

In this example, the candidate explicitly declares her difficulty, namely that she is not confident that her pronunciation of *probably* will be clear enough to be understood (even though her first attempt at the word is largely successful). So, she uses an alternative word (*perhaps*) to express her meaning. Although it does not have exactly the same meaning, it is close enough, and it allows the speaker to keep going.

Example

Candidate: I believe TV news more than Internet.
Examiner: Why?
Candidate: Because I think on television is, on air to everybody and every day but Internet is, is not so far – govern... I don't know how to say.

This candidate has difficulty expressing her meaning ('Internet is, is not so far – govern…') and then hesitates. She declares her difficulty ('I don't know how to say') but does not attempt to paraphrase. Perhaps her meaning is that the Internet is not as controlled (monitored or regulated) as TV news.

The first example highlights how paraphrasing can involve using different words to convey the same meaning. Fortunately, there are many ways to express the same idea or concept in English because the range of vocabulary is so large.

Exercise 23 Paraphrasing

For each of the following sentences, produce a sentence that expresses the same meaning without using the word(s) underlined. In some cases you might need two sentences to express the same meaning. The first one has been done as an example for you to follow. If possible, do this exercise quickly as a speaking exercise.

1. They postponed the meeting till Wednesday.
   They changed the date of the meeting to Wednesday.

2. My father retired a few years ago.

3. I do volunteer work in my spare time.

4. This dish is very nutritious.

5. I have a driver's licence but it's not valid here in Canada.

6. She submitted her assignment on time.

7. He couldn't finish his assignment in time so he requested an extension.

8. People who are highly motivated are generally more successful.

9. There are many arguments in favour of teaching your children foreign languages.

10. Many people argue that television has a negative effect on children, but the evidence is inconclusive.

continued ▶

> **11** I think newspaper reports <u>are more reliable than</u> news reports on television.
>
> ....
>
> **12** There has been <u>widespread condemnation</u> of the government's decision to <u>amend the legislation</u> without <u>community consultation</u>.
>
> ....
>
> Sample answers are provided in the answer key.

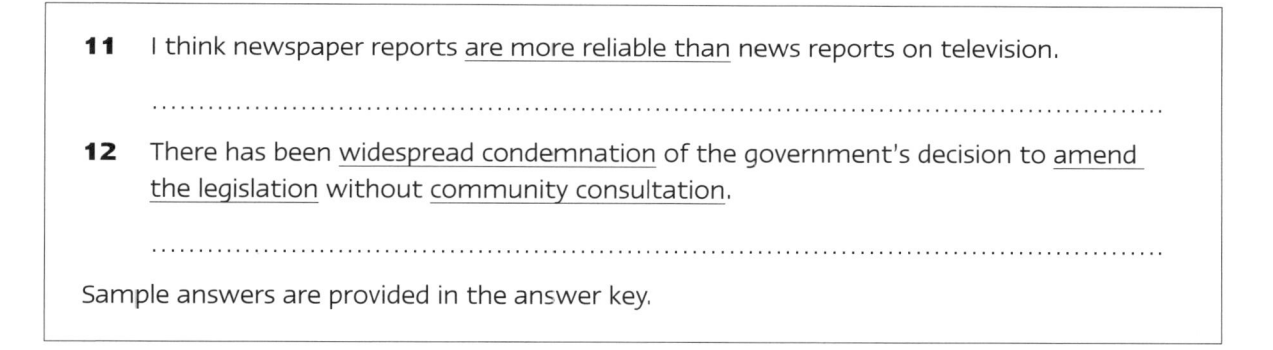

Paraphrasing for clarification

Another way paraphrasing can be useful in the Speaking Test is to clarify (make clear) a question you have been asked by the examiner. Especially in Part 3, there is a possibility that you will be asked a question that you do not understand. Maybe the topic is completely unknown to you, or the examiner uses a key word that you do not know. In this case *don't panic*. Instead, clarify what the examiner wants you to talk about.

There are several ways to do this. One way is to ask the examiner to rephrase the question in a different and/or simpler way. However, a more effective way would be to *guess* what the examiner is asking about and then use language to check whether this guess was correct. This will probably involve paraphrasing (putting in your own words) your understanding of the question you have been asked.

Here are two examples.

Examples

Examiner: Can you tell me what you think of government censorship of the media?
Candidate: So, censorship is a type of control or restriction of the newspapers and magazines – is that right?
Examiner: That's correct.

Examiner: Tell me the main differences between the educational system in your country and the system in this country.
Candidate: Ah – you'd like me to explain how education is organised in my country and then compare it to here?
Examiner: Exactly.

Other examples of ways to begin paraphrasing for clarification include:

So you're saying that ...

Just to make sure I've got this right. Are you saying that ...

Alright, so you want me to ...

Unit 2: Speaking

Exercise 24 — Paraphrasing for clarification

Listen for the clarification strategies used by a candidate in Part 3 of a Speaking Test. In the table below, note down the words they use and whether they were successful or not. Listen more than once if you need to.

How she asks for clarification	Successful?
1 Are you asking me about a city planning?	Yes
2	
3	
4	
5	

Now check your answers and read the evaluation of the candidate's performance in the answer key.

Now focus on your own vocabulary. In the next exercise your aim is to use vocabulary that is accurate, appropriate and varied. You should also concentrate on using paraphrasing where necessary.

Exercise 25 — Self-assessment of accuracy and range of vocabulary

1. Below are three practice topics for a Part 2 response. For each topic, take one minute to prepare what you are going to say. Record your response.

   a. Talk about your best friend. Who is it? How do you know each other? Why are you such good friends?

   b. Talk about a song that you think is typical of your country. What is it about? Why is it typical? How do people in your country feel about this song?

   c. Choose a sport that you find enjoyable. Do you watch it or play it? Why do you enjoy it? What skills does this sport require?

2. Listen to your recordings and assess them for vocabulary using the questions below. Tick the column that most applies to you.

Questions about your performance	Yes	No	Sometimes	Not sure
Are your words accurate? (i.e. Do they have the right meaning in this context?)				
Are your words appropriate? (For example, are they suitably formal for an examination or interview?)				
Do you use a reasonable range of words (avoiding repeated use of the same simple opinion words such as 'I think' or 'I like' or qualifiers such as 'very', etc)?				
Do you use a variety of idioms and collocations?				

If you answered 'not sure' to any of these it might be useful to ask other people (study partners, teachers, etc) to assess your vocabulary.

Grammatical accuracy and range

The examiner awards a score from 1 to 9 for your grammatical range and accuracy, which means your ability to speak accurately and appropriately.

Grammatical accuracy

Grammatical accuracy means using grammar correctly. For example, the examiner assesses whether you follow the standard patterns for sentence structure (word order), verb tense, (modal) auxiliary verbs, number (singular/plural), articles and so on.

Let's look at two examples of candidates describing where they live.

> **Example**
>
> **Candidate 1:** In my apartment have two bedroom and one bathroom. It really comfortable, but expensive. I live there for seven month now. It locate near university. I can to walk there just five minute.
>
> **Candidate 2:** There are three bedrooms and two bathrooms in my apartment. It's rather small, but very convenient. I've been living there for three months. It's located very close to my college so I can walk there in about ten minutes.

The first candidate does not use plural nouns accurately ('bedroom', 'month' and 'minute' should all be plural). The structure to express the existence of something is also not used accurately; the form should be either 'In my apartment **there are** two bedrooms' or 'My apartment **has** two bedrooms'. The candidate uses the wrong tense in 'I live', and the modal auxiliary verb *can* should not be followed by *to*. By contrast, the second candidate uses accurate grammar.

In the Speaking Test you are judged for your grammatical *performance*, not your grammatical *knowledge*. It is not enough to know the correct grammar terms or names: you must produce them consistently when you speak – forming tenses accurately, remembering to add plural endings on nouns when needed, forming the passive voice correctly, etc. Your aim throughout is to make minimal grammatical errors.

It is not possible to predict precisely which structures you will need to use in the Speaking Test, but it is reasonable to expect that you may have to use the following:

A describing things (places, buildings, food) and people: *there is/are*; nouns (singular and plural forms), passive forms of the verb (for example, 'it was built in 1900')

B describing events in the past: past tense and present perfect tense

C describing aspects of your life: simple present tense

D talking about plans: future tense, present continuous tense

E comparing things: comparatives, superlatives

F expressing opinions: modal auxiliary verbs

G discussing hypothetical situations: conditional expressions.

You need to be able to use these structures accurately, although of course you do not need to know the correct grammatical names for them. However, it is useful to know how these grammar areas could 'fit' into the test.

Exercise 26 — Using grammatically accurate structures

Using information from the list list opposite, match each question to the structure that would be needed to successfully answer it. Note: more than one answer may be possible for some questions. The first one has been done for you as an example to follow.

1. What did you do in your spare time when you were a child? ………..*B*…………..
2. Which did you find more enjoyable – primary school or secondary school? ……………
3. Who are better drivers – men or women? ……………………….
4. How did you feel when you finished high school? ……………………….
5. How would you spend your money if you won the lottery? ……………………….
6. Describe your best friend to me. ……………………….
7. Which do you find easier to understand: American English or British English? Why? ……………………….
8. What advice would you give to a young friend hoping to study overseas? ……………
9. How long have you been studying English? ……………………….
10. How many hours per day do you usually sleep? ……………………….
11. Describe a famous building in your country. ……………………….
12. When is your birthday? How do you usually celebrate it? ……………………….
13. Do you think that cash (that is, paper money and coins) will disappear in the future? ……………………….
14. What part of your country would you recommend every visitor see? ………………….

Exercise 27 — Speaking with grammatical accuracy

Now give full (extended) answers to each of the above questions. If possible, work with a partner for this exercise. Record your answers and then assess their grammatical accuracy by comparing them with the comments and sample answers in the answer key.

Exercise 28 — Using grammatically accurate past tense

Here are some notes about the life of a writer.

Part A

Read the notes and then write answers to questions 1 to 12 below. Most of the questions require an answer that uses the past simple tense. The first one has been done for you as an example to follow.

Name: Francis James Hatton

Born: Newcastle 1973

Family: Only child; abandoned by parents; raised by grandmother

Background: Extremely poor; worked part time (after school)

Education: Attended local school until 1989

Work experience: Worked in department store; quit work to write full time in 1992

Writing career: 'Black Morning' (short story) published 1992, three more short stories published 1993; *This Man* (novel) published 1995; *Eternity* (novel) published 1997

Film work: sold film rights to *Eternity* for $2.5 million in 1999; Academy Award (Best Screenplay) for *This Man*, 2002

Personal life: married Elizabeth Charles 2000; daughter Clara born 2004; son Andrew born 2006; daughter May born 2009

1. What is his full name?

   His full name is Francis James Hatton.

2. Why was he raised by his grandmother?

   ....

3. Does he have any siblings?

   ....

continued ▶

4 Why did he work part-time?

....

5 How old was he when he left school?

....

6 How many novels has he published?

....

7 Has he ever published any short stories?

....

8 How did he earn $2.5 million?

....

9 When did he win an Academy Award?

....

10 Who did he marry?

....

11 How old was he when he got married?

....

12 How many daughters does he have?

....

Sample answers are provided in the answer key.

Part B

Now use the notes and your answers above to give a full spoken biographical description of Francis Hatton. Record your description and then compare it with the sample in the answer key.

Part C

As a follow-up, give a spoken biography of three people: a famous writer in your country, a friend and yourself. In particular, focus on using past tenses correctly.

Exercise 29 — Assessing grammatical accuracy

(SPEAKING — CD 3 · Track 11)

Listen to a candidate attempting a Part 2 topic in a practice test and assess the accuracy of her grammar.

When making your assessment, consider how successfully she has used these structures:

- the verb *to be*
- the structure *there is/are*
- singular and plural nouns
- passive verbs
- simple present tense
- past tense and present perfect tense
- future tense and/or present continuous tense
- comparatives and/or superlatives
- modal auxiliary verbs
- conditionals.

Listen to the recording and make your assessment. Complete the notes below.

Things she has managed well: ....

....

Problem areas: ....

....

....

....

Listen again, this time reading the transcript at the same time and underline examples in the transcript which support your assessment.

Finally, compare your assessment with the one given in the answer key.

Exercise 30 — Writing with grammatical accuracy

Look at the transcript from Exercise 29 once again. Correct any errors by writing out a 'correct' version. You can do this individually or with a partner. Check your version against the sample answer in the answer key.

Improving the accuracy of your grammar is an important aspect of preparing for the Speaking Test. The best way to do this is to identify your weaknesses and develop a program of practice. See 2.5, pages 127–37, for more details about how to do this.

Grammatical range

In the Speaking Test, the examiner judges whether you use a variety of grammatical structures when you speak and how successful you are in using them. Specifically, the examiner assesses how you express spoken information using a range of clause and sentence structures.

Clauses

When we speak or write, we use clauses to connect parts of our speech together. A clause is any group of words that has a subject and a verb. A clause may or may not make up a complete sentence. There are two types of clauses: independent (main) and dependent (subordinate).

An independent clause includes a subject and a verb and expresses a complete thought. It is able to stand as a sentence by itself.

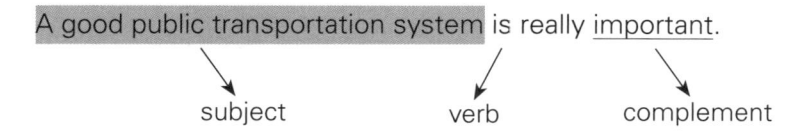

A good public transportation system is really important.
→ subject   → verb   → complement

A dependent clause usually begins with a subordinating conjunction (subordinator) such as *since*, *if* or *while* followed by a subject, verb and complement. Dependent clauses are commonly used to provide additional information about the subject of a sentence.

Even though a good public transportation system is important …
→ subordinator   → subject   → verb   → complement

A dependent clause is not a complete thought and it cannot stand by itself as a sentence. For this reason dependent clauses are sometimes called sentence fragments.

Sentences

There are three main kinds of sentences in English: simple, compound and complex. A **simple sentence** has one independent clause.

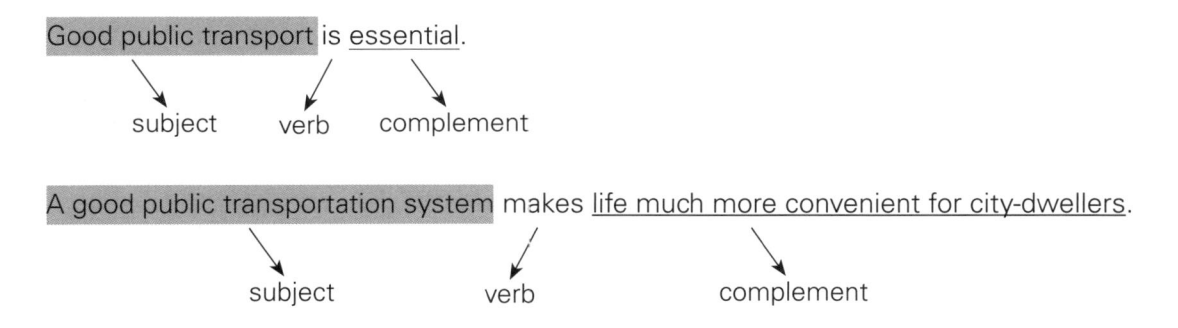

Good public transport is essential.
→ subject → verb → complement

A good public transportation system makes life much more convenient for city-dwellers.
→ subject   → verb   → complement

Unit 2: Speaking

Although simple sentences can be of different lengths, in natural spoken English they tend to be quite short.

A **compound sentence** has two or more independent clauses joined together. Each clause is *equally* important and could stand alone.

In speaking, there are two ways to form compound sentences:

1 with a **coordinating conjunction**
2 with a **conjunctive adverb**.

Coordinating conjunctions include such joining words as *and* (used to add ideas), *or* (to indicate alternative ideas), *so* (to introduce an effect) and *but* or *yet* (to contrast ideas).

Here is an example of a coordinating conjunction used to form a compound sentence:

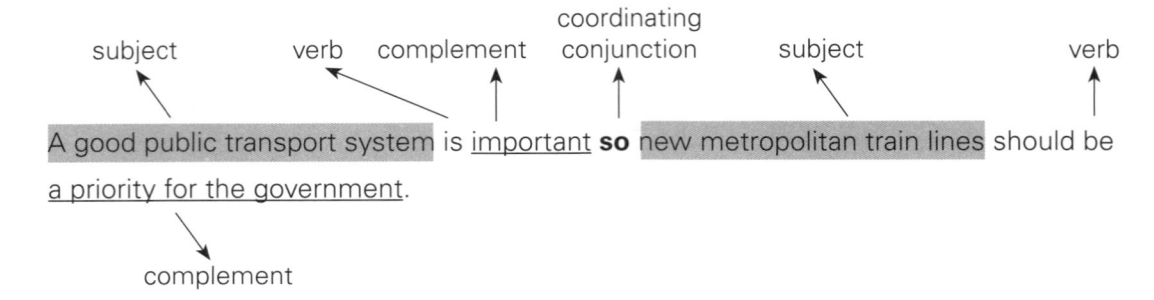

A good public transport system is important **so** new metropolitan train lines should be a priority for the government.

The use of conjunctive adverbs signals a different type of relationship between clauses. For example, *also* and *besides* are used to add ideas while *in fact* and *still* are used for emphasis. Conjunctive adverbs are also commonly used to compare or contrast ideas and indicate cause or effect relationships.

Here is an example of a conjunctive adverb used to form a compound sentence.

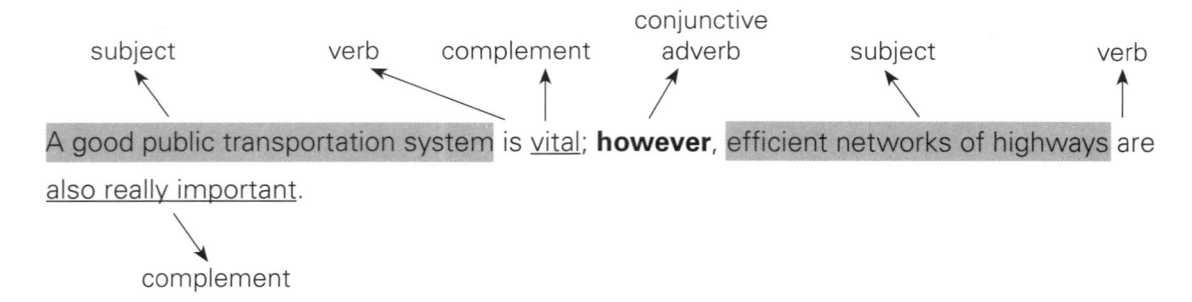

A good public transportation system is vital; **however**, efficient networks of highways are also really important.

A **complex sentence** has one independent clause and one (or more) dependent clauses. In a complex sentence, one idea is generally more important than the other one. The more important idea is usually found in the independent clause, while the less important one is placed in the dependent clause.

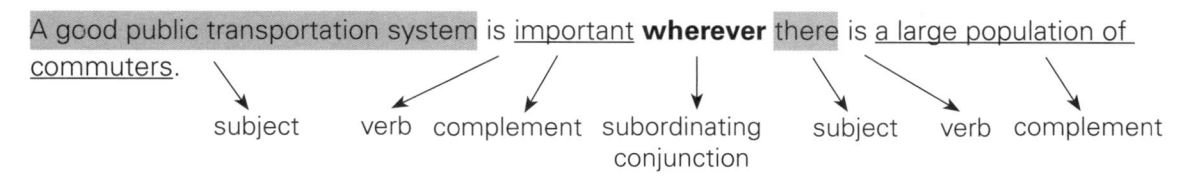

A good public transportation system is important **wherever** there is a large population of commuters.

- A good public transportation system → subject
- is → verb
- important → complement
- wherever → subordinating conjunction
- there → subject
- is → verb
- a large population of commuters → complement

Independent clauses can also be 'interrupted' by dependent clauses.

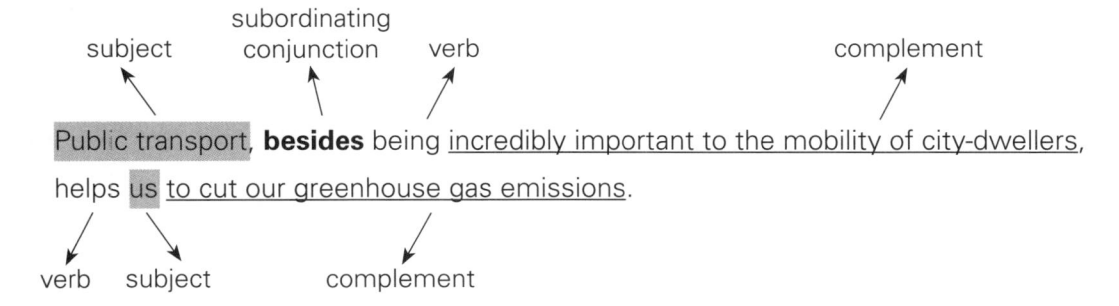

Public transport, **besides** being incredibly important to the mobility of city-dwellers, helps us to cut our greenhouse gas emissions.

- Public transport → subject
- besides → subordinating conjunction
- being → verb
- incredibly important to the mobility of city-dwellers → complement
- helps → verb
- us → subject
- to cut our greenhouse gas emissions → complement

Relative clauses

Another way to form complex sentences is to use a relative clause. This is a type of subordinate clause that begins with a relative pronoun such as *who*, *whose*, *which* or *that* and is very common in spoken English. These clauses are mainly used to give more information about a person, thing or group.

One popular tourist spot is a city called Taitung, which is located in the eastern part of Taiwan. → relative clause

The woman who became his partner worked for the same company. → relative clause

All three sentence types (simple, compound and complex) are used interchangeably in natural, spoken English. To achieve a higher band score in the IELTS Speaking Test you should aim to use a variety of sentence structures. You should use these with a range of **discourse markers** to make your message clearer and more precise. See 2.4, page 81, for more information on discourse markers.

Unit 2: Speaking

Responding to questions using a range of grammar

Each part of the Speaking Test provides you with an opportunity to display your grammatical range. For example, questions asking you to describe or assess something or somebody might enable you to produce compound sentences.

> **Example**
>
> **Examiner:** Do you enjoy your course?
> **Candidate:** My course is quite difficult but I really enjoy it.

Most basic 'why' questions can be answered using complex sentences. 'Why' questions lead you to give reasons.

> **Example**
>
> **Examiner:** Why was he such a good teacher?
> **Candidate:** I consider him a great teacher *because* he was able to inspire his students.

'When' questions ask you to indicate a time.

> **Example**
>
> **Examiner:** When did you meet your best friend?
> **Candidate:** I met him at university *when* we both joined the chess club.

'How long' questions are also concerned with time but could require the use of present perfect tense instead of past simple tense.

> **Example**
>
> **Examiner:** How long have you been a stamp collector?
> **Candidate:** I've been collecting stamps *since* I was about five years old.

Questions that seek higher-level responses can also be answered using complex sentences.

> **Example**
>
> **Examiner:** Why are you studying for an MBA?
> **Candidate:** I'm doing this degree so that I can learn how to manage my own business in the future.

Questions asking you to **specify** (for example, *which ... ?/what kind ... ?*) can be answered using relative clauses.

Example

Examiner: What kind of books do you read?

Candidate: I like books that make you think about life.

Exercise 31 Speaking with grammatical range

For each sentence beginning in the first column below, continue the sentence by adding two compound and two complex sentences. Do this by:

- ▼ linking it to other information
- ▼ giving a reason
- ▼ adding some detail

or

- ▼ expressing a contrast or concession.

The first one has been done as an example. When you have finished writing, practise saying the sentences you have created with a partner.

Sentence stem	Additional information
1 I'm planning to study French ...	(link to other information) *and go to France.* (give a reason) *because I feel it will be useful.* (add detail) *which I think is a beautiful language.* (express a contrast) *though I'm not very good at languages.*
2 I think we should reduce the number of cars in our cities ...	
3 I enjoy living in a small town ...	
4 I need to have a holiday ...	

continued ▶

Unit 2: Speaking

5 She would make an excellent manager ...	
6 Internet usage should be strictly monitored for all children and teenagers ...	

When you have finished writing, practice saying the sentences you have created with a partner. Sample answers are provided in the answer key.

Exercise 32 Practising grammatical accuracy and range

Answer questions 1 to 10 below. If possible, work with a partner. In your answers, focus on achieving accurate grammar and use a range of compound or complex sentence structures.

1. How long have you been studying English?
2. Why do you want to study at a foreign university?
3. What's your house (apartment) like?
4. Do you enjoy speaking English?
5. What kind of people do you like?
6. Should university education be free?
7. At what age do men usually get married in your country?
8. Why do so many people choose to learn English as a foreign language?
9. How do you keep up to date with current affairs?
10. What job would you like to be doing in five years?

Questions 11 and 12 are sample Part 2 cards. Respond to each card under test conditions, giving yourself one minute to prepare and then speaking for one to two minutes. If possible, record and transcribe your presentations.

11.
> Describe your best friend.
> You should say:
>   who it is
>   how long you have known each other
>   where you met
> and explain why you regard this person as your best friend.

continued ▶

12

> Describe a film you have enjoyed watching.
> You should say:
> > the name of the film
> > what the film is about
> > how it differs from other films
> and explain why you consider this a good film.

Sample answers are provided in the answer key.

Exercise 33 — Self-assessment of grammatical accuracy and range

1. Below are some questions of the kind you may be asked in Part 3. Give your spoken answer immediately to each question and record it.
   a. If you could, how would you change the education system in your country?
   b. In your view, what are the characteristics of a good friend?
   c. Do you think that there should be a minimum age and a maximum age for politicians?

2. Now listen to your recorded answers and assess them for accurate and appropriate grammar using the questions below. Tick the box that most applies to you. To help you assess more carefully, you may find it useful to write out what you have said.

Questions about your performance	Yes	No	Some-times	Not sure
Is the grammar associated with your verbs correct: for example, tense, subject–verb agreement, negative forms, modal auxiliary verbs, adverbs, adverbial clauses?				
Do you use the correct singular or plural form for nouns?				
Do you use comparatives and/or superlatives correctly?				
Do you use a range of sentence structures (i.e. compound and complex sentences as well as simple sentences) and do you produce them accurately?				

If you answered 'not sure' for any of these, it might be useful to ask other people (study partners, teachers, etc) to assess your grammatical accuracy and range.

Unit 2: Speaking

Pronunciation

The examiner awards a score from 1 to 9 for your pronunciation. Specifically, you are assessed on:

- production of individual sounds
- correct word and sentence stress
- use of stress-timed rhythm
- effective use of intonation and pitch.

This section deals with how to use these aspects of pronunciation to your advantage in the Speaking Test.

Throughout the Speaking Test, the examiner listens to your pronunciation and decides whether it is expert (band 9), excellent (band 8), good (band 7), acceptable (band 6), inadequate (band 5) or poor (band 4 and below). Specifically, the examiner will grade your performance on three main criteria:

1. how wide and how accurate is your range of pronunciation features
2. how effectively you use these features for communication
3. how difficult you are to understand.

Production of individual sounds

There are 44 phonemes (sounds) in the English language. Of these, 12 are vowel sounds, 24 are consonants and the remaining eight are diphthongs, which are a combination of two vowel sounds.

One way to identify and work on individual sounds is to use the phonetic alphabet. This is a special alphabet for pronunciation that has one symbol representing each phoneme in English.

For example, the symbol /ɛ/ represents the short 'e' sound in English – found in words like *egg* or *head*.

Phonetic chart

This version of the phonetic chart is for Australian English (from the *Macquarie Dictionary*). Other versions may use slightly different symbols.

Vowels					
i	as in 'peat'	/pit/	ʊ	as in 'put'	/pʊt/
ɪ	as in 'pit'	/pɪt/	u	as in 'pool'	/pul/
ɛ	as in 'pet'	/pɛt/	ɜ	as in 'alert'	/alɜt/
æ	as in 'pat'	/pæt/	ə	as in 'apart'	/əpat/
a	as in 'part'	/pat/	ɒ	as in 'pot'	/pɒt/
ʌ	as in 'but'	/bʌt/	ɔ	as in 'port'	/pɔt/
Diphthongs					
aɪ	as in 'buy'	/baɪ/	oʊ	as in 'slow'	/sloʊ/
eɪ	as in 'bay'	/beɪ/	ɪə	as in 'here'	/hɪə/
ɔɪ	as in 'boy'	/bɔɪ/	ɛə	as in 'hair'	/hɛə/
aʊ	as in 'how'	/haʊ/	ʊə	as in 'tour'	/tʊə/
Consonants					
p	as in 'pet'	/pɛt/	ʃ	as in 'show'	/ʃoʊ/
b	as in 'bet'	/bɛt/	ʒ	as in 'measure'	/mɛʒə/
t	as in 'tale'	/teɪl/	h	as in 'heal'	/hil/
d	as in 'dale'	/deɪl/	r	as in 'real'	/ril/
k	as in 'came'	/keɪm/	tʃ	as in 'choke'	/tʃoʊk/
g	as in 'game'	/geɪm/	dʒ	as in 'joke'	/dʒoʊk/
f	as in 'fine'	/faɪn/	m	as in 'mail'	/meɪl/
v	as in 'vine'	/vaɪn/	n	as in 'nail'	/neɪl/
θ	as in 'thin'	/θɪn/	ŋ	as in 'sing'	/sɪŋ/
ð	as in 'then'	/ðɛn/	j	as in 'you'	/ju/
s	as in 'seal'	/sil/	w	as in 'woo'	/wu/
z	as in 'zoo'	/zu/	l	as in 'last'	/last/

Problem sounds

If you have learnt English as a second or third language, your production of individual sounds and other aspects of your pronunciation *will always be influenced by your first language*. This is usually not a problem unless the influence of your first language leads

Unit 2: Speaking

you to mispronounce some sounds so that they cannot be understood, or if you have to produce particular sounds in English that do not occur in your first language. For example, many Thai English language learners have trouble with the sound /θ/ as they are unfamiliar with this sound in their own language.

Exercise 34 Producing individual sounds

Get a copy of a phonetic chart, from your dictionary or another source, of the variety of English you wish to speak (for example British English, Canadian English, etc).

With another learner of the same language background, agree on a list of sounds that cause problems for speakers of your language. Practise these problem sounds – first in isolation, and then as they occur in common words. Practise the sounds every day until you are more confident.

Exercise 35 Assessing individual sounds

Listen to an example of Part 2 from the Speaking Test. What sounds does this candidate have particular problems with? How do her problems affect her speech? Read the comments on her performance in the answer key.

Final consonant sounds

It is important to pronounce the final consonant sounds at the ends of words. Sometimes, if you don't pronounce this final sound, your listener may hear another word.

Example

A: My brother sent me a beautiful card for my birthday.
B: He sent you a new car? He must be rich!
A: Not car, a *card*!

It is particularly important to pronounce the final *-s* on the ends of words. The *-s* ending has two main purposes:

▼ (nouns) to indicate more than one: plant ⟶ plants
▼ (verbs) to agree with the third person: I paint ⟶ she paints.

Exercise 36 Listening for final consonant sounds

Listen and underline the word you hear. The first one has been done for you as an example to follow.

1	<u>bat</u>	batch					
2	sin	sing			7	seven	seventh
3	mole	mould			8	bring	brings
4	live	lives			9	expect	expects
5	pass	past			10	when	went
6	type	types			11	fall	fault

Now practise the word pairs by yourself. If possible, record yourself and make sure you can hear the difference between the two words each time you pronounce them.

Correct word and sentence stress

Word stress

Each different sound in a word is called a syllable, and each syllable has a vowel sound.

English words can have one or more syllables. For example, the word *vowel* has one syllable, while *pronunciation* has five (*pro/nun/ci/a/tion*).

When a word has more than one syllable, one syllable usually carries the main stress or accent. For example, the first syllable of <u>tele</u>phone is stressed, while in be<u>come</u> the second syllable is stressed, and the third is stressed in auto<u>matic</u>. Stress is indicated by saying the stressed syllable a little *louder* and/or holding it a little *longer*. Unstressed syllables are short and often have a reduced vowel sound.

There are no firm rules for word stress. However, more than 80% of two-syllable nouns and adjectives have their main stress on the first syllable. Stress patterns can differ for the same word – for example, whether it is being used as a noun or a verb.

Examples

Conduct (verb) The interview is recorded to ensure that the examiner conducts the test correctly.

Conduct (noun) Nathan was discharged from the military for unsatisfactory conduct during training.

The best ways to get to know the stress patterns of individual words are to note the individual stress markings for words shown in your dictionary and to listen carefully to English speakers. In the examples above, stress is indicated with a dot above the stressed syllable. It can also be indicated by a slash (/) before the stressed syllable, or by bolding or underlining the syllable.

Unit 2: Speaking

Exercise 37 — Identifying word stress

Below is a mixture of two-, three-, four- and five-syllable words. Before listening to the spoken words, write the words in the table depending on how many syllables you think they have. The first one has been done for you as an example.

~~combine~~   combination   academic   socialise   inspire
unemployment   vegetarian   arrangement   marriage   interfere
capitalism   probable   probability   eighteen

Two-syllable words	Three-syllable words	Four-syllable words	Five-syllable words
com/bine			

Now listen to the words as they are spoken and mark which syllable holds the main stress. Put a dot above the vowel in the stressed syllable. For example, the second syllable of *combine* is stressed, so the pronunciation is *com/bine*.

Exercise 38 — Predicting word stress

Read the following passage and guess where you think the word stress on the underlined words will be. Put a dot above the vowel in the stressed syllable. The first one has been done for you as an example.

Check-in of the future

Airport check-in times will be **1** drastically reduced as part of a plan by national **2** carrier ComfortAir to improve **3** customer service and increase **4** automation at airports. But while **5** passengers may welcome yesterday's **6** announcement by ComfortAir CEO, Alex Brand, **7** unions fear that it will cost jobs. The **8** proposed changes mean that by the end of the year, all ComfortAir **9** frequent flyer members will receive cards **10** embedded with microchips. These cards will act as boarding passes which also 'talk' to **11** luggage tags with chips to ensure that bags and owners do not part company. Instead of proceeding to a check-in desk, members will swipe their cards at a **12** kiosk, weigh their own luggage and put it on a **13** conveyor belt before passing through security to their **14** departure lounge.

Confirm your answers by listening to the passage as it is read aloud before checking the answer key.

116   Focusing on IELTS   Listening and Speaking Skills

Sentence (focus) stress

English speakers often choose to give more or less prominence to particular words in a sentence. Another name for sentence stress is focus stress because it tells you what the speaker wants to focus on. Stressed words usually give important or new information to the listener (for this reason they are sometimes called content words), while unstressed words simply join information together or provide less important information.

If you give all of the words that you use equal stress, someone listening to you may misunderstand what you mean or they may miss the most important information. You could also sound bored and uninterested in what you are saying.

Exercise 39 Identifying sentence stress

Listen to five examples of the same sentence said with different sentence stress. For each example, underline the word in the sentence that is stressed and carries the focus. What does the speaker want to focus on in each sentence? The first one has been done for you as an example to follow.

1 Could <u>you</u> help me with my preparation for the IELTS exam?

   Focus: *The speaker wants to focus on the listener rather than anyone else as a possible provider of help.*

2 Could you help me with my preparation for the IELTS exam?

   Focus: The speaker wants to ....

   ....

3 Could you help me with my preparation for the IELTS exam?

   Focus: The speaker wants to ....

   ....

4 Could you help me with my preparation for the IELTS exam?

   Focus: The speaker wants to ....

   ....

5 Could you help me with my preparation for the IELTS exam?

   Focus: The speaker wants to ....

   ....

Now check your answers and practise saying the sentence yourself with different sentence stress each time.

Exercise 40 — Using sentence stress

Listen to the following monologue twice. It is on the same topic as Exercise 38 ('Check-in of the future'). The first time just listen and read. The second time you listen, underline the words you think have been stressed by the speaker. Why have they been stressed? The first one has been done for you as an example to follow.

I am <u>delighted</u> to introduce <u>ComfortAir's vision</u> for the <u>check-in of the future</u>.

At the moment, check-in is a painful experience for too many of our valued frequent flyer members. It takes too long. It causes stress. Our own research points to what our customers want, and that is speed and ease at check-in.

To ensure this happens, we have commenced a bold new initiative.

Our frequent flyers will soon be able to use their existing card, embedded with a smart microchip. They'll be able to whiz through check-in, simply swiping their card through a reader. Next stop will be a simple bag drop before a final smooth walk through security to their flight gate. Instead of queues and stickers at the desk, the check-in of the future is all about convenience and speed.

With your personal boarding pass and permanent bag tag, checking your baggage will no longer be a tedious chore. Our plan is to halve check-in time – or better.

It's going to be a revolution at airport check-ins, with our staff freed to focus on customer care. And it's a revolution coming your way by year's end.

Check the answer key and read the comments on the speaker's use of sentence stress. Practise speaking the monologue yourself, paying special attention to sentence stress.

Stress-timed rhythm

Rhythm is the music of language – specifically it is the *beat* of the language. Rhythm mainly results from the pattern of stressed and unstressed syllables in speech. While all languages have their own particular rhythm, English is a *stress-timed language*, which means that strongly stressed words (normally content words that are nouns or verbs) drive the rhythm and occupy most of the speaker's time and effort. Weakly stressed words (often prepositions, articles and pronouns) are generally delivered rapidly in the time between the strongly stressed words.

To have good rhythm in English, you need to gain control over a number of areas. In addition to word and sentence stress, rhythm is affected by:

- use of linking
- use of contractions
- speed of delivery
- pausing.

Linking

English speakers do not usually pause between each word they speak; rather, they glide smoothly from one word to the next. When the words join together this is called *linking*, and it is an important part of English rhythm. Linking occurs in rapid, spontaneous speech when the sound at the end of one word joins together with the sound at the beginning of the next word. Normally, linking happens automatically, but it can be consciously exaggerated when speakers want to skip quickly over less important information, or it can disappear altogether when a speaker wants the listener to focus on one particular piece of information.

Examples

Switch‿on the light! How‿often do‿I have‿to‿tell you?

I thought you‿said you‿were going‿to do the washing‿up.

Contractions

Another way English speakers maintain a distinctive rhythm is through using contractions. These occur when two words join together in rapid speech and some letters are left out.

Examples

He said **we're** (we are) the best team in the school.

Hadn't (Had not) you better send her a present for her birthday?

Contractions are common in informal speech but less common in formal speech and writing. Contractions can make you sound friendlier, and it is a good idea to use some contractions in the Speaking Test. Your use of contractions could be assessed both for rhythm in pronunciation and for range in vocabulary.

Exercise 41 — Contractions

Write the contraction and an example sentence using the contraction in the table below. The first one has been done for you as an example. When you have finished, listen to how they are pronounced and then practise saying them. If possible, record yourself and compare your recording to the original.

Full form	Contraction	Example sentence
1 We have	We've	We've got a new textbook for AFC1000 this semester.
2 I am		
3 I will		
4 You had		
5 He has		
6 She had		
7 It will		
8 They are		
9 They would		
10 Cannot		
11 Will not		
12 Ought not		
13 Shall not		

Sample answers are provided in the answer key.

Speed of delivery

Speaking too fast or too slowly can make your listener feel uncomfortable and confuse your message. In the Speaking Test, there is a danger that you will feel anxious and speak too fast. This rushed delivery could affect your score for pronunciation. Instead, try to express yourself using a relaxed, comfortable rhythm.

Example

Listen to this example of Part 2 from the Speaking Test. As you listen, notice how the rapid speed of delivery makes the candidate difficult to understand.

Pausing

The number and length of stops or breaks in your speech affects your rhythm in English. These pauses can help listeners distinguish between important and background information and can also give dramatic impact to speech. In writing, we use punctuation to break up parts of speech, but in speaking we rely on pausing. However, if you pause too often – for example, between most words – your English rhythm will be disrupted and your listener may find it uncomfortable to listen to you for long periods.

Speaking too fast or too slowly, or with too many or not enough pauses, will also affect your fluency in English. See 2.4, pages 77–80, for more information on this.

Exercise 42   Evaluating use of rhythm

Listen to two extracts from Part 2 of a Speaking Test. While you listen, note which candidate delivers their talk with a more noticeable English rhythm. Consider the use of stress, linking, contractions, speed of delivery and pausing in your evaluation.

Complete the sentence below.

   I think Candidate ………… has better English rhythm.

Check your evaluation by reading the comments in the answer key.

Exercise 43 — Practising English rhythm

This exercise is in two parts. First, listen to the following extract from Part 1 of a Speaking Test and note the candidate's use of rhythm.

Examiner: Thank you, Jason. Now let's talk about food. What are your favourite kinds of food?

Candidate: My <u>favourite</u> kind of food is / <u>Mauritian food</u>.

Examiner: OK, and do you generally like sweet or savoury food?

Candidate: Sweet food.

Examiner: Why?

Candidate: Oh, I like cakes, I like, ah, everything sweet, like fruits and yes.

Examiner: When do you generally eat more – during the day or at night?

Candidate: Sorry?

Examiner: When do you generally eat more – during the day or at night?

Candidate: At night.

Examiner: And why?

Candidate: Ah, like in my culture, ah, we eat, ah, rice every day, so we eat rice every night, like a big amount of rice during at night.

Examiner: Does the weather generally change how much food you eat?

Candidate: Sorry?

Examiner: Does the weather generally change how much food you eat?

Candidate: Yes, of course, in winter I, I eat more than in summer, yeah.

You may have noted that the rhythm was rather slow, with a lack of sentence stress and many pauses in the answers given. Now, think about how the candidate's rhythm could be improved. <u>Underline</u> words in the transcript you think should be stressed and put a slash (/) where you think the speaker should pause. The first one has been done for you as an example.

Now practise saying the dialogue with this new rhythm. Substitute different words for the answers if you wish. Finally, check the answer key for a suggested answer.

Intonation and pitch

English speakers change the pitch of their voices as they speak, sometimes making it higher and sometimes lower. This rising and falling melody is called *intonation*. Movement in pitch can be sudden or gradual and can be put together in various tone combinations. Intonation and pitch can be used to show a speaker's attitude or opinion about a topic, to help structure ideas or to alter meaning. In the Speaking Test, you should use intonation and pitch to help you send or reinforce precise messages about what you mean.

English tones and their specific uses include:

1 level or low rise intonation ⟶ to give incomplete information, information of minor importance

2 high or rising intonation ↗ used for questions that can be answered with a simple *yes* or *no* and for clarification questions

3 falling tone ↘ used for commands, statements or questions where we are not sure what answer we will get.

4 fall–rise tone ↘↗ to show uncertainty, hesitation or contrast

5 rise–fall tone ↗↘ used for exclamation or surprise, or to display a strong attitude towards a subject.

In Exercise 44, we consider the example of the word *Tuesday*. The word only has one meaning, but the use of different tones can greatly alter its significance.

Exercise 44 Recognising intonation and pitch

Listen to five ways 'Tuesday' is said and then match them with the interpretations below. The first one has been done for you as an example to follow.

1	Tuesday	A	Rise-fall to indicate surprise
2	Tuesday	B	Falling tone to indicate a statement
3	Tuesday	C	Strongly rising tone to indicate a question
4	Tuesday	D	Low rise tone to indicate incomplete information
5	Tuesday	E	Fall-rise tone to indicate hesitation or uncertainty

Here is an example of a candidate using intonation and other pronunciation features in Part 3 of the Speaking Test.

Example

Examiner: Why did you choose this particular course?

(level tone) ⟶

Candidate: Um, because, ah, when I was teaching and I thought I should learn something

(slight fall) ↘

more about the linguistics, and that's why I, I chose this, um, area to study.

Unit 2: Speaking

The candidate answers this question using a low, level tone. A slight fall occurs when the speaker makes her final statement on the question. She uses focus stress on the words 'teaching', 'learn' and 'linguistics'. Exercise 45 gives you practise at analysing intonation and pitch.

Exercise 45 Analysing intonation and pitch

Listen to a few more sentences from Part 3 of this Speaking Test. Using arrows, as in the example above, indicate the candidate's intonation. Then write notes on how the candidate uses intonation and other pronunciation features, following the example above.

1 **Examiner:** Mm hm, what are the most challenging or difficult things about your course?

  Candidate: Well … I think the most difficult part is, um, the reading part, because, um, quite a lot of a new concepts involved in, and, ah, that the things I didn't know before. So I think that's the most difficult part for me.

Intonation used: ....
....
....
....

Other features: ....
....
....
....

2 **Examiner:** And what will you do when your course finishes?

  Candidate: Um, teaching, I guess. I would go back and I'm still, I'm doing teaching and I will … I would prefer actually, prefer to use the, the knowledge I learnt here, so back to teaching again.

continued ▶

Intonation used: ....
....
....
....

Other features: ....
....
....
....

Check your notes against the sample comments in the answer key.

Exercise 46 Identifying problems with intonation and pitch

CD 3 · Track 27

First, read the transcript below and predict the intonation and pitch this candidate will use in this extract from Part 3 of a Speaking Test. Then listen and identify problems with intonation and pitch – underline any problem areas in the transcript below.

Examiner: So, firstly, let's look at truth and printed information. So, do you think people generally believe what they read online or in print?

Candidate: Yes, I think so.

Examiner: Why do you think they believe what they read?

Candidate: Because that's the only way they can get the information, of course they can rely on to the material of the newspapers and magazines also on the radio but that's quick way easy way to get the information from the printing way. And I, yeah, I depend on the Internet most of the time.

Examiner: You do? OK. Um, which of the different media, online or print, gives more reliable or truthful information, do you think?

Candidate: I can say that printing but Internet is more quick, so that's why the printing one is like for example the newspaper the next day on the news but for the Internet that day very quick. So people feel more depend, mm, rely on to the Internet, I feel.

Read the comments provided in the answer key.

Unit 2: Speaking 125

Exercise 47 — Self-assessment of pronunciation

1 Below are three practice topics for a Part 2 response. For each topic, take one minute to prepare what you are going to say. Record your responses.

   a Describe a difficult journey you have taken. Explain what made it so difficult.
   b Describe the national flag and/or emblem of your country. What do these things mean to you and other people from your country?
   c Describe a nature reserve or wilderness area that you know about and like. Why does it attract you?

2 Listen to your recordings and assess them for pronunciation using the questions below. Tick the box that applies to you.

Questions about your performance	Yes	No	Some-times	Not sure
Do I produce the individual sounds (phonemes) in words accurately?				
Do I pronounce final consonant sounds?				
Do I use correct word stress?				
Do I give prominence to important or new information in sentences?				
Do I link some words in sentences?				
Do I use enough contractions?				
Do I speak at a good speed – not too fast or slowly?				
Do I use pausing to good effect?				
Do I have a good overall rhythm?				
Do I use intonation and pitch to make my meaning more precise?				

If you answered 'not sure' for any of these, it might be useful to ask other people (study partners, teachers, etc) to assess your pronunciation.

2.5 Developing an independent study program

To prepare for the IELTS Speaking Test, you need to devise a study program that will help you develop your speaking strategies and skills independently. The first step is to identify your needs.

Identifying your needs

Think about what you need to work on in your study program and tick those items in the checklist below.

Speaking checklist ✓

1 **Do you need to improve your general listening?**
   - [ ] General listening

2 **Which aspects of the Speaking Test do you need to find out more about and practise?**
   - [ ] The format of the test (number of parts, types of topics, etc)
   - [ ] Part 1: Introduction and interview
   - [ ] Part 2: Individual long turn
   - [ ] Part 3: Two-way discussion

3 **Which specific strategies and skills do you need to improve for the Speaking Test?**
   - [ ] Speaking fluently
   - [ ] Speaking coherently
   - [ ] Using discourse markers and other cohesive features
   - [ ] Using vocabulary accurately and effectively
   - [ ] Using a range of vocabulary when you speak
   - [ ] Paraphrasing when you speak
   - [ ] Speaking with accurate grammar
   - [ ] Speaking with an appropriate range of grammar
   - [ ] Pronouncing individual sounds correctly
   - [ ] Using word and sentence stress appropriately
   - [ ] Speaking with an effective rhythm
   - [ ] Speaking with appropriate intonation and pitch

When you have completed the checklist, note the section(s) where you have the most ticks and read the relevant section below to discover how you can develop an effective and relevant program of independent study. You can also check the Speaking skills and strategies summary on page ix to make sure you've completed the relevant exercises.

Improving your general speaking

The following resources and suggestions will help you improve your general spoken English.

English-language radio and television stations

Find national and international English-language radio and television stations. Listen to them as much as you can and record some programs so you can play them back for transcription and more detailed practice. If you want to practise your awareness of pronunciation, don't listen so much for the content of the speech – rather, listen to the sounds and 'flow' of the language.

Books, websites and multimedia

Books, websites and multimedia resources are the best sources of material for structured speaking practice. Choose material that will help you practise the skills that you identified in the checklist as needing work.

To improve spoken fluency, it is important to have a reasonably wide, general knowledge so you have enough ideas to talk about in the IELTS test. You can use a range of material to improve your knowledge about the world but a program of general reading is a good start. Become an enthusiastic reader and develop a 'need to know' about all sorts of things. Start with the country or region you are from – find out which is the highest mountain, the longest river, the driest place and the biggest city. You could gather information from an encyclopedia, a travel guidebook or a promotional website for tourists. Read something informative every day to build your own ideas about different topics.

Your first resource for vocabulary practice is a good, advanced-level English–English dictionary. A comprehensive thesaurus to build your knowledge of synonyms would also be useful. Use a reliable search engine, such as Google, <www.google.com>, to find vocabulary practice resources on the Internet. For example, you can access the Academic Word List – a useful resource for improving your spoken academic vocabulary at <www.victoria.ac.nz/lals/resources/academicwordlist>.

A comprehensive grammar book is the foundation for speaking accurately and appropriately. Use a resource that focuses on practical language usage and addresses authentic spoken grammar, rather than just a language 'rulebook'.

Find pronunciation resources that cover all areas of pronunciation, not just sounds. These resources should use voices from the English-language culture you want to enter. For example, if you are planning to study or live in Australia, try to find resources that feature Australian accents. You can also find many excellent pronunciation sites on the Internet. Use a search term such as 'English language pronunciation' to see what you can find.

Practise speaking with other people

Regular practice in expressing your ideas in English with other English speakers is the best way to improve your spoken English. Try to speak in as many authentic situations as possible every day. If you live in an English-speaking country it should be relatively easy for you to find situations in which to practise your English.

Finding situations to practise the more structured English of Part 2 of the Speaking Test is more difficult; however, you could join an organisation such as Toastmasters, or even start your own speaking group for further practice in this area.

Practising for specific sections

Your first resource for finding out more about the Speaking Test is the recording accompanying this book. If you haven't already done so, make sure you do all the exercises in the unit.

You can also find out more about the demands of the test by interviewing people who have already successfully completed IELTS. Ask them what they did to prepare for the Speaking Test and ask for their advice. If possible, record what they have to say.

Practice Speaking Tests

Use the three Practice Tests in 2.6 of this book. By doing these, you can familiarise yourself with the layout and appearance of the IELTS test, and get used to the flow of the test as it progresses from Part 1 to Part 3. The tests start on page 136.

Practice for Part 1

In Part 1, the focus of the test is on casual, conversational English. For this section of the test you need to be able to handle simple questions and give straightforward answers without too many pauses. Try to find situations where you can practise this type of short exchange of information in English. If you don't have easy access to an English-speaking environment, you could analyse how English speakers on television or film conduct this type of conversational exchange.

Practice for Part 2

Part 2 requires you to give a one- to two-minute talk in English about a general topic. It is important to get the timing right for this long response. Record yourself giving talks using the topics listed in the box under 'Just a minute or two' on page 134 with a timing device. Listen to the recordings and transcribe what you have said. Mark any problem areas, such as grammar errors or unclear pronunciations, and re-record your talk with corrections.

Practice for Part 3

You are expected to participate in a discussion, or longer conversation, in Part 3 of the Speaking Test. In this section, you may need to defend your ideas and consider other points of view about potentially controversial issues. Practise speaking at length about topical issues in the English-speaking world to prepare for Part 3. Try to gain some knowledge about current issues through reading newspapers and magazines, or by speaking to English speakers about topics that people are currently discussing in their countries.

Practising specific strategies and skills

If you need to practise the specific strategies and skills required for the Speaking Test, the following suggestions will help you.

Find speaking models

You should collect as many good speaking 'models' as possible. Models are examples of *effective speaking*. Listen to as many models as you can and, if possible, record them. By listening to models and carefully focusing on their pronunciation, fluency, vocabulary, etc, you can set a good standard for how you want to sound when you speak in English.

Speaking fluently

When you listen to your speaking models, focus on how fluently they speak. Notice how they maintain their pace of speaking and any techniques they use to gain thinking time. Also notice how, if they cannot find a particular word to express their meaning, they find other words to keep their speech flowing smoothly. Repeat key parts of their speech, then record your versions and compare them to the models.

When you are involved in authentic conversations (or presentations) try to focus on your fluency. Speak as smoothly as you can and, for this practice, don't be too concerned about your accuracy. Make sure that you do not stop communicating simply because you cannot find a particular word – quickly find a different way to say it and keep going. *Don't translate word for word from your first language*, as this will slow you down.

Speaking coherently

Listen to how coherently your models speak. Pay particular attention to how the speakers relate their answers to the questions. For example, notice how they use pronouns to refer back to nouns in the question. When you are involved in authentic conversations, pay particular attention to answering questions coherently. Make it very clear that you have understood the question and make sure that your answers are completely relevant. For example, if the question asks you *why*, ensure your answer gives a *reason*.

Using vocabulary effectively

While listening to your models, focus on the vocabulary they use. If you think the words you hear are useful, try to use them yourself in situations where you have to speak. In real-life conversations, notice the vocabulary that people use. Don't hesitate to ask people the meaning of the words they use and what words you could use to express the meaning you want to convey. Also, when you are involved in authentic conversations, try to vary your vocabulary as much as possible. Make *diversity* your goal.

Vocabulary development should be an ongoing, regular part of your study plan. Collect all of your new vocabulary together in a notebook and organise this book by theme or category. For example:

- words that describe emotions
- words connected with study
- words describing towns or cities
- words describing houses, apartments or buildings
- words describing festivals and customs in my country
- words connected with expressing opinions
- words to express likes, dislikes and preferences.

Organising your vocabulary learning in this way will help you remember useful words for the Speaking Test.

For each word you list, also record the following:

▼ what other words they are commonly used with, that is, collocation information

▼ synonyms from a dictionary or thesaurus

▼ words that belong to the same word 'family', for example, *nation, national, nationality*, etc.

Set yourself a specific target: for example, five new words per day. This way, you can measure how much you have achieved and feel more positive about your progress.

Speaking accurately and appropriately

When listening to your models, focus on their use of grammar. Each time you listen, adopt a different focus: for example, 'I'll listen to all of the nouns and pay attention to singular or plural' or 'This time I'll listen to the tenses they use'. If you can, read transcripts of their speech as you listen.

It is also important to listen to recordings of your own practice answers and presentations. Transcribe exactly what you said, and analyse it for grammatical accuracy. If possible, ask someone else to check your assessment. From this, you should be able to make a shortlist of weaknesses in grammar and highlight specific areas to improve. Use grammar resources that both explain grammar rules and have grammar exercises to practise.

Another way to assess your grammatical accuracy is to use grammar tests. For example, standard multiple-choice or gap-fill grammar tests are easy to find online. Analyse your errors to pinpoint problems in your use of English grammar.

Also assess your transcripts for grammatical range. Does your speaking show a range of simple, compound and complex sentences? When you extend your Part 1 and Part 3 answers, or when responding to the prompt in Part 2, do you link related points by, for example, adding a detail, a reason or a contrast? Doing this should help you to form more complex structures.

As well as listening to your models, you can develop your grammatical accuracy and range by reading and writing as much as possible. Reading in particular will give you ideas about the many ways we can connect and extend ideas in English.

Speaking clearly

Pronunciation is one of the most challenging areas to work on independently. Your main priority should be to determine your *target* – what specific aspects of your pronunciation do you need to improve? For example, if you want to concentrate on the production of different sounds, you first need to find out which English sound(s) give difficulty to speakers of your first language. Then, listen to recordings of yourself speaking and assess your pronunciation of these individual sounds. Finally, ask other people to assess this area of your speaking.

One effective way to become a better speaker is to note the different ways of expressing things when you hear them. Note the way people say things – the sounds, stress, rhythm and intonation they use. In the days that follow, try to use what you have learnt when you are speaking.

If you are speaking with people you trust, ask them to check your pronunciation and give you feedback. Learn ways to ask for feedback politely (for example, 'Is that how you say it?' or 'Is that the right way to say it?'). Also notice when people misunderstand you or ask you to repeat what you have said. This may be caused by particular aspects of your pronunciation, and should be noted in your notebook.

Once you have identified your priorities in pronunciation, you will know what to practise. Choose the part of the day when you feel most alert and systematically work through your priority list. Here are some specific techniques you can use when practising pronunciation.

- Get a list of difficult words (that is, words that include sounds which you find difficult to pronounce), and practise saying them aloud on a *regular basis*. As you practise, speak slowly and carefully, and exaggerate the movements of your mouth and jaw. A good way to practise is to regularly pronounce all English vowels, consonants and diphthongs using a phonetic chart. While practising, it is important to use a good English–English dictionary, so that you can be sure you are following accurate models of pronunciation.

- To practise your intonation and pitch, experiment with *varying your intonation and pitch* and note what effect it has on the message you are giving. Repeat the same sentence with varied intonation and pitch. For example, try to sound interested or bored, kind or cruel, friendly or unfriendly. Ask someone to listen to a recording of your different sentences and note their feedback.

- Talk aloud to yourself as a *rehearsal* for spoken language. Doing this will force you to predict all the important pronunciation features of words and sentences, and it will give you confidence when you produce the 'real' language later.

- *Shadow reading* can also help you prepare for spoken language. This involves reading along with a recorded speaker, following the pace, rhythm and intonation of the original speaker. This can help with pronunciation, and also with fluency and cohesion.

- Practise *projecting* your voice, so that the examiner does not have to strain to hear you. When you listen to recordings of yourself speaking, ask yourself: can my voice be easily heard? Keep practising until your voice is sufficiently loud.

More exercises for independent study

Even when you don't have anyone to speak with, you can still have a regular program of independent speaking practice. It is important to find a regular time to work on your speaking and to practise as much as you can.

First, you need to build up a stock of practice questions. There are sample Part 1, 2 and 3 questions throughout 2.4 and 2.5, and in the Speaking Test question bank on pages 138–41. You can also generate your own questions. Look at old photos and your CV (resumé) to think of Part 1 questions, and use television, radio, the Internet and books to help you think of Part 2 and Part 3 questions. Write each question on a separate card or piece of paper, and mix them all together in a container. Then, at regular times in your study schedule, select a question from your container to practise.

Record your performances – if possible, make video recordings of them. At a later time, listen to or watch the recordings and judge them according to the IELTS assessment criteria discussed in 2.4. Assess only one criterion each time you listen. Then self-assess to decide what your main needs are and adjust your study plan accordingly.

If possible, keep all of your recordings and note the date on each. Later you can listen to older recordings and judge how your performance has changed (for example, 'My pronunciation is getting better and my structure is more accurate'). Assessing your progress over time will motivate you to keep practising. Improving your speaking skills is a matter of *regular, long-term practice*.

Exercises for study partners

Having a study partner to practise English with is an efficient way to improve your English. If possible, choose a partner who is at the same English language level – maybe someone in the same class who wants to do the IELTS test at the same time as you. It would be best if this person spoke a different first language from you, so you can work solely in English. The following are some suggestions for exercises that you can do with your study partner.

Just a minute or two

This is an activity that improves fluency. Choose one of the topics in the box or one of your own. Talk for one to two minutes on the topic without any repetition or long pauses. If your partner notices any repetition, hesitation or simply can't understand what you're saying, they should say 'stop' and then you should start again. Once you have successfully finished, it is your partner's turn to speak on a topic.

Possible topics

Birthdays	Something that scares me
My favourite restaurant	Dangerous games
Developments in personal communication	The last book I enjoyed
	Technology and education
A perfect weekend	Noise pollution
Student fees	Diet and health
My best travel experience	Universities in my country
A person I really admire	The future of banking
An interesting person I have met in the last week	What makes a good teacher

You can adapt the game to focus on other aspects of speaking: for example, say 'stop' when you hear a grammar mistake or a pronunciation error.

Oral summary of a written text

Both of you read the same short passage from a magazine or newspaper, then think about how you would *summarise* it orally to an audience. Remember that written English is different to spoken English, so you will have to change the vocabulary and make it simpler so your audience can digest it. If possible, get another person to listen to each of you deliver your talks so he or she can say which one was more successful and why.

Cartoons without words

In this activity, each person draws a cartoon of two or three frames without any words. They then swap this cartoon with their partner, who has to fill it in with captions and/or speech balloons in their own words. You should use all the clues you can find in your partner's cartoon to make the cartoon clearer.

Reading aloud

Read a text aloud to your study partner. Because you will be reading to an audience, you will need to incorporate all the features of *delivering a presentation*. Before you begin, read the text privately and mark it up with word and sentence stress. While doing this, try to hear the sounds in your head before you voice them aloud.

Practising English sounds

This is best done with three or four other people. Each person has to write ten sentences using minimal pairs of vowel sounds: for example, 'I lost my pack/pick' or 'Quick, the boss/bus is coming'. Each person then marks the word in each pair that they intend to pronounce. Writers then read their sentences aloud and the other group members have to write the words they hear. If the listeners are unable to detect accurately which word the writer said, it may be because the word was mispronounced.

2.6 Practice IELTS Speaking Tests

Three different, complete practice IELTS Speaking Tests have been provided for you on the recording accompanying this book. They have been written to simulate the real IELTS Speaking Test in style, format and length.

- **Practice Test 1:** Korean female (Jade)
- **Practice Test 2:** Indian male (Jimmy)
- **Practice Test 3:** Taiwanese female (Madeleine)

There are two main ways to use these practice tests:

1. If you have a study partner to help you, he or she could help you take the practice tests before you listen to the models, by using the question bank (pages 138–41).
2. If you do not have a study partner, you can listen to the three tests and assess the performance of the candidates.

Doing the practice Speaking Tests with a partner

If you would like to use the tests for active practice, first find a study partner and ask them to take the role of the examiner. The 'examiner' should select one of the three practice tests from the question bank on the following pages. You should simulate the conditions of the IELTS Speaking Test by sitting opposite each other at a desk and by using a recording device to record the test. Make sure that the 'examiner' times each part of the test.

When you finish, listen to your recording. Assess your own performance using the same assessment criteria as in Exercise 48. Also ask your study partner to assess your performance.

Assessing other candidates doing the practice Speaking Tests

Listen to the complete recording for each of the three candidates without reading the transcript or making notes. As you listen, make a general assessment of the candidate's performance using the assessment grid in Exercise 48. Then listen to each recording again, this time reading the transcript as you listen. This will help you to understand more clearly what the candidate and examiner are saying. You will then be able to confirm (or change) your initial assessment. Listen and read for a third time, but this time underline examples that support your assessment.

Exercise 48 — Practice test assessment

SPEAKING
CD 4
Tracks 1–3

In the table below, score the three practice-test candidates using the simplified four-point scale below. Circle one number for each skill area.

1 = poor   2 = satisfactory   3 = good   4 = excellent

	Jade CD 4, Track 1	Jimmy CD 4, Track 2	Madeleine CD 4, Track 3
Speaking fluently	1 2 3 4	1 2 3 4	1 2 3 4
Speaking coherently	1 2 3 4	1 2 3 4	1 2 3 4
Speaking with effective vocabulary	1 2 3 4	1 2 3 4	1 2 3 4
Speaking with effective grammar	1 2 3 4	1 2 3 4	1 2 3 4
Speaking clearly	1 2 3 4	1 2 3 4	1 2 3 4

Check the answer key to compare your assessment and read extensive notes on each candidate.

Unit 2: Speaking

Speaking Test question bank

Practice IELTS Speaking Test 1

Do you work or study?

Why did you choose that particular type of job?

Are you friends with the people you work with?

Would you still like to be doing the same job in five years?

Part 1

Now, let's talk about **sport and leisure.**

What is your favourite leisure activity? Why do you like doing this so much?

Do you do anything that involves a lot of physical activity (such as jogging, tennis)?

Do you think all children should play some kind of sport at school? Explain why or why not?

Why do you think some sports are only popular in certain countries while other sports are enjoyed across the world?

Let's go on to discuss the topic of **holidays.**

Where do you usually spend your holidays?

Who do you prefer to spend your holidays with? Why?

Are public or national holidays in your country similar or different to the ones in this country?

What do children usually do in their school holidays in your country?

Part 2

> Describe something that you read on the Internet or in a newspaper that surprised you.
> You should say:
> - what you read
> - when you read it
> - where you were when you read it
>
> and explain why it surprised you.

Do you think this was written by a professional writer?

Part 3
Truth and printed information

Do you think people generally believe and trust what they read online or in print? Explain why or why not.

Which of these different media – online or print – gives more reliable or truthful information do you think?

Would you agree or disagree with the idea of fining or even jailing people who were found printing false or misleading information in newspapers or on the Internet? Why do you hold that view?

Citizen journalists

We have recently seen the emergence of citizen journalists – ordinary people who report on events and publish their stories and photographs – usually on news sites on the Internet.

Why would a newspaper or news website publish a story by a citizen journalist? What could be some risks involved?

Do you think citizen journalists provide a good service to the public? Should they be paid for their work?

Do you think citizen journalists will one day replace traditional writers (that is, full-time journalists on a salary)?

Would you enjoy being a citizen journalist?

Practice IELTS Speaking Test 2

Let's talk about where you're living now

Where do you live exactly?

Why did you choose to live in that area?

Do you think other people in your area chose to live there for the same reason(s)?

What kind of recreation facilities are there in your local area?

Part 1

Now, let's talk about **food**.

What are your favourite kinds of food?

Do you generally like sweet or savoury food?

When do you generally eat more – during the day or at night? Why?

Does the weather change how much food you eat?

Let's go on to discuss the topic of **clothing**.

What colours do you prefer to wear? Why?

Do you ever wear very formal clothes or a uniform? When?

When shopping for clothes, do you prefer to go alone or with a friend? Why?

What type of clothes would you wear to a party? Why?

Part 2

> Describe a significant event from your teenage years (that is from 13 to 19 years old).
> You should say:
> - what the event was
> - when it happened
> - where it happened
>
> and explain why you still remember this particular event.

Are you happy that your teenage years are over?

Part 3

Characteristics of teenage life

Could you explain why the teenage years are so different to other stages of life?

When you compare your teenage years with young childhood, what are some major differences between those two stages of life?

In your life, did you enjoy your young childhood or your teenage years more?

Teenagers are often attracted to new technology, such as computer games and iPods. Do you think this interest is good for their personal development?

Were you interested in technology as a teenager?

Difficulties of being a teenager

Would you agree or disagree that the teenage years are the most difficult years in a person's life?

What are some particular things parents can do to help their children make that transition from teenage years to adulthood?

What sorts of new challenges will face teenagers in the coming generations?

Practice IELTS Speaking Test 3

Are you currently studying or do you work?

Why did you choose this particular course/job?

What are the most challenging or difficult things about your course/job?

What will you do when your course finishes?

Part 1

Now, let's move on to talk about **learning languages**.

Would you say you are good at speaking other languages?

Why do you think some people are better at learning languages than other people?

Are some second languages easier to learn than other second languages?

What do you think is the most effective way to learn a language?

Let's talk a little about **your country**.

Have you travelled around it much?

What's the most popular region in your country for overseas tourists?

And why is it so popular?

Does the government encourage tourism to your country? How does it do this?

Part 2

> Describe somewhere you have enjoyed living
> You should say:
> where it was
> what the place looked like
> what the weather was like
> and explain why you enjoyed living there.

Would you go back to live there again?

Part 3

City planning

Let's consider the recent development of a city you know well. To what extent was this development a result of planning?

What do you think is the importance of planning in shaping development in urban areas?

Do you think large cities will become more or less planned in the future?

Gated communities

We've seen the development of a lot of communities called 'gated communities' recently, which are guarded by private companies and restrict entry to non-residents so only residents can go in. Why do you think people choose to live in these kind of communities?

What kind of people do you think would choose to live in these gated communities?

Transcripts

Unit 1: Listening

Exercise 1

Listen carefully and answer questions 1 and 2.

A: Morning. Can I help you?

B: Hi. Yes, I'm thinking about buying a computer. Do you sell secondhand computers? You know, computers that have been reconditioned so they're like new again.

A: No, we find there's a limited market for them, to be honest. We only sell new computers here. Brand new.

B: OK. Well, let's have a look.

A: Sure.

B: Oh, and what about renting? Do you rent computers at all?

A: No, we don't rent, I'm afraid.

B: OK.

A: You might be surprised how good the prices are these days, though.

B: I hope so.

A: OK. What kind of computer? Desktop or laptop?

B: Laptop. I want to be able to take it with me to the university. I've got a desktop at home, but it's really old and I can only use it when I'm there.

A: And you wouldn't consider a mini-notebook, you know, like one of these small ones that are very portable?

B: No, I don't think so. I want a full-size keyboard.

Exercise 2

Listen carefully and answer questions 3 and 4.

A: OK. A laptop. Well, they're the most popular these days.

B: Really?

A: Yes. We sell more laptops than desktops and mini-notebooks combined.

B: I suppose that's not surprising.

A: And what are you going to use your computer for? You have to think about your specific needs.

B: Well, mainly word processing.

A: OK. Anything else? Internet, games, graphics?

B: Yeah, all those things sometimes, I guess. But most of the time I'll just use it for word processing.

A: Well, you can get all of those functions easily with any of these laptops.

Exercise 3

Listen carefully and answer questions 5 and 6.

B: OK. Great. How heavy are laptops anyway?

A: They're really light nowadays. Here, hold this one.

B: Yes, I see what you mean. It's really light. Incredible.

A: Of course, you'll generally find that the really light laptops are more expensive than the heavier ones.

B: Mm, I see.

A: This one, for example, the Apex. It's by far the lightest of the three laptops we sell, and that's why it's the most expensive.

Exercise 4

Listen carefully and answer questions 7 and 8.

B: I should write all this down. So, what have we got? Apex, Sunray and Nu-tech. And how much do they weigh?

A: The Apex is 1.7 kilograms …

B: 1.7.

A: … the Sunray is 2.4 kilograms.

B: 2.4.

A: And the Nu-tech is the heaviest at 3.1.

B: 3.1. And what are the main differences between them?

A: Well, you'd have to say that the Apex is the most convenient, because of its light weight. If, like you said, you're going to carry it around a lot, to and from university, that might be a factor for you. The Sunray, on the other hand, is the most powerful, there's no doubt about that.

B: So … it will handle the Internet OK?

A: Sure. It's well named. It's like the sun, really powerful. It'll handle all your needs. And the Nu-tech is the cheapest, which …

B: … which could also be a factor.

A: Yes.

Exercise 5

Listen carefully and answer questions 9 and 10.

B: I like the look of the Sunray.

A: Yes, I do too.

B: And what are all these?

A: Well, here on the left-hand side is the in-built CD/DVD drive.

B: The what?

A: You know, the place to put your CDs or DVDs.

B: Oh, yes. I'm with you.

A: You just press here.

B: Yes.

A: And over on this side are the different media ports … and this is the microphone.

B: Microphone?

A: Yes, if you want to record your voice.

B: Where? Here?

A: No, that's the on/off button … Here next to it, you see the microphone?

B: Oh, yeah.

A: And the mouse, of course.

B: Oh so … the Sunray has a mouse.

A: Yes, just like the desktop computer.

Exercise 6

Listen carefully and answer questions 11 to 13.

B: Do all the laptops use a mouse, or should I say mice?

A: Yes, they all do but there are different types. If you look here, you can see that the Apex has a cordless laser mouse … see, you just move it and that moves the cursor in the direction you want.

B: That looks pretty easy.

A: And this one has a very similar one except it's called an optical wireless mouse.

B: Yep.

A: And of course, the other type is a traditional mouse. You can see one on the Nu-tech here with its standard cord. You just move it like this.

B: I'm not so keen on that type. Hmm …

Exercise 7

Listen carefully and answer questions 14 to 16.

B: And tell me, what happens if there are problems with the computers – do they have a guarantee?

A: Oh, yes, all of these three models have guarantees. The Apex and the Sunray are guaranteed for 12 months and the Nu-tech for six months. You can see it here on the labels. I suppose the Apex gives you the best arrangement, though, because it guarantees both parts and labour.

B: What do you mean?

A: Well, they will cover the cost of any parts in the computer that need to be changed, and also their labour – their time in fixing it – is covered. You don't have to pay anything.

B: Oh, I see.

Transcripts Unit 1: Listening

A: But the Sunray guarantees parts only.
B: Parts only? Oh, I see. I would have to pay for the labour.
A: Exactly. And the Nu-tech is the same as the Sunray.
B: OK. Right. That's great. I think that'll do for the moment. Thanks for all your help.

Exercise 8

A: Have you finished your assignment?
B: Almost. I'll be finished tomorrow.
A: That's a relief.
B: Actually, I really enjoyed this assignment, to tell the truth.
A: How come?
B: It was interesting. I'd never thought about all this stuff.
A: Like what?
B: Well, like all of the data on gender. Did you know that females make up 52% of university students? Who would have expected that? I was sure that there would be more males than females at university.
A: Yes, me too. That's great.
B: Yes, well, it's not all great. Things are very different at the top, believe me. Do you know how many female Vice-Chancellors there are in the entire country?
A: No idea.
B: Guess.
A: Ten?
B: Three!
A: That's not very good, is it? Anyway, your assignment looks good. Very impressive.
B: I still haven't done the references. Once they're done, it'll be finished.
A: I hate doing the references too.

Exercise 9

A daring daylight robbery has stunned the small community of Roseville. At nine o'clock this morning, just after opening, two men wearing face masks entered the Central Bank and brandished shotguns. The terrified staff handed over the money, and the robbers fled the bank. Fortunately, there were no customers in the bank at the time. The robbers made their getaway in a blue Toyota sedan, driven by a third person. Bank officials have yet to confirm the amount of money stolen, but it is understood that the thieves may have got away with close to half a million dollars.

The two suspects are described as being in their late teens or early twenties, both of slim build and approximately 175 centimetres tall. There is no description of the driver, although one witness has suggested that this person may have been a woman. This is the first major robbery in the small fishing-industry township, and residents are extremely upset. The manager of the Central Bank, Elaine West, has announced that the bank will conduct a comprehensive and immediate review of its security procedures. If anyone has any information possibly relating to the robbery, please call the police hotline on 9357799.

Example, page 16

A: Have you seen our new lecturer?
B: No.
A: That's her over there.
B: Gee, she's tall.
A: Don't worry about her height. Let's just hope she's a good lecturer.

Exercise 10

A: Hello, can I help you?
B: Yes. I need to see an original edition of a rare book in your collection.
A: Of course, that should be fine. Can you tell me some details about the book?
B: Right, it's the *The Theory of Moral Sentiments* by Adam Smith. It's by the same guy who wrote *The Wealth of Nations*.

A: Ah yes, I think we have a number of copies of that text. Let me check our catalogue.

B: Thank you. It's for a philosophy assignment.

A: OK ... yes, we have three copies of very early editions of that work. Which one would you like to request?

B: Well ... I'm not really sure. Are they all in good condition?

A: Let me look. Because they are rare books, we have a copy of their front covers here on the WebCat. Right ... here they are. Yes, they all appear to be in excellent condition.

B: Umm, I can see they're all well preserved. Were they all published in the same year?

A: Let's have a look. Well, no, two of them were and the other one was published a little later. Yes ... the one with the cover title in the larger font was the third edition – published in 1767.

B: I need the earliest edition, so I guess that leaves these two ...

A: Let me see. Ah ... there is a small difference. Yes, the quality of the covers is different.

B: Really? They look exactly the same to me.

A: No. If you look closely, you see this one has some irregular shading along one side.

B: I can't really see that. You mean this darker patch on the left?

A: No, no, I think that's the image quality. I mean this area on the top right-hand side – maybe it's been discoloured through heavy use.

B: Oh, I see. Anyway, if they are both the same edition – it doesn't really matter, but maybe I'll take the better-looking one.

A: So, the one without the stain?

B: Yes, that's right.

Exercise 11

Now, before you go, let me give you the details of your next assignment. Yes, I know you're busy studying for your exams, but this is the last essay for the semester – and it has to be done. I've written the topic on the board. Can you all see it? Please copy it down and please make sure that you get it right: 'Attitudes towards public transport'. Now, as you can see, it's a very straightforward topic and you shouldn't have too many difficulties with it. And you'll be happy to hear that it doesn't have to be very long. Ten pages. That's all, OK? Don't give me less than that and please don't give me more. Remember: I don't want a postcard and I don't want a thesis. As for methodology, well, I'm going to leave that open to you to choose. You can conduct a telephone survey, for example, or maybe a series of face-to-face interviews, or maybe you can do an in-depth case study and draw your conclusions from that. It's up to you, but please do think about it carefully before you decide which way to go. Now, you haven't got a huge amount of time to get this in to me. I want it submitted to me by the 11th of September. Is that clear? The 11th of September. And as usual, I won't consider any extensions unless there are really exceptional circumstances. Now, please also make a note of a few more points. As you know from before, it's an absolute requirement that the essay be word processed. No options here, I'm afraid. I don't want to be sitting up all night trying to decode your handwriting. Also, there must be a title page. Some of you failed to do this last time, so please make a note of it to remind yourself this time. And finally, please make sure that you include a statement of your methodology. Clear and concise, no more than say half a page. OK. That's about it. Any questions?

Transcripts Unit 1: Listening

Exercise 12

(**S** = Speaker; **R** = Recording; **M** = Mia; **O** = Operator)

S: You're going to listen to a telephone conversation. Mia is telephoning an airline company. She wants to change her flight reservation.

R: Welcome to Sky Air, the friendly airline. If you would like flight arrival information, press 1. If you would like to make a domestic reservation, press 2. Please note that it is not necessary to confirm domestic flights. If you would like to make an international reservation, press 3. If you would like to speak to one of our sales officers, please hold the line.

M: Hm. Number 3, I guess.

R: You have reached international reservations. All of our operators are busy at the moment. Please hold and an operator will be with you as soon as possible.

M: Oh, come on. I'm in a hurry.

O: Good morning. Andrew speaking. Welcome to Sky Air. How can I help you?

M: Yes, I'd like to change my reservation, please. I can't travel on the day I booked. I have to work.

O: And what was your name, please, madam?

M: Mia Torres. T-o-double-r-e-s.

O: And what was the flight number, Ms Torres?

M: Yes, I have it here. SA233.

O: And do you have the date?

M: Uh … January 21st.

O: Right. I have it here. Sydney to Honolulu.

M: Yes, that's right.

O: Now, what would you like to change it to?

M: Well, what's available? Is there a flight on the 22nd?

O: No, I'm afraid not. There are only three flights a week direct to Honolulu. Mondays, Thursdays, and Fridays.

M: What time does the Friday flight leave?

O: All the flights leave at the same time: 5.45 pm.

M: OK. Well, I'll take Friday the 25th. Do you have seats available?

O: Yes, we do. Would you still like a window seat?

M: Yes, please. I like sitting near the window – you can see everything.

O: OK. That's fine. Friday the 25th. The same flight number as before: SA233. And please remember to be at the airport two hours prior to departure.

M: Do I have to ring again and reconfirm?

O: No, Ms Torres. There's no need to reconfirm.

M: And I'd like to know … how much luggage can I take on the flight?

O: The allowance is 22 kilos.

M: So, if I have more than that I have to pay extra, right?

O: Yes, that's right … So, can I help you with anything else?

M: Ah … let me think … I wanted to change the date of my reservation … ask about reconfirming … and check the regulations about the luggage allowance … They were the main things, I think.

Exercise 13

A: Good morning. Ace Security. Can I help you?

B: Yes, I'd like some information about the alarm system in this house. I've just moved in and I don't know how to use it. The previous owner left me a code number, but that's about all I know about it. I've got no experience with using alarms.

A: Sure. Can you see the monitor on the wall?

B: Yes, I'm looking at it right now.

A: Good. What does it say on the screen?

B: 'Disarmed. Ready to arm.' Whatever that means.

A: Well, to arm is to 'activate', to 'switch on', I suppose.

B: So, disarmed means 'deactivated', I guess.

A: Yes, that's right.

B: Fair enough. So, how do I arm it then?

A: Well, you mentioned that you have a code, right?

B: Yes.

A: A four-digit number, right?

B: That's right.

A: Well, all you have to do is enter that code number on the key pad and press 'away'.

B: What does 'away' mean in this case?

A: It simply means 'go out', as in you want to go out of the house and therefore you want to activate the alarm system while you're away.

B: OK, I see. I thought it meant something like wipe it away. OK. So that's when I want to go out. What about when I come back into the house? Do I press the key with 'C' on it?

A: No. Actually, you enter your code again and press the 'off' button. Can you see it on the left-hand side of the pad?

B: Oh, yes. So what is the 'C' button then, on the far right? I thought it was 'C' for 'clear' like you get on a calculator.

A: No. Actually it stands for 'change code'. That's the key you press when you want to change your four-digit code. For security reasons, for example.

B: Oh, I see. Well, I really had that one wrong. ... So, OK. What's the asterisk just below it? Is that for emergencies or something?

A: No. That's what we call the 'fault check'. When you press that, the screen will tell you if there are any faults in the circuit – you know, faults as in 'problems', like you've left a window open somewhere or there's a problem with one of the sensors, for example. Anything that needs to be checked before you're ready to arm.

B: Oh, I see. I guess it's not that complicated.

Exercise 14

To illustrate this phenomenon, let us look at a practical example. I'm sure you will have noticed that nowadays competitive swimmers typically wear full-length body suits, from neck to ankles, instead of the traditional briefs. Why do they do that? It certainly has nothing to do with appearance. In fact, some people don't like the look of them at all. Rather, the reason they wear these swimsuits is a matter of physics, and hence of interest to us in this course. The suits, you see, are specifically designed to improve performance by reducing drag. Drag, of course, refers to contact which slows down forward movement. The issue of drag is important in many sports, including speed skating, cycling and running.

Sports scientists have long worked on reducing drag by getting swimmers to shave their bodies. In experiments conducted in 1990 – you can follow up these experiments in the reading I've assigned for next week – in these experiments, they found that swimmers consumed something like 10% less oxygen after they shaved their body hair. The experiment was limited to shaving body hair, not head hair, although some studies conducted the following year also had similar results. Of course the experiments do not prove that shaving body hair will automatically help people swim faster, but it is clear evidence of the impact of reducing drag.

Scientists have extended their concern with drag in swimming even further and have collaborated with swimsuit manufacturers to produce a swimsuit which is like a new skin for the swimmer. They've done this by emulating the skin of one of the swimming superstars of the world, one of the fastest swimmers in the world: the shark. The new swimsuits are usually called 'shark-skin suits' because, of course, that's exactly what they look like: shark skin.

Sharks are a miracle of evolution who have ensured their survival by becoming faster swimmers than their prey or competition. But why are sharks so fast? Quite simply, because of tiny ridges all over their skin. Even though their skin looks remarkably smooth, their skin is, in actual fact, covered with these almost invisible ridges. And that is what the manufacturers have managed to put on the swimsuits: tiny ridges. And it's these ridges which reduce drag and help the swimmer glide through the water faster. At least, that is the theory. It is impossible to prove scientifically that these suits lead to better performance, and indeed some commentators are sceptical.

Exercise 15

Tutor: OK. We've looked at the issue of the quality of our politicians and you've all been rather critical of their performance. So, how can we as a country improve the quality of our politicians? Do you have any practical suggestions? Yes, Mark?

Mark: Well, I really feel that politicians should be required to have a certain level of education.

Tutor: And what level of education would you require?

Mark: Well, at least a university degree.

Sally: I can't see the sense in that, I'm afraid.

Tutor: Why not, Sally? What's wrong with the idea?

Sally: Well, I don't think there's any evidence that university graduates are actually any better than less well-educated politicians. I mean, what's the connection between a university education and the quality of political leadership? We need politicians with good hearts and good ethics, not clever brains.

Anna: I can't see any connection either. I mean, I don't feel any more intelligent now that I'm studying at university.

Tutor: Well, I'm not sure that intelligence is the issue, Anna.

John: Exactly. It's not about intelligence.

Tutor: Would you care to elaborate, John?

John: University graduates have analytical skills and are better able to distinguish between facts and opinions, and that's really important, I think. Having those kinds of skills can't possibly hurt, and it might actually help raise the quality. I reckon we should make it a requirement. Some of our politicians are really pathetic.

Sally: Well, I certainly agree with that. They're totally out of touch. Just dead wood. I reckon we should get younger politicians, not better educated ones.

Tutor: You think we should have younger politicians, Sally?

Sally: Yes.

Anna: No way. I think it's the other way round. We should put a minimum age requirement on people running for political office. We need people with

Transcripts Unit 1: Listening

more maturity, more life experience. Not younger people.

Tutor: And what minimum would you suggest, Anna?

Anna: Forty, I think.

John: That sounds reasonable to me.

Tutor: What about you, Mark? Do you agree? Is establishing an age requirement one way of improving the situation?

Mark: Not as far as I can see. You're not going to get better politicians by worrying about their age. I don't know. Maybe the only way to get better quality is to pay more. Give politicians higher salaries and you'll attract better candidates.

Sally: You're joking!

Exercise 16

He currently works as a tutor in molecular science at one of the local colleges. Apparently he earns around 50% more than he used to. The workload is oppressively heavy, but he has a reasonable amount of annual vacation. By and large, he's satisfied with his new position and responsibilities.

Exercise 19

1 **A:** Do you like my new radio?
   B: Yeah, it looks great.
   A: Actually, it's not a new radio. It's an antique.
   B: I love the colour. What's it made of?
   A: Bakelite.

2 **A:** Look, Jane, isn't Dr Metwali great with kids?
   B: Oh, yes, kids adore her. Look at them all crowding around her. Mind you, it's no wonder.
   A: What do you mean it's no wonder?
   B: Well, she is a pediatrician, after all.
   A: Is she? Someone told me she was a surgeon.
   B: No, she's definitely a pediatrician.
   A: Well, as you said, no wonder. I really admire pediatricians.
   B: Why?
   A: Well, it must be terribly hard for them, treating little kids who are seriously ill, you know, with terminal cancer or something.
   B: Yes, I know what you mean. That must be hard.

3 **A:** Turn that radio off, will you. It's driving me crazy.
   B: Don't you like the music?
   A: No, it's not the music. It's all the ads, with all those dreadful jingles. I can't bear them. I can't get them out of my head.
   B: Well, all stations have ads, so you can't escape them. Anyway, jingles are music.
   A: Please don't call jingles music.

4 **A:** The former Senior Accountant at Universal Machines, Alicia Trent, has been found guilty of embezzlement and has been sentenced to four years jail.

5 **A:** What a beautiful garden!
   B: Thanks. Yes, it's coming along quite well. There's still a lot of work to do, though.
   A: Like what?
   B: Well, this wall for example. It's totally bare. I'm going to put a trellis here and I'm thinking of planting an allamanda.
   A: That'd be nice. The yellow would look great against that wall. Does it grow quickly?

B: Yes, that's one of the reasons I chose it, actually. It should reach the top of the wall within a year.

6 A: What are you going to plant in this corner?

B: Yes, it's very empty. I don't know what to plant. It's really hot in this corner, and the soil gets extremely dry.

A: Yes, you're going to need something really hardy.

B: How about agave? They're hardy, aren't they?

A: Yes, they are. They don't need much water or food, and they can stand really hot temperatures. They can survive just about anything.

B: That's what I think I'll have, then.

Exercise 20

As the train slows to enter the station on this clear Friday morning, I'm suddenly aware of the huge central bank building. Its twin, thirty-nine metre towers and giant central dome momentarily overshadow the train's passengers.

Example, page 30

The crisis in handwriting began with the first computer.

Exercise 21

The way a person writes displays individual style and personality. In previous centuries, children were taught techniques to write properly and letter-writing became an art form. However, with the emergence of computers and mobile phones, many children are no longer capable of producing good handwriting. This is a great pity for several reasons. Firstly, a piece of well-ordered script written with flow and flair is pleasing to the eye – kind of like a firm handshake or a nice smile when you meet someone new. Mastery of handwriting also assists young people to control their hand and promotes hand–eye coordination. Finally, it teaches them to slow their thinking and reflect before writing.

Example, page 31

A: Professor, can I talk to you about my research project?

B: Let's talk about your *essay* first.

Exercise 22

Devices such as notebooks, interactive whiteboards and e-book readers have all secured a place in our schools and universities. Texting and social networking sites like Facebook completely dominate our lives outside of work. But as we continue to embrace new technology, what role do we leave for traditional forms of text construction, such as handwriting? Are we disadvantaging our young people with this blind acceptance of digital technologies? Indeed, many young people struggle to form words by hand and can't even spell. This has already become a significant problem both in school and tertiary education, as handwritten exams still form the main method of assessment.

Example, page 32

This year I'm studying chemistry – in fact I've just bought the main textbook – and physics.

Exercise 23

Good morning, class. Today, I'd like to talk about producing educational multimedia.

This particular type of multimedia – as distinct from entertainment multimedia – is an area of interest for educators everywhere. I'd particularly like to discuss the process of producing this type of multimedia. Your first consideration, apart from deciding what medium you're going to deliver your product through, is your audience. Who they are, what they expect and, most importantly, what they need. After you have determined this basic information about your users, then you can go on to the all important area of content.

Example, page 33

I think we're ready. We've got pens, pencils, erasers and a stapler.

Exercise 24

1. Cacti are part of a group of plants called succulents.
2. I'd like you to meet my friend, Vanessa.
3. We have a wide variety of language courses, including Arabic, Tagalog, Thai.
4. Educational multimedia can be delivered via CD-ROM or over the Internet.
5. Flight number 823 from Kuala Lumpur is delayed.
6. I'd like to speak to the Managing Director, please.

Exercise 25

1. Hi, Lek. How are you? Long time no see.
2. Excuse me. Does this bus go to the State Library?
3. Excuse me. Could you press the bell for me, please. I can't quite reach it.
4. **A:** I think you should just go to her and explain exactly what happened. Just tell her everything and ask her to forgive you.
   B: Really? Do you think I should?
5. **A:** I didn't.
   B: Yes, you did. You know you did!
   A: No, I didn't! I wasn't even there that day!
6. That's really kind of you. I'd really love to come, but I've got a huge assignment to do this weekend and I'm going to be really busy. I really wish I could come.
7. It'll be fine, believe me. You'll find it really easy.
8. It's huge and it's got a really flat screen. And the picture is so clear, it's like being at a cinema.
9. Why don't you come around on Friday night? We're having a few people over to celebrate Mark's promotion.
10. I won't take 'no' for an answer.

Example, page 35

A: Excuse me. I'd like to speak to the manager, please.

B: I'm the manager. How can I help you?

A: Well, I'm really unhappy about this carton of milk.

B: And what's the problem, madam?

A: Well, look at it. I bought it here yesterday. See, here's my receipt. And look at the use-by date! It's expired for over a week. Look! The 15th it says, and today's the 23rd. How come you still have old milk in your refrigerators? It's disgusting. I want my money back, and I'm never coming to this supermarket again, I can assure you.

B: Well, Madam, I can see why you would be upset. We do always try to …

Exercise 26

1. **Woman:** Hey, I heard the good news. That's wonderful. Well done. I'm really happy for you.
   Man: Thanks. Yes, I'm really pleased … and relieved that it's all over.
   Woman: Oh, I never had any doubt that you'd pass. And look, you got a 'distinction'. Well done. You really deserve it.

Man: Thanks. I'm heading over to the student union. I'm going to ring my parents. You coming with me?

2 **Woman:** Come on.

Man: I don't want to.

Woman: Oh, come on. I don't want to go by myself. And it's only $25 for students. That's great value. Look, how about this? I'll pay for half of your ticket if you come. Will you come then?

Man: But I'm not that keen on their music.

3 **Woman:** It's really four machines in one. It's got a telephone, a fax machine, an answering machine, and a copier. And it's guaranteed for two years.

Man: How much does it cost?

4 **Woman:** The thief is described as being short and stocky with bleached blond hair. Anyone with any information about the robbery should contact the police hotline on 131 800. And now for today's highlights in sport, here's Jim. Hi, Jim.

5 **Woman:** Hi. I'm interested in the property for sale at Days Road, but I just wanted to check what it says in the advertisement.

Man: Sure. What can I help you with?

Woman: Well, it says the property is being sold with 'vacant possession'. What does that mean?

Man: It simply means that the property will be empty – there won't be any tenants in it – when you buy it.

Woman: Oh, I see.

Exercise 28

Most people assume that ornamental gardens have always existed since the beginning of time. However, this is [*pause*] not true, at least as far as Western civilisation is concerned. Although the Chinese were growing plants for aesthetic pleasure at least two thousand [*pause*] years ago, in the West, plants were grown for purely practical purposes, such as [*pause*] for food, medicine, or for ceremonial use. Well into the 15th century, gardens were largely limited to crops, orchards and herb gardens. Monasteries in particular had herb gardens where they raised many of the plants which we still use today to [*pause*] add flavour to our food. It was only the very wealthy who cultivated anything which was not of practical use. In 16th century English such people were called 'curious gardeners', both because [*pause*] they wanted to learn more about plants and because most people regarded them as rather strange.

Examples, page 38

times a quarter past four, ten to nine, half past twelve

dates the 5th of March, the 21st of November, the 13th of February

numbers three point five, seventeen, seventy, fifth, three quarters, eight-and-a-half million

letters UN, USA, S-t-e-v-e-n, IBM, c-a-t-e-g-o-r-y, M-a-r-i-a, c-l-i-c-k

Exercise 30

Listen carefully and answer questions 1 to 5.

A: Kingscliffe Library. Can I help you?

B: Yes. Good morning. I just wanted to … um … My library book is due back, but I can't come to the library to return it. I had a bit of an accident and I can't walk at the moment.

A: That's no problem. We can extend it for you. Have you got your library card there?

B: Yes.

A: And what's your membership number? It's on the front, in the bottom, right-hand corner. Can you see it?

B: Oh, yes. It's 0-1-0-3-0 6-9-double-7.

A: Great. Jacqueline Smithies, is that right?

B: Yes, that's right. Well, yes and no. It isn't right strictly speaking. There's always been an error on my card. That's not how you spell my name. My surname.

A: Oh, isn't it? Sorry about that. I'll change it now on the computer while we're here. So, what is it?

B: Well, you've got Smithies, right? S-m-i-t-h-i-e-s.

A: Yes, that's right.

B: Actually it should be Smithers: S-m-i-t-h-e-r-s.

A: I see. OK. I've changed it now. But Jacqueline is spelled correctly, is it? J-a-c-q-u-e-l-i-n-e.

B: Yes.

A: OK. We'll post you out a new card with the correct spelling on it.

B: That'd be great.

A: Your postal address is right, isn't it?

B: I think so.

A: 17A Heeley Street, H-double-e-l-e-y.

B: Yes, that's it.

A: Clapham.

B: Yes. SW11.

A: SW11. Yes, that's right. OK. Well, all that's in order now.

Listen carefully and answer questions 6 to 10.

A: Now, what was the book that's due? Oh yes, I see it – yes, it's due tomorrow, the 12th of August.

B: Yes, that's it.

A: Well, I can extend that to the 30th of September. Will that be enough time for you to get it back?

B: Oh, that's plenty of time. Yes, that'll be fine. Thanks.

A: No problem.

B: Listen. While I've got you …

A: Yes?

B: There's a book I'd like to find.

A: Sure. What's the title?

B: Well, that's the problem. I'm not sure. It's about 'hardanger'.

A: Sorry?

B: 'Hardanger'. H-a-r-d-a-n-g-e-r. It's a kind of craft, like crocheting, or … sewing, I suppose. I'm not real sure to be honest. It's for my mother. It's her hobby. But I know the author's name.

A: Fine. That's all we need. What's the author's name?

B: Liebke. L-i-e-b-k-e.

A: Do you know when it was published?

B: 1989, I think.

A: Oh, yes. Here it is. *Hardanger Patterns and Techniques* by Liebke. Is that the one?

B: Yes, I'm sure that's it.

Listen carefully and answer questions 11 to 15.

A: It's out at the moment, I'm afraid. It's due back on the 13th – the 13th of August. You could come in and pick it up then if you like. Would you like me to reserve it for you?

B: I could come in at the end of next month. Could you reserve it for then?

A: Done. You can pick it up on the 30th.

B: Thank you. By the way, what times are you open?

A: During the week we open at half past nine and we close at seven o'clock.

B: Seven?

A: Yes. On Saturday and Sunday we close a bit later, at eight thirty.

Transcripts Unit 1: Listening

B: But the same opening time?
A: Yes. The same.
B: Great. Thanks for all your help. What was your name?
A: Axel.
B: Sorry?
A: Axel. A-x-e-l.
B: Thanks a lot, Axel.
A: A pleasure. Bye now.
B: Bye. Thanks.

Exercise 31

One of the most widely occurring processes in the world is the production of refined flour from wheat, through a process called *milling*. There are four main stages in the process. In the first stage, the cleaning stage, the wheat grains, or *kernels* as they are called, are placed in large bins which contain revolving blades. These remove any dirt or debris, leaving clean kernels for further processing. In the next stage, known as *conditioning*, the kernels are placed under large sprinklers. In this way they are treated with water to *condition* them – that is, to soften them, to make them soft enough to break in the next stage of the process. The next stage is the actual milling itself. In this *milling* phase, as we call it, which of course is the key process in the whole operation, the grains are passed between rollers – enormous round rollers. This action splits the kernels and produces the finely ground grains that we know as *flour*. The flour moves to the *bleaching* stage, where it is placed in large vats and treated with bleaching agents. This makes the flour white. Traditionally, this process was achieved through natural aging. The flour is then mechanically packed in a process known as *sacking*, so called because the flour is placed into large sacks. The flour is then ready for use in baking bread and cake products, and for use in cooking.

Exercise 32

Mr Lee: Here, I'll show you what I mean. Have a look at this. Can you all see this? Come a bit closer, you three over there. Yes, that's it. Can you see?

Ben: What is it?

Mr Lee: Well, what do you think it is?

Ben: I don't know. Looks like a thermometer.

Colin: No, it's a barometer.

Mr Lee: That's right. A barometer.

Ben: I thought it was a watch.

Mr Lee: Actually it's an aneroid barometer, to be precise.

Ben: A what?

Mr Lee: Aneroid.

Ben: Sounds like a robot.

Mr Lee: Aneroid. A-n-e-r-o-i-d. Don't worry about writing it down – I'll give you a handout on it in a moment. OK. It means non-liquid – that is, it doesn't have any liquid, any mercury, which is what is used in the other type of barometer. And of course you know what a barometer is for, don't you?

Colin: Measuring … um … moisture in the air, measuring humidity … air pressure.

Mr Lee: Yes, that's close enough. This … here, I'll show you … this is the critical part inside … it's the vacuum chamber. Can you see it? Some of the air has been taken out of this chamber – that's why it's called a vacuum of course – so that it reacts to air pressure.

Ben: But how does it work?

Mr Lee: Any changes in air pressure make this chamber contract or expand. This shift is transferred along this series of levers – you see there are two of them, one here connected to another one here.

Ben: Why are they called 'leaders'?

Mr Lee: No, I'm not saying 'leaders', Ben. Levers.

Ben: Oh, sorry. Yes, I see.

Mr Lee: So, the move is transferred along the levers to this chain – just a regular chain, and then the chain wraps around this spindle. 'Spindle', Ben. I don't want you to get it wrong again. Spindle. S-p-i-n-d-l-e.

Ben: Got it. Thank you, sir.

Mr Lee: Which, as you can see, in turn drives the needle.

Colin: It moves the needle across the dial.

Mr Lee: Precisely. That's how a barometer measures. And there are three ways to make this measurement – you can use millibars, millimetres or inches. What does this one use? What's written there on the dial, Ben? Can you see it?

Ben: Where?

Mr Lee: Just near the head of the needle.

Ben: Oh, yes. I can see. 'Inches'.

Colin: What's a millibar?

Mr Lee: Don't worry about that just now. Let's take a look at this handout first.

Exercise 33

1 **A:** How come he arrived so late?
  B: Because his flight was delayed

2 **A:** Did you hear about that awful car accident?
  B: Yes, I heard. Apparently it was all due to driver fatigue.
  A: Really?
  B: Yes. She'd been driving for ten hours, and fell asleep at the wheel. Sad, isn't it?

3 **A:** The five-per-cent fall in the New York stock exchange has led to similar falls in other markets internationally.

4 **A:** How come there are so many birds in your garden?
  B: It's those trees I planted last spring – they attract the native birds.

5 **A:** The warmer temperatures have meant more loose sea ice as the ice sheet begins to melt.

6 **A:** And of course as a result of these endless delays we're now ten days behind schedule.

7 **A:** How come her visa application was rejected?
  B: She didn't pass the medical test.

8 **A:** Environmentalists attribute the recent, record-breaking floods to the erosion which has accompanied the destruction of forests in adjacent foothill areas.

Exercise 34

Another English-speaking country in this region is Trinidad and Tobago. The official name of this country is 'the Republic of Trinidad and Tobago', reflecting the fact that the nation comprises two islands: Trinidad and Tobago. Trinidad is the larger of the two islands, with an area of 4,828 square kilometres, whereas Tobago, which is located to the north-east of Trinidad, has a mere 300 square kilometres. As well as in size, the two islands are very different in shape. Trinidad is round in shape, while the latter is long and thin. Trinidad is also the higher of the two islands, reaching a maximum elevation of 940 metres, while Tobago reaches a height of only 576 metres. Both islands are densely inhabited, with an estimated 96% of the total population of the country living on Trinidad, and a mere 4% on Tobago. Now united and independent (since 1962), both islands passed through many colonial hands. Trinidad was confirmed as a British possession in 1797, while Tobago was confirmed in British hands in 1814. The two colonies were linked in 1888.

Exercise 35

1. There are three fares available. The first class fare is $1,350, the business class fare is $1,030 and the economy fare is $650.

2. There are two different types of test. One is the so-called Academic Test. This is for candidates seeking to enter university, and it comprises three subjects: English, Computer Literacy and Mathematics. The other test is the Technical Test. This is for candidates wishing to enter technical college. It is the same as the Academic Test, except candidates do not have to take the English component.

3. Broadly speaking, writing can be divided into two kinds: non-fiction and fiction. In non-fiction writing, for example, biographies, textbooks and dictionaries, the content is factual. On the other hand, fiction, such as novels or poems or cartoons, uses imaginary characters and events.

4. Languages can be divided into three main types according to their structure, in particular the order of the constituent elements in a sentence. The first (and most common) type contains SOV languages. Here 'S' stands for *subject*, 'O' stands for *object* and of course 'V' then refers to *verb*. The second type (and English is an example of this second type) contains SVO languages. The third type contains VSO languages.

5. One of the most fascinating birds in the world is the emu. Emu. E-m-u. This large, flightless bird can reach up to 2 metres in height. There are two varieties of emu: the Western emu and the Eastern emu, the names of the varieties reflecting their geographical distribution. There are two features which distinguish the varieties. The first feature is colour, with the Western variety typically having a darker colour. The other feature relates to seasonal change. The Western emu develops a white 'ruff' (like a white collar around its neck) when it is breeding, whereas the Eastern emu does not change colour at all during breeding.

Exercise 36

Mrs Blake: More coffee anyone?

All: No, thanks.

Mrs Blake: Another piece of cake, Julie?

Julie: No, thanks, Mrs Blake. It was great.

Tom: Hey, Diane. Have you finished your assignment yet?

Diane: Yes. I handed it in this morning. What about you?

Mrs Blake: No, of course he hasn't. He's always running late.

Tom: Thank you very much, Mum.

Mrs Blake: Well, it's true, isn't it?

Tom: Yes, I have to admit it. I haven't quite finished it yet. How much is it worth?

Diane: 10% of the final mark, I think.

Tom: All that hard work for just 10%? I hate continuous assessment! The never-ending pressure.

Mrs Blake: What's 'continuous assessment'?

Diane: Well, instead of just having one exam at the end of the year, they give you a mark for each of your assignments throughout the year. And sometimes they give you a mark for how well you participate in tutorials too.

Mrs Blake: Mmm. Sounds like a good idea to me. I'm sure it makes you study harder throughout the year. I can just imagine how lazy Tom would be if his assignments didn't count.

Tom: Thank you very much, Mum. Of course Diane loves continuous assessment, don't you?

Diane: No, I don't. I hate assignments just as much as you do, but it's still better than just having one formal examination. There's too much stress that way. I get really nervous having to do an exam. This way I've got a better chance of getting a reasonable mark.

Mrs Blake: What about you, Julie? Which method do you prefer?

Julie: Oh, you know me, Mrs Blake. I'm a risk-taker. Give me an exam any day. Do or die, I say.

Tom: Exactly. And an exam is over in a couple of hours. It's much less painful than all these endless assignments.

Julie: And I think it's very fair. Everybody takes the same exam on the same day.

Diane: Well, we'd better leave you alone, Tom, so that you can finish your assignment.

Tom: Oh, come on. Don't leave. Have another coffee!

Exercise 37

1 Solar power is our future. It is renewable, it is safe, it is clean. You can't say that about the other major forms of power, such as fossil fuels or nuclear power. No wonder that in 1999 the United Nations described it as, quote, the preferred source of power for the 21st century, unquote. Solar power is our only way forward.

2 Anti-drug television commercials are a waste of time and money, and they should be stopped. The nation-wide survey which our agency conducted throughout April 2001 indicates that the majority of young people do not like the commercials and are not frightened by their message. Also, in the survey interviews, over 60% of young people felt that the commercials were unbalanced, because they did not also target alcohol and tobacco, the drugs used by their parents.

3 At the moment I'm doing a business degree via the Internet. When you study in distance mode like this, it's great. You feel that you have more control over your study. You can study when you like. You can also manage the pace of your study: you can go more quickly or more slowly. You can pause, repeat, or you can skip things and go ahead. And you can tell that distance study suits me better. I study much harder nowadays than when I went to university. I feel really motivated. I love it.

4 Marine pollution has reached crisis level around the world, and yet governments appear totally unable or unwilling to acknowledge the extent or significance of the problem. Studies undertaken at our monitoring station at Port Fortitude in the Antarctic indicate a staggering 150% increase in marine pollution since we began taking measurements just three years ago. This rate of increase is frightening. Similar studies conducted by the South African government confirm these fears, and the studies by the Icelandic government, at marine locations the same distance from the pole as in the southern hemisphere studies, show increase rates of over 200% per year.

5 Critics of the ancient sport of boxing completely miss the point when they call for it to be banned. They claim that it is too dangerous and cite the most recent boxing-related fatality as proof of their claim. I know, and most of you know, that

the reality is different. In fact, there are fewer deaths associated with boxing than with just about any other major contact sport, and that includes rugby. In 1999, for example, boxing deaths worldwide were estimated at less than half of rugby deaths. Quite apart from that, boxing is a very positive and much-loved sport. For one thing, it represents an excellent opportunity for young athletes, especially from disadvantaged backgrounds, to excel, to achieve self-esteem, and to achieve a satisfying and lucrative career. And boxing brings great pleasure to millions of fans around the world. Did you know that the most recent world heavyweight championship bout reached a worldwide television audience of over a billion people? What are you going to say to these people? Tell a billion people they are wrong? What are you going to do? Switch off boxing? No, don't be ridiculous.

Exercise 38

Our challenge is to produce graduates who are able to go into the workplace and get on well enough with their fellow employees to complete projects successfully. There is also a need to turn out graduates who have superior interpersonal and negotiation skills. It is strongly recommended that tutors carefully organise their classes so that students develop these skills.

One way to do this is to organise more group work. However, tutors need to pay very careful attention to how they put these groups together. The traditional approach is to let students choose their own groups. Unfortunately, this rarely leads to achievement of target skills, as students will choose their friends and won't develop their interpersonal skills with strangers. My advice would be to go with random group allocation but making sure there is a balance between local and international students.

Now you have your groups but how can you make sure students work together effectively? First, you need to point out the benefits of working with 'strangers' – particularly in the context of preparation for the workforce. Then make sure the group members are able to connect with each other through exchanging each others' details, such as phone numbers and email addresses. Urge them to schedule regular meetings and agree on common expectations for the group assignment related to quality of work and expected grades. It is also important to allocate responsibilities within the group so that the work gets done. This could involve matching personalities to roles. For example, someone who likes organising could be assigned the role of 'task master'.

Exercise 39

A: Hey, Gayle, how did the conference go?

B: Not bad, quite interesting, but I had a few dramas while I was there.

A: Really? What happened?

B: Well, you know I had to present a poster?

A: Yeah, saw you working on it before you left. How did it go?

B: Well, I got there on time and registered and that was all fine.

A: Mmm.

B: Then I went next door to the conference hub to find out where I had to put my poster up, but they told me there that their program had me listed as doing a presentation!

A: Oh, dear! What did you do?

B: Well, I just said that I hadn't prepared a presentation but had a poster instead.

A: Did that put them out?

B: Not too much, considering. They asked me to go to the poster hall straight away and see if they could fit it in there.

A: And did you end up displaying it there?

B: Well, first I had to find it. It was the building furthest away from the main conference venues and no, when I got there and they told me there was no room. So they sent me back to another building. The one where the delegates had their coffee break. Kind of like a cafeteria in the centre of the cluster of conference venues. So I ended up sticking my poster on the wall there.

A: Goodness!

B: It wasn't really ideal, but at least I got it up somewhere.

A: And did you have to stay next to it for the rest of the conference?

B: No, I was lucky. After that, I could slip out to the main presentation hall just next door and listen to all the talks. It was a huge auditorium – the biggest on the campus. I just had to make sure I was standing beside my poster during the tea breaks.

A: Not much time to drink tea and socialise though.

B: You're right about that!

Practice IELTS Listening Test

You will hear four different recordings and you will have to answer questions on what you hear.

There will be time for you to read the instructions and questions before the recording is played. You will also have the opportunity to check your answers.

The recordings will be played ONCE only.

The test is in four sections. Write your answers on the question sheet as you listen. At the end of Section 4, you have ten minutes to transfer your answers onto the answer sheet, which is on page 60. When you finish, check the answers at the back of the book.

Now turn to Section 1 on the next page.

Section 1

You will hear a conversation between a real-estate agent and a man who wants to rent a flat. First, you will have time to look at questions 1 to 5. You will see that there is an example that has been done for you. On this occasion only the conversation relating to this will be played first.

Jill: Hello. Are you Mr Lee?

Michael: Yes. Michael Lee. Sorry, I've forgotten your name.

Jill: It's Jill Brown, nice to meet you.

The name of the woman is Jill Brown, so 'Jill Brown' has been written in the space. Now we shall begin. You should answer the questions as you listen, because you will not hear the recording a second time. Listen carefully and answer questions 1 to 5.

Jill: Hello. Are you Mr Lee?

Michael: Yes. Michael Lee. Sorry, I've forgotten your name.

Jill: It's Jill Brown, nice to meet you.

Michael: You too.

Jill: Now, you wanted to rent a flat, is that right?

Michael: That's right. My wife and I will be moving here soon and so I need to find us somewhere to live.

Jill: Oh, lovely. Do you have any particular area in mind?

Michael: Well, we don't really know the city very well but I have a job at the university, so I'd like to live near there.

Transcripts Unit 1: Listening

Jill: Well, there are some lovely flats in Toowong.

Michael: I'll write that down. How do you spell it?

Jill: T-double-o … w-o-n-g.

Michael: Got it.

Jill: It's a lovely little area. It's very quiet with lots of lovely trees and it's got a very good shopping centre.

Michael: Sounds great. What is the public transport like near there? I know the city has a good ferry service, I'd love to be able to travel on that rather than the bus!

Jill: Yes, it's on the river so you'll be able to catch the ferry and it is so much nicer than the bus or train.

Michael: Great! How close is it to the city centre? My wife will be looking for work and may need to travel into the city. I'd like to be no more than 10 kilometres away if possible.

Jill: Let's see, it's 5 kilometres to the centre of the city and only 2 kilometres to the uni, so you're close to there as well.

Michael: Great! What's the best way to get into the city? Would you recommend we get a car?

Jill: Parking is so expensive. And the bus can take too long because of the traffic.

Michael: So the train would be the best idea for my wife then.

Jill: Definitely.

Before you hear the rest of the conversation, you have some time to look at questions 6 to 10. Now listen and answer questions 6 to 10.

Michael: So do you have many units available in the area?

Jill: Yes, I've got two really good ones at the moment. Do you want me to tell you about them?

Michael: That would be great.

Jill: The first one is on the ground floor. It's got two bedrooms. The main bedroom is nice and large, the second bedroom is only small but it would make a nice office, which would be good if you have to work at home. That flat is $250 per week.

Michael: Sounds great. Though I think I don't like the idea of being on the street level.

Jill: Well, I have got another one in the same apartment block. It's on the seventh floor.

Michael: Good. Does it have a view of the river or anything?

Jill: Yes, it has actually, and it would be so relaxing sitting out on the balcony watching the river.

Michael: I like the sound of that one.

Jill: It's the same size as the other one, with two bedrooms and a fairly typical living area. The kitchen has been renovated recently, so no problems there, and it has the standard laundry and bathroom.

Michael: Hmm. It sounds promising. Is the rent the same?

Jill: No, it's $75 a week dearer, so you'd be paying $325. Is that a problem?

Michael: No, I'd actually budgeted for up to $350 a week, so that's fine.

Jill: Good. When would you like to see the property?

Michael: As soon as possible really.

Jill: I don't have any appointments on Thursday. Would that suit you?

Michael: Actually, I have to go to the university that day. Could we make it earlier? I know my wife is free on either Tuesday or Wednesday and she would love to see it as well. We'd both prefer Tuesday if possible, because that would give us Wednesday to go to the bank and organise a deposit.

Jill: Good, let's do that then. I'll see you …

That is the end of Section 1. You now have half a minute to check your answers.

Now turn to Section 2.

Section 2

You will hear the boss of a company giving a welcome talk to new staff. First you have some time to look at questions 11 to 15. Now, listen carefully and answer questions 11 to 15.

Good morning everyone, and welcome to Global Shopping. My name is Paul Cullen and I'm the owner of the company and your new boss! Your job here is to take as many telephone orders as you can each day. As we are such a large organisation, we always like to get our new employees together to meet important staff members and fill you in on some of our systems. Firstly, I'd like to introduce you to Mark Rogers. Mark was recently promoted from our sales and marketing department and is now office manager. You should see him if you need any particular equipment or office supplies. Next, we have Lucy Scott, she runs our accounts department and more importantly looks after any of your pay issues. She also handles payments for any orders you take. You'll find her office on level two, opposite the photocopiers and fax machines. Next, we have Janet Bowden, my very efficient personal assistant. She organises all of my appointments so if you need to see me for anything at all, you will need to see Janet first! Then, there is James Ferguson. James works on reception and meets and greets all of our visitors. James also handles all calls that aren't from customers, so if you are going to be away from your desk for any reason then you need to let James know and he can leave a note about any missed calls. And finally, I'd like to introduce Peter Harding. Peter oversees all of the orders and makes sure that they are all dispatched quickly. So you need to pass any orders on to him as soon as you receive them.

Before you listen to the rest of the talk, you have some time to look at questions 16 to 20. Now listen and answer questions 16 to 20.

Right now, I'd like to talk about some of the day to day systems we have here that you need to know about. Firstly, this is a very secure building so you can only enter each day if you show your ID card. You'll be issued with one of those this afternoon. I mentioned visitors earlier: they have to go to the security office where they will be given a day pass that they can then use in the same way. Now, you'll find sitting and answering the telephone all day can be very tiring, so we try to make our staff feel as comfortable as we can. Mark is coming around now handing out your own headphones. These allow you to move your hands about freely so you can take notes while you talk. We also recommend you get up and stretch as often as possible. To make sure this happens, you are allowed to take a break of ten minutes every two hours. You are also allocated a 30-minute refreshment break every four hours, so please make sure to eat and drink during the day.

Your job here, as I have said, is to take telephone orders for all of the products we offer. These products change on a regular basis. They are advertised on TV each Monday and they appear in magazines issued every Thursday. To help you get to know these products, we hold an information session on the Friday before the new items are released. Once you have received an order, you will need to send it to the relevant department, which may be overseas or in the same building. To do this, you need to complete our special online order form and email it to the relevant department. We manage all our orders this way now, as it is so much more efficient than filling out order forms by hand or sending them by fax.

Ok, so that's our ordering system and now we'll take a tour of ... [fade]

That is the end of Section 2. You now have half a minute to check your answers.

Now turn to Section 3.

Section 3

You will hear a student and a university lecturer talking about a new car design. First, you will have some time to look at questions 21 to 26. Now, listen carefully and answer questions 21 to 26.

Lecturer: Hi, Colin. Come in and sit down.

Colin: Hello, Dr Sims. Thanks.

Lecturer: I wanted to hear all about this car you've been working on. Sounds amazing!

Colin: Yes, we're really proud of what we've managed to do.

Lecturer: It's a racing car you've built, is that right?

Colin: That's right. But it's unlike any other racing car you'll ever see.

Lecturer: So I've gathered! Now, it's got the nickname of 'The Flying Carrot'. Is that because of the colour of the paintwork?

Colin: No, that's actually white. Our aim was to make a car out of totally recycled materials. We've even managed to use plant materials, and the steering wheel was actually created out of processed carrots – although funnily enough it turned out purple for some reason!

Lecturer: That's quite amazing. So what materials did you use for other parts of the car? I heard you'd managed to use plastic bottles?

Colin: That's right. We wanted to ensure the body of the car was as light as possible so we combined old bottles with waste aircraft materials. We're really pleased with the results.

Lecturer: And what a great way of saving money. But what about the internal workings? Surely the engine couldn't be made from vegetables or plastic?

Colin: No. We had to use a standard engine but we did manage to adapt it so that it can run on chocolate waste products.

Lecturer: Wow, that must save a lot on running costs and I'd imagine it's the only racing car that can run on biofuel.

Colin: That's right, it is.

Lecturer: I know some manufacturers have already tried making their racing cars greener by replacing petroleum-based products in the tyres with orange oil.

Colin: Yes, and that's great but we wanted to go further than that. For example, with the car's radiator.

Lecturer: Oh? Is it made from vegetables as well?

Colin: [*laughing*] No, what we did with it was to coat it with a special material so that it actually eliminates ozone in the air and converts it to oxygen while it is still at ground level.

Lecturer: What a great idea. Maybe 'Smog Eater' would have been a better name for it then!

Colin: [*laughing*] I suppose we've used so many strange and unusual materials that it's going to get called lots of odd names! We even found a way of using potatoes to make the wing mirrors, and the seats are filled with a soya-based material.

Lecturer: I can't wait to see it. What about the brakes? They're often a problem in racing cars because they wear out too quickly. But I was told you used cast iron, why was that?

Colin: Well, we wanted to get away from the carbon that standard cars use and find something more efficient, so that's what we came up with. We have been trying to come up with a brake system using cashew nuts but we're not quite there yet!

Lecturer: Well I think you and your team have done an amazing job.

Before you hear the rest of the conversation, you have some time to look at questions 27 to 30. Now listen and answer questions 27 to 30

Lecturer: So tell me how you came up with this idea in the first place. Why did you decide to make a car?

Colin: Well, we wanted to design something that would really draw attention to the idea of using recycled materials.

Lecturer: But you chose some very strange materials. Are you hoping these same materials will be used in ordinary cars?

Colin: I imagine some of these materials might not be commercially viable but using them helped us to make our point. We've designed a car that can race at 125 kilometres per hour. It might not win any competitions, but no one can deny it's a racing car.

Lecturer: Yes, but why did you decide to make a *racing* car and not something simpler? Was it just because no one else has done it before?

Colin: Well, there's been a lot of controversy in the media about Formula 1 cars lately and that's what made us come up with the idea. You see, the running costs are so great that sponsors are questioning whether Formula 1 racing has any future. We thought we could show them one way to solve their problems.

Lecturer: So what's next? I know you've already taken the car for a test drive. How did that go?

Colin: It went really well, as I said the driver managed to reach 125 kilometres an hour, which is a pretty respectable speed. It actually has a top speed of 140.

Lecturer: Did he comment on any safety issues?

Colin: That's something we would like to continue working on and improving. Although the driver said he felt very comfortable driving it.

Lecturer: That's good. What are you hoping the car will be used for? You've said it can reach pretty good speeds, are you aiming to enter any races? It would be a great way to promote the uni's engineering department!

Colin: Well, I don't think we're quite up to Formula 1 standards just yet but we're hoping to get permission to showcase it at that type of event.

Lecturer: So, before the actual race takes place you'd drive it around the track then let people have a look at it?

Colin: That's right. It will hopefully make them think twice about the way they are travelling around, the type of vehicle they buy or the fuel they use.

Lecturer: Well it should certainly do that. Look, I think you've all done an amazing job and …

That is the end of Section 3. You will now have half a minute to check your answers.

Now turn to Section 4.

Section 4

You will hear an expert giving a talk about evolutionary biology. First, you will have some time to look at questions 31 to 40. Now, listen carefully and answer questions 31 to 40.

Good morning, everyone. My name is Marco Archetti. I've been asked to talk to you today about a branch of biology you may not have heard of, namely evolutionary biology. We evolutionary biologists study the origin of different species, and how they change and evolve over time. To give you a better idea of what we do, I thought I would describe a recent study I conducted.

This particular study involved an attempt to answer an age-old question in biology: why do the leaves of some trees change colour in autumn? My own theory was that the brilliant red and orange colours we see in autumn in colder climates act as a warning in the same way as tropical frogs or butterflies use bright colours. The meaning of the colour is 'stay away from me, I'm dangerous'. For example, the colour might signal to an insect that the leaf contains a chemical that has the potential to harm it. Or it might simply mean that the leaves contain very little nutrients and so should be avoided.

So, what kind of tests can we do to establish whether or not these theories are correct? Well the ideal test of a hypothesis such as this is to let populations of trees evolve with and without insect pests for many generations. If autumn colours were intended to scare off insects, we might expect red colouration to be lost in areas that are protected from insects, because with no insects present, that system would no longer be needed.

An experiment like this would take too long to perform, of course, but we are very fortunate in that this test was really begun two thousands years ago when we began to domesticate apple trees by farming them and defending them from insects with pesticides. So my study involved checking the results. I looked at wild apple trees in Central Asia, which were the ancestral stock for the domestic varieties we eat today, and I found that while 60% of these wild trees turn red, just 40% of domestic trees in that region do. We also tested 2,170 domesticated varieties in Britain and the results were even more convincing, with less than 3% of trees turning red.

We wanted to be really sure of our findings and so we carried out a second test. We found that yellow or green leaves had twice the number of insects on them than the red or orange leaves. We also found that the insects on the yellow or green leaves were much healthier. This suggests to me that the red and orange leaves pose some kind of threat to the insects.

Of course, not everyone is convinced by my conclusions and there are several other theories as to why the leaves change colour. The first of these suggests that the red pigment is produced as a chemical sunscreen, which shields the leaves from the harmful effects of sunlight at cold temperatures. Other studies have shown that the red pigment helps trees to reabsorb nutrients from the leaves before they drop off. This theory proposes that this allows the trees to stay healthy right up until they lose their leaves, perhaps aiding in survival through the harsh winter ahead. Still other scientists believe that the red pigment might help plants to retain water in their leaves, thus helping them to survive the winter for longer. Another theory is that the red colour makes green insects more visible to their predators and so helps the tree stay free from pests. Whichever theory is correct, it is evolutionary biology that will eventually help to find the answer.

That is the end of Section 4. You now have half a minute to check your answers.

That is the end of the Listening Test. You now have ten minutes to transfer your answers to the listening answer sheet.

Unit 2: Speaking

Exercise 3

Examiner: Let's talk about your study or work. Are you currently studying or do you work?

Candidate: I am a student, yes, studying.

Examiner: And why did you choose this particular course?

Candidate: You mean, the course in the university?

Examiner: Mm hm.

Candidate: Yeah, because, actually it's more easy to find a job becau … if you are an accountant. Yeah, I'm studying accounting.

Examiner Mm hm. And what are the most challenging or difficult things about your course of study?

Candidate: Yeah, I think the most difficult thing is there a lot of difference in different company. I mean, the situation is quite different, and use which kind of method to data the … the, to data the figures or something else, I mean, as well use different methods. It is a big challenge because, um, different situation in different situation you need to use different methods, so maybe this method is especially suitable for that company. Yet you need a lot of experience, yeah.

Examiner: Mm hm. And what do you think you'll do when your course finishes?

Candidate: I think I will find a job in Australia and to earn more, ah, experience, because become accountant experience is much more important than the degree.

Examiner: Mm. Now let's move on, ah, to talk about, um, learning languages. Ah, would you say you are good at speaking other languages?

Candidate: Um … I think that's OK if you keep on practising and practising, will be better.

Examiner: Mm hm. Why do you think some people are better at learning languages than other people?

Candidate: I think that's their talent. Yes, some people they are born to be good at learning some languages. I think … that's it.

Examiner: And do you think some second languages are easier to learn than other second languages?

Candidate: Mm, I don't think so, but I have no experience, I just, that's just my opinion.

Examine: OK. What do you think is the most effective way to learn a language?

Candidate: Effective? I think, um … more listening, um … more practice. I think you can, um … use a tape there, for example, when you listen to English and you follow them sentence by sentence and speak much quickly and quickly each time. Then you keep going every day, I think, is most effective.

Examiner: Let's talk a little, um, about your country. Have you travelled around it much?

Candidate: Um, I think just a small part of our country because China is a large country. And I just travel about some big cities.

Examiner: What's the most popular region in your country for overseas tourists?

Candidate: Region? Mmm, I'm sorry, I know but I don't, I don't know how to describe in English. I don't know that, the name of that region.

Examiner: Is there a particular city that's, um, that's popular for tourists?

Candidate: Oh yes, mmm … yeah, the big cities, for example, the Beijing, Shanghai, Guangzhou, Sindran and Hong Kong nowadays.

Exercise 5

1   **Examiner:** Can you start speaking now please?

   Candidate: Yes, Ah, the thing I wo … own that's most important from me, it's my car, which is in Brazil. Ah … my father gave me this four years ago and it is the most important thing because I … I have a few problems travelling by bus or train. Because of the movement I have a problem here in my labyrinth so I feel a little bit sick for the whole trip. And … it's the best thing, because I can … not only because of this disease, if I can call like this, but it's the moment I can stay alone, listen to my music in peace without a lot of people bother me. Not exactly bother me but I feel more comfortable because I can think of my day, I can think of everything happen and listen to my music, but it's always more comfortable and … than travelling by train or bus.

2   **Candidate:** I'm going to talk about my iPod because I rarely go anywhere without it. I have a million things stored on it like songs, photos and some videos. I use it everyday when I'm travelling on public transport and walking to work. However, it's not my first one. I did have one before but lost it on an overseas trip. I really love my little pink Pod since it gives my ears such a lot of pleasure and is so cute.

Exercise 6

The city I would like to visit is Rome, the capital of Italy. It's a city that has always attracted me because of its culture. I'm particularly interested in its architecture since it has examples from all major European styles of building. Besides, it was the capital of the Roman Empire, so it has a wonderful collection of public buildings from that time. What I think is great about Rome is that many of the beautiful and historic buildings are still in use – as galleries, public offices and even houses. They are not all locked up as museums, so it's really living history there. Even though it's an expensive city to stay, I'd like to go there for at least a month, as there's so much to see and do. During my time there, I'd have to be careful that I didn't spend too much on Roman food! I'd find a cheap *pensione* – sort of a low budget hotel. It would probably be in the *centro storico*, the old centre of the city, probably within walking distance of the River Tevere. Most visitors to Rome would agree that it is a very special place but for me, it's Europe's most historic and romantic city. While cities like Paris, Vienna and Madrid are lovely too, I think Rome beats them all.

Exercise 10
Candidate 1

Candidate 1: I like, I like living there because, um, because, um, the culture is ah, is similar, similar to, ah, my culture. Um, the language is the same language. Um, we are all, we all say, ah, Cantonese. And it's, and we, it's and, ah, and Hong Kong is when, is, is near, um, is near my, ah, home town, Guangzhou. So, um, if I live there, if I live there, ah, I think, ah, it will be, ah, very convenience. And I, I like, I like living in Hong Kong because, um, ah, everything is very convenience, ah, and I, I can, I can eat, ah, I can eat cheaply and I can, ah, bought many things because Hong Kong is a shopping heaven.

Candidate 2

Examiner: OK. Remember you have one to two minutes for this. I'll stop you when the time is up. Can you start speaking now, please?

Candidate 2: Yes. Mm, I think my recent unit is a very good place for living and I, when I arrived Australian I, I rent this unit from my agent, agent, as you say. Yeah, it's apartment on the floor see ... on the second floor and, um, it is on the corner of the Fontenoy Road and the Lane Cove Road. Ah, it's a bed, it has two bedroom and a laundry and a kitchen and a bathroom. Mm, I like it because, mm, I think, firstly, I can, I live here very comfortable and secondly, I think the view is very good. You know, in front of, in front of my unit it's a park. And the bus stop just at the, at the corner so I can take buses very convenient. And, ah, secondly, and ah, I think this and the rent is very cheap, so it save me a lot of money. Mm, I think another thing is I, my friend, my flatmate is very friend and kind, real kind. It's very easy to get along with her, so I'm like my unit very much and I, I enjoy the living very much.

Exercise 11
Candidate 1

Examiner: Ah, let's first consider the design of modern cities. Can you describe, um, the recent development of a city that you know well?

Candidate 1: Recent development? [*unclear*] OK. Ah, when I, when I visit United States it was very, ah, modern, modern city, and, ah, and was why, you know, ah, in Japan it's very, the city is very messy. So ... So the airport is always entrance for the foreigners but ah, in Japan, ah, the access to the airport is very, ah, hard, and ah, unconvenient.

Examiner: Ah hah.

Candidate 1: But in United States, ah, it different. So ah ...

Examiner: So to what extent do you think, um, the development of these two cities was a result of planning? How would you compare them?

Candidate 1: Yes, maybe, ah. Mm ... United States is, is not so old country and it was, the city has been developed, ah, for, for within 100 years or so. Or something.

Examiner: Mm hm. Yeah.

Candidate 1: And it was planned to, to be comfortable for the people.

Examiner: OK. How important is planning in shaping development in cities?

Candidate 1: Cities? Mm, maybe, ah, like Australia, ah, there are m... if there are many natures, trees, it be a very comfortable for the people who are living.

Examiner: Mm hm.

Candidate 1: And, mm, and also we need big street, yeah, and, ah, that, ah, good access to the downtown area.

Examiner: OK. What do you, what do you think large cities will be like in the future? Um, will they be more planned or less planned?

Candidate 1: Less planned?

Examiner: Yeah. Will there be more planning or less planning in cities in the future?

Candidate 1: Ah, it's ... maybe more planning is necessary for the future cities. Mm, I don't know how to, how should, how they should plan to the city but, ah, mm, planning is always necessary.

Candidate 2

Examiner: OK. We've been talking about places where people live. I'd like now to discuss one or two general questions relating to this topic.

Candidate 2: Yes.

Examiner: Firstly, ah, let's consider the recent development of a city you know well. To what extent was this development a result of planning?

Candidate 2: Ah, OK. This one is a little bit difficult, um. I will try, if I can put it this way. The city I know, I would like to use the example of, um, the capital city I'm coming from, Taipei.

Examiner: Mm hm.

Candidate 2: Um, the government has, ah, planning to build the city of Taipei as one of the, ah, international city. So the government have been putting quite a lot of the public transportation, for example. Um, so, and also, um, knocking down some old buildings and they put quite a lot of parks. And ah, some very big shopping centre, for example, as well.

Examiner: And do you think large cities will become more or less planned in the future?

Candidate 2: I think they will become more planned and actually that is the, one of the needs that people actually want, because I think more and more people want to, um, doing their business in their commercial area. And when they want to relax, when they want to enjoy their family life, they don't want to hear some, um, like, a commercial, um, you know, like announcement all the time, the people are doing business or they will put very loud music. I think they would just like enjoy their own family life in the com... residential area.

Example, page 81

Examiner: In what day, way does a good system of public transportation affect the quality of life for city dwellers?

Candidate: Yeah. Public. Mm, public transportation? For the, ah, public buses I, ah, sometimes very confused to, how to use the buses and h... which bus is going which, ah, which place, you know. And, ah, so, how to pay a fee is different from the each cities. It's very confusing.

Example, page 83

Examiner: Why do you think some people are better at learning languages than other people?

Candidate: Ah, I think that some people do better in some languages because if the languages that they are studying has got, like, ah, the same, um, language structure, this will be much more easier for them to, to, um, handle with the language.

Example, page 95

Candidate: Um, I think security probably the major reason. Ah, so if people uh... who choose to live in the gated community, they plobably, plobably (oh, sorry, I have the problem with that word). Um, they perhaps, ah, the reason for them to choose is for the concern of security, as I just say earlier.

Example, page 95

Candidate: I believe TV news more than Internet.

Examiner: Why?

Candidate: Because I think on television is, on air to everybody and every day but Internet is, is not so far – govern... I don't know how to say.

Exercise 24

Examiner: Ah hah. OK, we've been talking about places where people live. I'd like now to discuss one or two general questions relating to this topic. First, ah, let's consider the recent development of a city you know well. To what extent was this development a result of planning?

Candidate: Mm ... I'm not so sure. Are you asking me about a city planning?

Examiner: Yes, that's right.

Candidate: So ... ah, you mean that, ah, what do I think about ...

Examiner: Yes, to what extent was the development of this city the result of planning?

Candidate: Mm … I think ah, … if the city have got a very good planning, the way people live will be more organised, so I think that, um, planning city planning is important for people who live in.

Examiner: Mm hm. And was, um, the city that you know well, was, was, um, the development of this city a result of planning?

Candidate: Um, I'm not so sure about this because, um, I haven't been to many places, but I can give you an example in Australia because I got like a, a direct experience here. I think that in Sydney, especially in the, in the… um, how can I say, the, the area nearby the city are quite well organised. For example, in, in, North Ryde, Epping, there are, there are, um, parks. So people can enjoy their free time over there.

Examiner: Ah ha.

Candidate: Yeah, but for in Thailand, we haven't got that much space, especially in the, in the central part of Bangkok.

Examiner: Ah ha. We've seen the development of 'gated communities', um, quite a lot recently. Um, those are communities that are maintained and guarded by private companies, and they're restricted, um, to non-residents. Why do you think people may choose to live in these kind of communities.

Candidate: Mm, ah, it's … it's very challenging question but I'm not so sure the word that, that you ask me. Ah, the 'gated community', is that mean the, um, private property?

Examiner: Yes, that's right, guarded by private companies. And only residents are allowed in, normally.

Candidate: Ah ha, yes. Um, you ask me whether this is good for people to live there or what?

Examiner: Why do you think people choose to live in these kind of communities?

Candidate: Ah, I think that it will be more safe for people, ah, to live over there because it had been guarded perfectly, I think. So people who would like to be secured, they prefer to live there but I think for that, that, that place you've got to pay a lot in order to live there.

Exercise 29

Um. Where is the place that I have enjoyed living? Um, there are many places that I have been visited and Sukhothai Province is one of the place that I have, um, enjoy living in over there. Ah, there are many reasons why I like to live there. First, ah, first reasons it is, ah, its environment and its, um, surroundings. Second reason is, ah, people over there are really nice and friendly. Thirdly, Sukhothai Province is not located far from Bangkok where I live. Is what … it is about, ah, 500 kilometres from Bangkok and it is located, ah, northern part of Thailand. Ah, Sukhothai Province, um, was the first, um, dynasty, ah, of Thailand. So over there, there are many, many, ah, historical sites so that Sukhothai is a very popular place for foreigner. Secondly, ah, I liked Sukhothai because, um, I met many, ah, friendly people over there. For example, like five years I went to Sukhothai to do some my research, to collect the data, with, um, religious, ah, in one village at Sukhothai. Over that period of time I had a lot of good experience with the, with people over there.

Exercise 35

Candidate: Last today I read the newspaper, um, about Europe very angry that Japan copycat the car. At first I very surprised the word 'copycat' because I haven't seen this word so I asked my host family about this. And Europe very angry because they produce the car and desi... the shape, colour and, and, ah, light in front of car. But Japan always copy each part and I think is, is about copyright so, but they can not do anything because is not whole of, whole part of the car but is only a little of part. So now. But they very angry about this.

Exercise 36

1	bat	2	sing	3	mole
4	lives	5	past	6	type
7	seventh	8	brings	9	expect
10	when	11	fault		

Exercise 37

combine, combination, academic, socialise, inspire, unemployment, vegetarian, arrangement, marriage, interfere, capitalism, probable, probability, eighteen

Exercise 38
Check-in of the future

Airport check-in times will be drastically reduced as part of a plan by national carrier ComfortAir to improve customer service and increase automation at airports. But while passengers may welcome yesterday's announcement by ComfortAir CEO, Alex Brand, unions fear that it will cost jobs. The proposed changes mean that by the end of the year, all ComfortAir frequent flyer members will receive cards embedded with microchips. These cards will act as boarding passes which also 'talk' to luggage tags with chips to ensure that bags and owners do not part company. Instead of proceeding to a check-in desk, members will swipe their cards at a kiosk, weigh in their own luggage and put it on a conveyor belt before passing through security to their departure lounge.

Exercise 39

[*repeated five times with different intonation*]
Could you help me with my preparation for the IELTS exam?

Exercise 40

I am delighted to introduce ComfortAir's vision for the check-in of the future.

At the moment, check-in is a painful experience for too many of our valued frequent flyer members. It takes too long. It causes stress. Our own research points to what our customers want, and that is speed and ease at check-in.

To ensure this happens, we have commenced a bold new initiative.

Our frequent flyers will soon be able to use their existing card, embedded with a smart microchip. They'll be able to whiz through check-in, simply swiping their card through a reader. Next stop will be a simple bag drop before a final smooth walk through security to their flight gate. Instead of queues and stickers at the desk, the check-in of the future is all about convenience and speed.

With your personal boarding pass and permanent bag tag, checking your baggage will no longer be a tedious chore. Our plan is to halve check-in time – or better.

It's going to be a revolution at airport check-ins, with our staff freed to focus on customer care. And it's a revolution coming your way by year's end.

Examples, page 119

Switch on the light! How often do I have to tell you?

I thought you said you were going to do the washing up.

Examples, page 119

He said we're the best team in the school.

Hadn't you better send her a present for her birthday?

Exercise 41

1. We have
   We've
   We've got a new textbook for AFC1000 this semester.

2. I am
   I'm
   I'm so happy it's Friday today.

3. I will
   I'll
   It's raining, so I'll bring the car to the front door.

4. You had
   You'd
   You'd better close the curtains to keep the house warm.

5. He has
   He's
   This is Jim. He's got a few orders for you.

6. She had
   She'd
   She'd better be home when I get there.

7. It will
   It'll
   It'll be cool and cloudy for the remainder of the week.

8. They are
   They're
   Can you move over? They're coming to sit here.

9. They would
   They'd
   They'd probably want to stay about a week if they came.

10. Can not
    Can't
    Sorry – I can't help you with that.

11. Will not
    Won't
    No, I won't do that.

12. Ought not
    Oughtn't
    I really oughtn't be here with you.

13. Shall not
    Shan't
    That's right. She shan't be arriving until midnight.

Example page 121

Examiner: Could you start speaking now, please?

Candidate: Yeah. So I'm going to describe of my, ah, unforgettable event in my teenage so I met my wife in a marriage party so it's my [*unclear*] so I like to discuss about that event. I met her in a marriage party – that's where we see each other in the marriage party and, ah, he and we exchanged number he likes, she likes me and I like her then we talk, ah, talk on the phone. And just it goes, ah, this goes for the one month and then suddenly that's when we decide to get married and, ah, this we get married after one month and it was an unforgettable event for me. But it's a bit hard for me because at that time I was studying, so I find difficulties to settle down in the life, then … then for after one year I got [*unclear*] it's too hard, I find too hard for me to settle down. Ah, then finally I decided to, ah, to ah turn off from the studies, then I think about the business, then I open a business. Then, then after two years I decided to go abroad and then I give [*unclear*] test so then I come over Australia and, ah, now I'm happy here I'm doing good and everything is going good. And ah.

Exercise 42
Candidate 1

Candidate 1: OK, ah. Well, ah, I think it's a notebook which is very important for me. Ah, well, a notebook you can find everywhere, every store. Ah, I have been actually I have two of them, and around four years ago, and I'm still losing them. I use it to write a lot of them, in here, to write my poems and about me. That's the reason because it's very important. It's not …

Examiner: So if you lost one, would it be very hard to replace?

Candidate 1: Yeah, very hard, because it's a lot of work in that, in that notebook, so, yeah, should be very hard.

Examiner: So is it like a diary as well or, or mainly poems?

Candidate 1: Well, you can, it's not, yeah, maybe you can call diary but it's not the typical diary that you say 'today I did this and I met my friends'. It's more, it's more different, it's like a kind of know you, yourself. So it's more, I don't know, deep.

Candidate 2

Candidate 2: Yeah, sure, ah, the signifent event, the significant event was when I graduated from high school, ah, I was 18 at that time and, ah, I thought after that I thought I finished my study, then I, I realised I'm, I'm just going to start my life. Ah, I was a, a bit lost because I was thinking which major I should study and, ah, in my bachelor. Then ah, ah, I've chosen the management, management information system because it's, ah, so important and I like to manage, ah, I like, I prefer to manage my time I manage, ah, the things.

Examiner: So are you happy that your teenage years have finished now?

Candidate 2: Yeah, yeah, I did spend you know the teenage years I was a bit quiet for most teenagers.

Exercise 43

Examiner: Thank you, Jason. Now let's talk about food. What are your favourite kinds of food?

Candidate: My favourite kind of food is Mauritian food.

Examiner: OK, and do you generally like sweet or savoury food?

Candidate: Sweet food.

Examiner: Why?

Candidate: Oh, I like cakes, I like, ah, everything sweet like fruits and yes.

Examiner: When do you generally eat more – during the day or at night?

Candidate: Sorry?

Examiner: When do you generally eat more – during the day or at night?

Candidate: At night.

Examiner: And why?

Candidate: Ah, like in my culture, ah, we eat, ah, rice every day, so we eat rice every night, like a big amount of rice during at night.

Examiner: Does the weather generally change how much food you eat?

Candidate: Sorry?

Examiner: Does the weather generally change how much food you eat?

Candidate: Yes, of course, ah, in winter I, I eat more than in summer, yeah.

Exercise 44

[*repeated five times*] Tuesday

Example, page 123

Examiner: And, why did you choose this particular course?

Candidate: Um, because, ah, when I was teaching and I thought I should learn something more about, ah, the linguistics, and that's why I, I chose this, um, area to study.

Exercise 45

1

Examiner: Mm hm, what are the most challenging or difficult things about your course?

Candidate: Well ... I think the most difficult part is, um, the reading part, because, um, quite a lot of a new concepts involved in, and, ah, that the things I didn't know before. So I think that's the most difficult part for me.

2

Examiner: And what will you do when your course finishes?

Candidate: Um, teaching, I guess. I would go back and I'm still, I'm doing teaching and I will ... I would prefer actually, prefer to use the, the knowledge I learnt here, so back to teaching again.

Exercise 46

Examiner: So, firstly, let's look at truth and printed information. So, do you think people generally believe what they read online or in print?

Candidate: Yes, I think so.

Examiner: Why do you think they believe what they read?

Candidate: Because that's the only way they can get the information, of course they can rely on too the material of the newspapers and magazines also on the radio but that's quick way, easy way to get the information from the printing way. And I, yeah, I depend on the Internet most of the time.

Examiner: You do? OK. Um, which of the different media, online or print, gives more reliable or truthful information, do you think?

Candidate: I can say that printing, but Internet is more quick, so that's why the printing one is like, for example the newspaper, the next day on the news, but for the Internet that day very quick. So people feel more depend, mm, rely on to the Internet, I feel.

Practice IELTS Speaking Tests (Exercise 48)

Practice Test 1

Examiner: Good morning.

Jade: Morning.

Examiner: Could you tell me your full name, please?

Jade: Yeah, my name is Hanji Kim and my friend call me Jade.

Examiner: OK, Jade, ah, can I see your passport, please?

Jade: Yep, sure.

Examiner: Thank you. That's fine. Now in the first part of the test I'd like to ask you some general questions about your everyday life and interests. Let's talk about what you do with your time, Jade. Do you work or study?

Jade: I'm at this moment I'm working.

Examiner: OK, what do you do?

Jade: Ah, I'm a welfare worker and I'm working with the people with disabilities.

Examiner: Why did you choose this particular type of job?

Jade: Um, I always interested in, um, helping other people and I could see so many disabled people got disadvantaged by social system so that was my reason to choose work in this field.

Examiner: And are you friends with the people you work with?

Jade: Sorry?

Examiner: Are you friends with the people that you work with, your colleagues?

Jade: Yeah, absolutely, they are more likely my family.

Examiner: Would you like to still be doing the same job in five years?

Jade: Yeah, absolutely. I love to work in this field rest of, um, rest of my life.

Examiner: Now let's talk about sport and leisure.

Jade: Yep.

Examiner: What is your favourite leisure activity?

Jade: Um, I should say I don't do, but, um, I do enjoy walking in the bush and walking in the park as well.

Examiner: Why do you like doing these things so much?

Jade: I love the smell of trees and bushes, and that it is so peaceful and you don't have to say anything when you are walking, so that was my reason.

Examiner: And do you do anything that involves a lot of physical activity like jogging or tennis?

Jade: No, I do not run, so I enjoy to watch them, but I just don't do it.

Examiner: Do you think all children should play some kind of sport at school?

Jade: Yeah, absolutely, sport is the best way to learn, cooperative, cooperate with other friends and then, um, give them more freedom express their feelings, emotions. So that's really good for children.

Examiner: And why do you think that some sports are only popular in certain countries while other sports are enjoyed across the world?

Jade: Um, I don't know. It was so interesting when I came to Australia I saw cricket and footy's a really big deal in Australia but I never heard about it in my country. It's based on their culture because Australia adopts English culture and I do understand, um, cricket comes from UK, so, yeah, depends on culture.

Examiner: Oh thanks, Jade. Let's go on to discuss the topic of holidays now, where do you usually spend your holidays?

Jade: Um, these days I don't have any holidays to be honest but when I have any holidays I love to go into the mountains.

Examiner: OK, and who do you prefer to spend your holidays with?

Jade: With my family. Um, in Australia, I love to go with my friends and my colleagues.

Examiner: And what do children usually do in their school holidays in Korea?

Jade: In Korea, um, well parents wants their want their children to go to library or exhibition and museums. And then children love to go to the pool or playground. Things like that, yep.

Examiner: Thank you, Jade, now I'd like to move on to the second part of the test.

Jade: Yes.

Examiner: I'm going to give you a topic card, and I'd like you to talk about it for one to two minutes.

Jade: Yes.

Examiner: Before you start, please take one minute to think about what you're going to say. If you'd like to, you can write some notes in this preparation time. Is that clear?

Jade: Yes, thank you.

Examiner: Please use this paper to make notes, and here's your topic.

Jade: And my topic is …

Examiner: I'd like you to describe something that you read on the Internet … or something that you read on the Internet or in a newspaper that surprised you.

Jade: Oh, yep.

[*silence*]

Examiner: Could you start speaking now please, Jade?

Jade: Yes, um, I do not remember exactly when I read, but I read about a article about refugees. And it was some Internet news website and it was about how refugee affect Australia and, um, what I, I'm sorry, economics … And then I was pretty much surprised cause, um, the fact they describe was a kind of twisted fact so I was pretty disappointed by the fact they twisted. Cause I always believe the newspaper or news on the media they should be very, um, objective not focus on twist the fact so, yeah, that's about it.

Examiner: Do you think that this article was written by a professional writer?

Jade: Yeah, definitely, I could see that was written by professional but who knows how to use the fact what the way they want.

Examiner: You've been talking about something you read that surprised you, and now I want to discuss some wider questions linked to this.

Jade: Yes.

Examiner: Firstly, let's look at truth and printed information.

Jade: Yes.

Examiner: Do you think that people generally believe what they read online or in print?

Jade: Oh, yes, of course, um, especially old generation, I hope it's not any stereotype things but I believe more like, ah, old generation rely on newspaper and news on the TV. And young people focus on searching the information by themselves.

Examiner: But do you think they should believe and trust everything they read?

Jade: Um … they should accept that is some there information, however believe and trust that information, no, I don't think that's a good idea.

Examiner: Why not?

Jade: Cause some said like they have the power to alter real fact to, they are just saying the truth however the way described, it sounds like it's not the way it should be.

Examiner: OK. Um, comparing different kinds of media, um, newspaper, online media, television, um, which do you think gives the most reliable or truthful information?

Jade: Personally I trust, I try to trust the newspaper and, um, I do not have any trust on the television shows cause they tend to get people's attention, so they like to have 'hot potato' types of facts. I mean the altered facts.

Examiner: OK, now we'll move on to the topic of citizen journalists, so recently we've seen the emergence of lots of citizen journalists, and these are just ordinary people who write stories about things that they see, different events, um, sometimes they take photographs. And these stories and photographs are published, usually on news sites or on the Internet. Why do you think that a newspaper or, um, website, um, would want to publish these kinds of stories and photos from citizen journalists?

Jade: Cause, um, normal people accept the citizens, citizens, um, as themselves. They put more trust on ordinary people who report specific news. That's a reason I think.

Examiner: Do you think that this can be a bit risky for the newspapers to do this?

Jade: Um, yes, um, it is very risky I think, cause they haven't trained well enough to report any, um, news or incident whatsoever, so yeah.

Examiner: So do you think that this is a, a good service for the public?

Jade: I don't believe it is good service but the way it should be balanced – you need to use the general people who report just normal news and what's going on in your society, however, if you rely on too much, mmm, it, well, doesn't, um, keep that objectivity to deliver the news its I think, yep.

Examiner: Do you think that these people should be paid?

Jade: Um, if they pay what's the difference to being an ordinary citizen and then being a professional? What was it, I forgot the word, sorry, being a professional there's nothing much difference. So … [*unclear*]

Examiner: Do you think that, um, there's a possibility that in the future these citizen journalists will replace the professional writers?

Jade: I do not think so. They will have more power, I believe, however, it should be, no, it will be, um, um, there will be any, um, sorry, there will be a difference between professional and just, um, citizens.

Examiner: OK, and last question now, Jade. Do you think that you would enjoy being a citizen journalist and having your stories, um, online?

Jade: Um, it's hard question. Um, yes, I love to in specific topics, for instance like refugees who are being international students, things like that, but I wouldn't deliver any news what really happens just normal society like car accidents or politics or so ever, it depends on topics.

Examiner: OK, thank you very much, Jade, we've come to the end of your speaking test.

Jade: You're welcome.

Practice Test 2

Examiner: Good morning.

Jimmy: Good morning.

Examiner: Please tell me your full name?

Jimmy: Judesh Metta.

Examiner: What would you like me to call you?

Jimmy: Jimmy.

Examiner: Thanks, Jimmy, and can I see your passport?

Jimmy: Here you go.

Examiner: Thank you. That's fine. Now in the first part of the test I'd like to ask you some general questions about your everyday life and interests. Let's talk about where you're living now. Where do you live exactly, Jimmy?

Jimmy: I'm living in North Melbourne.

Examiner: Why did you choose to live in that area?

Jimmy: It's very close to city, and I'm working in city. My, my college is in the city. That's why I choose to live in North Melbourne. Very close to city, that's it.

Examiner: Do you think other people in your area chose to live there for the same reasons?

Jimmy: No, no, there is no reason behind it because they living there before maybe you can say from long time, so, yeah. Some people maybe could be the same reason because they working in city or, you know, it could be one reason, but, but not everybody.

Examiner: What kind of recreation facilities are there in your local area?

Jimmy: Um, its everything is there. The

supermarket close to my home. We have a laundry in my, in my apartment with a free laundry, um, there's a cinema close to my home, like Melbourne Central its very close to for my place, and the Victoria Market, it's a big market, veggie market, its close to my home. So it's everything is close to us, we all love that place.

Examiner: Thank you. Now let's talk about food, what are your favourite kinds of food, Jimmy?

Jimmy: Ah, I like to eat Indian food, but I love to cook Spanish food, yeah.

Examiner: Do you generally like sweet or savoury food?

Jimmy: Ah, sweet.

Examiner: Why?

Jimmy: Ah, I like sweet things, desserts, I love to make desserts, that's what I love eating here.

Examiner: And when do you generally eat more, during the day or at night?

Jimmy: During the day because I'm working as a chef so I have to taste every time, yeah.

Examiner: Does the weather generally change how much food you eat?

Jimmy: Ah, when the weather changes I eat less food because, yeah, because the weather that's why, yeah.

Examiner: Let's go on to discuss the topic of clothing. What colours do you prefer to wear?

Jimmy: Bright colours.

Examiner: Do you ever wear very formal clothes or a uniform?

Jimmy: No, not really. I use just wear my uniform at work, after very casual, yeah.

Examiner: When shopping for clothes do you prefer to go alone or with a friend?

Jimmy: Alone. I always go alone because I don't like, I can't, I want to choose my own clothes by myself, I don't want anyone opinion like this colour suits you, no, I don't like this.

Examiner: What type of clothes would you wear to a party?

Jimmy: Ah, casual, yeah.

Examiner: Now, Jimmy, I'd like to move on to the second part of the test. I'm going to give you a topic card and I'd like you to talk about it for one to two minutes. Before you start, please take one minute to think about what you're going to say. If you'd like to, you can write some notes in this preparation time. Is that clear?

Jimmy: Yeah.

Examiner: Please use this paper to make notes, and here's your topic. I'd like you to describe a significant event from your teenage years, that is from 13 to 19 years old.

[*silence*]

Examiner: Could you start speaking now, please, Jimmy?

Jimmy: Yeah, the event was my birthday. It happened on 20th March and the place was, it's next to my home there's a big hurdle over there. Um, its I still remember this time because I remember the time, ah, I ring my dad, I said Dad I want to celebrate my birthday but due to some reasons my dad, that is working in different state, so he said, oh Jimmy I can't come back home. So they send me money and they said you can celebrate your birthday and you can call your friends over there. And I remember the time I was just, ah, missing my dad when I was on the birthday and at the same time I saw my dad came. It was surprise for me and all the tears came in my eyes, said 'Oh, Dad, how come you come back?' And he said 'Now my son had a birthday I could leave everything.' And another thing when my dad clutches my hand and took me outside and he showed he gave me a motorbike on my birthday. Which I'll remember all the time because I can't forget this time, it's really, really good time for me and I really enjoyed the party because my dad came back for my birthday, yes it was really good time for me.

Examiner: Thank you. Are you happy that your teenage years are over?

Jimmy: Mm, yeah, yeah.

Examiner: OK, we've been talking about a significant event from your teenage years and now I want to discuss with you some wider questions linked to this. Firstly, let's look at characteristics of teenage life. Can you explain why the teenage years are so different to other stages of life?

Jimmy: Yeah, because a teenager is a young stage of your life. You no need to worry about what you have to do because they have someone behind you like your parents, they can teach you, they can worry about your future. But when you grow like you be 22 or 24 you have to be more responsible. You have to choose a good career for you. You have to, to think about your life. You have to find a partner for you, good partner for you because if you do mistake in your, in your, you know, young age you can't get a good life. That's why I think so the teenager is very important for you. To choose a good, good career, good life partner, yeah, that's it.

Examiner: And when we compare your teenage years with younger childhood, very young childhood, what are some of the major differences between those two stages of your life?

Jimmy: The major difference is responsibilities. When you're younger you don't need to worry about anything. Your parents are totally, as I told you before, your parents are doing everything for you. But when you younger, when you grow you have to think about your own responsibility. You have to more, let's say, more careful about the things and you, yeah, I think.

Examiner: In your own life did you enjoy your young childhood more or your teenage years more?

Jimmy: Ah, young, yeah.

Examiner: OK. Ah, teenagers are often attracted to new kinds of technology, such as computer games, iPods. Do you think that this interest is good for their personal development?

Jimmy: Yeah, it's true, because, ah, if the child is really interested in Internet this is different way he can get a good knowledge from them and he can be use in a wrong way. So it's up to the child what kind of the information he want. Because some children like they want to be a networking engineer, they can get, ah, plenty of knowledge from the Internet. They, if they use Internet every day, they can get a lot of information, but at the other hand some child they don't want to do these things but they just want to use their own things on the Internet. So it's depends on the child what he exactly want.

Examiner: And in your case, Jimmy, were you very interested in technology as a teenager?

Jimmy: Yeah, um, when I was in my teenager year I wanted to come to Australia for my further study. So I used to go to Internet café and always find the information, what kind of information I really need to, what other requirement, what kind of document I really need for the, my student visa. It's true it's, ah, its really good thing for if you want to for own development you can say.

Examiner: OK, the next topic is the difficulties of being a teenager. Do you agree or disagree that your teenage years are the most difficult in your life?

Jimmy: Not really, it's not really very difficult because, um, my opinion if you're, um, living with your family then it's not really hard because they gonna pay your expenses, they gonna pay your college fees, school fees, whatever. But, yeah, if you are living by yourself, you left your home and you living by yourself it's a bit hard. If you want to choose a good career for you, you have to spend a lot of money for you study. So you have to work hard, you have to do things by own. You have to do your cooking own. You have to study, so in my opinion you should leave your parents by if you want to study. Because you can get a lots of things from your parents. I mean to say like good they can teach you, they can teach you good things. Because if you living on own you don't know about the good things maybe it could be good or it could be right because not every time you will be right. You choose the right things, so that's why I think so.

Examiner: What are some particular things that your parents can do to help you make that transition from teenage years to adulthood?

Jimmy: Yeah, the main thing my dad, ah, I always before my dad actually I really didn't know when I was child what have to do, my dad told me every time you have to do these things. So they always told me you have to do this thing, they always, I always follow my dad that's why I'm here. Otherwise, if I do things by my own maybe I could choose something different thing. Which I was not really interested in that or maybe I could choose wrong things, so in my opinion your parents are always, you know, to help you to get, ah, a good part.

Examiner: Now the last question, Jimmy. Looking to the future, what sorts of new challenges do you think that teenagers will face in coming generations?

Jimmy: Can you repeat this question again, please?

Examiner: So in the future what sort of new challenges do you think there might be for teenagers?

Jimmy: Regarding jobs you mean to say?

Examiner: Ah, could be jobs ... or with technology.

Jimmy: Yeah, technology if we talk about. There are lots of things, lots of vacancies coming in future because it's a totally computerised everything. And, yeah, but, yeah, people can get lots of job with that like in the supermarkets everything is on computer. But in my country there's, it's not very developed, like you can't say, but when the new technologies come in everybody's doing networking things and regarding computer things. So, yeah, it's probably, you can say it's a good thing because everybody can have good job and like if I can talk about, ah, 90, you can say 82, very few people doing the computer things you know. They was not aware about these in there but in there a four-year child still using computer. So he can get a lot of information for, for his career and he can, he can do lots of things on Internet, he can get a lots of information, yeah.

Examiner: Thank you very much, Jimmy. We've come to the end of the speaking test.

Jimmy: Thank you.

Practice Test 3

Examiner: Good morning. I'm Clare. Could you tell me your full name, please?

Madeleine: Yes, ah, my name is Dai Fen.

Examiner: And what should I call you?

Madeleine: Ah, if you don't mind, you can call me Madeleine, that's my English name.

Examiner: OK. And could you tell me where you're from?

Madeleine: I'm from Taiwan.

Examiner: Can I see your ID, please?

Madeleine: Yes, here it is.

Examiner: Yes, that's fine. Let's talk about your study or work. Are you currently studying or do you work?

Madeleine: Ah, when I'm studying I'm a applied linguistic student.

Examiner: Ah ha, and why did you choose this particular course?

Madeleine: Um, because, ah, when I was teaching and I thought I should learn something more about the linguistics, and that's why I chose this, um, area to study.

Examiner: Mm hm, what are the most challenging or difficult things about your course?

Madeleine: Well, I think the most difficult part is, um, the reading part, because um, quite a lot of a new concepts involved in, and, ah, that the things I didn't know before. So I think that's the most difficult part for me.

Examiner: And what will you do when your course finishes?

Madeleine: Um, teaching, I guess. I would go back and I'm still, I'm doing teaching and I will ... I would prefer actually, prefer to use the, the knowledge I learnt here, so back to teaching again.

Examiner: Mm. Now, let's move on to talk about learning languages. What do you say you are good at speaking ... sorry. Would you say you are good at speaking other languages?

Madeleine: Mm, not really, I don't think so.

Examiner: Ah ha. Why do you think some people are better at learning languages than other people?

Madeleine: Um, possibly because their, the needs. I mean, people, some people, they are more interested in other cultures – then they had the motivation to learn the other languages. Then possibly that's the reason they are a better speakers than the others.

Examiner: Mm hm. Are some second languages easier to learn than other second languages?

Madeleine: Ah, I don't know. I have tried to learn French but that is very difficult for me. And English, because I have been learning English for quite a long time, so English is – for me, it's easier than French. If I put them to compare together.

Examiner: Mm. What do you think is the most effective way to learn a language?

Madeleine: To practise, to use it, to – yep, just to use it, um, with the people from that language, from that culture. I think that's the best way.

Examiner: Let's talk a little about your country. Have you travelled around it much?

Madeleine: Not really, I have been to, um, some cities but not that much.

Examiner: What's the most popular region in your country for overseas tourists?

Madeleine: Mm, I think there are two spots. One is, um, a city called Taitung, which is located in the eastern part of Taiwan.

Another part, it's called Kenting, is in the northern part of Taiwan.

Examiner: And why is it so popular?

Madeleine: Um, I think because, um, those two – OK, for example, like Taitung is, um, the city hasn't been developed too much. It's still quite natural, so, and also people are really, really kind there. And less, um, people like, um, to go hiking because there is mountains, quite a lot of, ah, mountains and the oceans. So they can do, the tourists, the tourist can do many different activities there.

Examiner: Does the government encourage tourism to your country?

Madeleine: I think so.

Examiner: How does it do this?

Madeleine: They probably just put a commercial in other countries, I don't know. But, um, I also know that our government tried to encourage our people to travel around in our own country. That's what I know.

Examiner: Mm hm. Now I'm going to give you a topic and I'd like you to talk about it for one to two minutes.

Madeleine: Mm hm.

Examiner: Before you talk, you have one minute to think about what you're going to say. You can make some notes if you wish. Do you understand?

Madeleine: Yes.

Examiner: Here's the topic, and here's a pen and some paper to make notes.

Madeleine: Yep.

Examiner: I'd like you to describe somewhere that you have enjoyed living.

Madeleine: Mm hm.

[*silence*]

Examiner: OK. Remember you have one to two minutes for this.

Madeleine: Yes.

Examiner: I'll stop you when the time is up. Can you start speaking now, please?

Madeleine: Yes. Um, the place that I have enjoyed living is called Armidale. It's, um, in Australia. It is actually about eight hours away from Sydney, and, um, it's a very small town. Um, the reason I like Armidale is because, um, they got … Armidale got a different face, let me put it in this way, in every season. Like, in spring, um, we can see the different types of flowers along the street and summer is very, very green. And, ah, it's not that hot, as well. It's not as hot as Sydney. And my favourite season is in the autumn because of the trees. And I heard from my friends that those trees are originally from England. And that's why the university there called the University of New England, I think. And, um, the winter – it's quite cold, I would say, compared with my country. Um, but seldom snow. Ah, actually, I haven't seen snow there yet.

Um, also, it's very conven… although there is no many, um, shopping centres there, but I would say it's very convenient for me if I want to do any, any kind of shopping there. Also, um, what else, mm?

Examiner: Would you go back to live there again?

Madeleine: Probably not. I don't think that's a very good place for doing business and, ah, the most people live there are students from other countries and also from other cities from Australia.

Examiner: OK. We've been talking about places where people live. I'd like now to discuss one or two general questions relating to this topic.

Madeleine: Yes.

Examiner: Firstly, ah, let's consider the recent development of a city you know well. To what extent was this development a result of planning?

Madeleine: Ah, OK. This one is a little bit difficult. Um, I will try, if I can put it this way. The city I know, I would like to use the example of, um, the capital city that I'm coming from, Taipei.

Examiner: Mm hm.

Madeleine: The government has, ah, planning to build the city of Taipei as one of the, ah, international city. So the government have been putting quite a lot of the public transportation, for example. Um, so, and also, um knocking down some old buildings and they put quite a lot of parks. And, ah, some very big shopping centre, for example, as well.

Examiner: Do you think the importance of, um ... What do you think is the importance of planning, um, in shaping development in urban areas?

Madeleine: I think that gives, um, if the place is designed well, that it, it will, um, help that each individual areas with a different functions, so we won't mix like residential areas with the commercial areas. That won't be a good ideas.

Examiner: And do you think large cities will become more or less planned in the future?

Madeleine: I think they will become more planned and actually that is the, one of the needs that people actually want, because I think more and more people want to, um, doing their business in their commercial area. And when they want to relax, when they want to enjoy their family life, they don't want to hear some, um, like, a commercial, um, you know, like announcement all the time, the people are doing business or they will put very loud music. I think they would just like enjoy their own family life in the com... residential area.

Examiner: Mm. We've seen the development of a lot of communities called 'gated communities' recently, which are guarded by private companies and, um, you don..., um, it restricts the entry to non-residents so only residents can go in. Why do you think people choose to live in these kind of communities?

Madeleine: Um, gated community. Ah, just let me check if I got the idea right. Does that mean the people live in the area, then there's a main entrance that everyone they, they want to go in and leave, they have to go through that main gate?

Examiner: That's right, yes.

Madeleine: All right. Um, I think security probably the major reason. Ah, so if people who choose to live in the gated community, they plobably, plobably (oh, sorry, I have the problem with that word). Um, they perhaps, the reason for them to choose is for the concern of security, as I just say earlier. Ah, they were think that, um, some people, if they want to pass or go into the community, they would have to pass some, some guard or things like that.

Examiner: Mm hm. And what kind of people do you think would choose to live in these gated communities?

Madeleine: Rich people?

Examiner: Mm hm.

Madeleine: And if I know, maybe I'm not completely correct. But in my country the people who choose to live in a gated community, usually they are quite rich. And they also require more protection, I think.

Examiner: OK.

Answer key

Unit 1: Listening

Exercise 1
1 B   2 A

Exercise 2
3 laptop / a laptop computer
4 word processing

Exercise 3
5 more expensive   6 lightest

Exercise 4
7 2.4 kg   8 most powerful

Exercise 5
9 CD/DVD drive   10 microphone

Exercise 6
11 OWM   12 CLM   13 TCM

Exercise 7
14 C   15 A   16 B

Exercise 8
1 Answer: Tomorrow
2 Information needed: A reason (for enjoyment)
   Answer: It was interesting and he learnt a lot.
3 Information needed: A percentage
   Answer: 52 (fifty-two) per cent (%)
4 Information needed: A number
   Answer: 3 (three)
5 Information needed: A part of the assignment
   Answer: The references

Exercise 9
Suggested underlining
1 At <u>what</u> <u>time</u> did the <u>robbery</u> take place?
2 <u>What</u> is the <u>name</u> of the <u>robbed</u> <u>bank</u>?
3 <u>How</u> <u>many</u> <u>customers</u> were in the <u>bank</u> which was robbed?
4 <u>How</u> <u>many</u> <u>people</u> were involved in <u>robbing</u> the bank?
5 <u>What</u> <u>telephone</u> <u>number</u> should people call to <u>give</u> <u>information</u>?

Answers
1 9 (nine) o'clock (9 am)
2 Central Bank
3 none (zero; no customers)
4 3 (three)
5 9357799

Exercise 10
B

Exercise 11
1 10 (ten) pages   2 methodology
3 11 (11th of) September   4 a title page

Exercise 12
1 SA233
2 January 21 (21st)
3 3 (three)
4 near the window
5 22 (twenty-two) kilograms (kg)
6 pay extra
7 yes

Exercise 13
1 deactivated   2 go out
3 change code   4 fault check

Exercise 14
1 C   2 B   3 A   4 B

Exercise 15
1 M   3 J and S   4 S   5 A and J

Exercise 16
Suggested answers
Versatile words: currently, local, apparently, reasonable, annual
Specific words: tutor, colleges, workload, vacation, responsibilities
Words/expressions probably not worth learning: molecular, oppressively, by and large

Exercise 17 (sample answers)
2 man: fellow, guy, chap
3 good: great, terrific, fantastic

4 **bad:**   awful, horrible, terrible
5 **big:**   large, huge, enormous
6 **to reduce:** to lower, to decrease, to lessen

Exercise 18

2 B   3 G   4 F   5 D
6 A   7 C   8 F

Exercise 19

2 **pediatrician:** a physician (doctor) who specialises in the study and treatment of diseases in children
3 **jingles:** simple, repetitious, catchy rhymes set to music
4 **embezzlement:** to appropriate fraudulently to one's own use, as money or property entrusted to one's possession
5 **allamanda:** a tropical woody vine (plant) with funnel-shaped flowers
6 **hardy:** capable of enduring fatigue, hardship, exposure, etc

Exercise 20

As the train slows to enter the station on this clear Friday morning, I'm suddenly aware of the huge central bank building. Its twin, thirty-nine metre towers and giant central dome momentarily overshadow the train's passengers.

Exercise 21

The way a person writes displays individual style and personality. In previous centuries, children were taught techniques to write properly and letter-writing became an art form. However, with the emergence of computers and mobile phones, many children are no longer capable of producing good handwriting. This is a great pity for several reasons. Firstly, a piece of well-ordered script written with flow and flair is pleasing to the eye – kind of like a firm handshake or a nice smile when you meet someone new. Mastery of handwriting also assists young people to control their hand and promotes hand–eye coordination. Finally, it teaches them to slow their thinking and reflect before writing.

Exercise 22

Answer

Devices such as notebooks, interactive whiteboards and e-book readers have all secured a place in our schools and universities. Texting and social networking sites like Facebook completely dominate our lives outside of work. But as we continue to embrace new technology, what role do we leave for traditional forms of text construction such as handwriting? Are we disadvantaging our young people with this blind acceptance of digital technologies? Indeed, many young people struggle to form words by hand and can't even spell. This has already become a significant problem both in school and tertiary education as handwritten exams still form the main method of assessment.

Comments on the use of focus stress

Devices: focusing the listener on technology
schools, universities: where these devices are found
Texting, social networking: particular form of technology
completely dominate: exaggerated to engage listener
traditional, handwriting: setting up the speaker's main point of view
disadvantaging, blind acceptance: the speaker's main point of view
Indeed: intensifying the speaker's main point and setting up an example
struggle to form words, can't even spell: an example illustrating the speaker's main point
significant problem, school, tertiary education, handwritten exams, main method of assessment: the results of the main point being discussed

Exercise 23

Good morning class. Today, I'd like to talk about producing educational multimedia. This particular type of multimedia – as distinct from

Answer key Unit 1: Listening **187**

entertainment multimedia – is an area of interest for educators everywhere. I'd particularly like to discuss the process of producing this type of multimedia. Your first consideration, apart from deciding what medium you're going to deliver your product through, is your audience. Who they are, what they expect and, most importantly, what they need. After you have determined this basic information about your users, then you can go on to the all important area of content.

Exercise 24
2 I   3 I   4 C
5 I   6 C

Exercise 25
2 asking for information
3 requesting   4 giving advice
5 arguing   6 declining
7 reassuring   8 describing
9 inviting   10 insisting

Exercise 26 (sample answers)
2 a insistent, forceful
   b two people discussing going to a concert
   c 'come on' 'how about this?', 'I'll pay'
   d persuading, trying to convince someone (to come to a concert)
3 a calm, matter-of-fact
   b two people discussing a machine, possibly in an office supplies shop
   c 'it's ... four machines in one', 'it's guaranteed'
   d describing, demonstrating

4 a calm, matter-of-fact, she sounds as if she is talking to an audience
   b one person, perhaps reading the news on television or on radio
   c 'described as', 'contact the police hotline', 'today's highlights in sport'
   d describing, explaining
5 a calm, curious
   b two people talking about a property advertised for sale
   c 'property for sale', 'just wanted to check' 'what does that mean?', 'it simply means', 'I see'
   d asking for information, clarifying

Exercise 27
2 F   3 B   4 D   5 A
6 E   7 D   8 D   9 B
10 E   11 D   12 C

Exercise 28
See transcript (page 154).

Exercise 29
1 Tuesday   2 Wednesday   3 Saturday
4 February   5 June   6 October
7 December
8 two hundred and fifty thousand
9 50th   10 six point four
11 4,600,000   12 two-fifths   13 9,076

Exercise 30
1 010306977
2 Smithies
3 Smithers
4 Jacqueline
5 17A Heeley St, Clapman, SW11
6 August 12 (12th of August)
7 September 30 (30th of September)
8 hardanger
9 Liebke
10 1989
11 September 30 (30th of September)
12 9.30 (half past nine; nine thirty)
13 7 (seven) o'clock
14 8.30 (eight thirty; half past eight)
15 Axel

Exercise 31
1 conditioning   2 milling
3 rollers   4 white
5 sacking

Exercise 32
1 aneroid   2 liquid   3 lever
4 spindle   5 dial   6 inches

Exercise 33
2 C   3 C   4 E   5 E
6 C   7 C   8 E

Exercise 34
1 round   2 long and thin
3 940   4 576
5 96   6 4
7 1797   8 1814

Exercise 35
2 A Technical; B Computer Literacy; C Mathematics
3 A fiction; B textbooks; C poems
4 A SOV; B SVO; C VSO
5 A emu; B varieties; C features

Exercise 36
1 M and D   2 T and J

Exercise 37
1 Agree   2 Disagree   3 Agree
4 Disagree   5 Disagree

Exercise 38
1 interpersonal   2 traditional
3 random   4 connect
5 expectations

Exercise 39
1 C   2 B   3 D   4 E

Practice IELTS Listening Test
Section 1
1 Toowong   2 shopping centre
3 ferry   4 5 (five)
5 train   6 C
7 B   8 B
9 A   10 A

Section 2
11 F   12 C   13 B
14 G   15 D   16 day pass
17 headphones   18 10 (ten) minutes
19 Friday(s)   20 email

Section 3
21 B   22 H   23 D   24 G
25 I   26 C   27 A   28 B
29 B   30 C

Section 4
31 warning
32 chemical
33 protected / insect-free
34 apple trees
35 Britain
36 red / orange (any order)
37 sunlight
38 healthy
39 water
40 (green) insects / pests

Unit 2: Speaking

Exercise 1 (sample answers)
Questions about home:
▼ Can you tell me something about your home town?
▼ Is it a historic place?
▼ What is the population?
▼ Does it have many attractive buildings?
▼ What are the main industries there?

Responses about home:
▼ I come from Sydney.
▼ My city is just over two hundred years old and has a population of over four million people.
▼ It has many attractive buildings – the older ones are made of the local yellow sandstone and the newer ones are glass and metal

- Sydney's main industries include services, such as transport and tourism, and some light manufacturing.

Questions about job or studies:
- What is your occupation?
- How long have you been in your job?
- What are you studying? Do you enjoy it?

Responses about job or studies:
- I am a vet and have been one for 16 years.
- I am studying to become a mechanical engineer. I mostly enjoy it, but hate the end of semester exams.

Exercise 2 (sample answers)

Note: It is *not advisable* to memorise these questions and answers, as it is extremely unlikely that you would be asked these exact questions in the IELTS Speaking Test.

2 Your daily routine
   Q: What do you do on Monday nights?
   A: I usually watch TV and go to bed early.
   Q: What time do you go to work?
   A: I usually leave for work just after eight.

3 Your leisure or free-time activities
   Q: What do you enjoy doing in your free time?
   A: I really enjoy playing with my baby brother.
   Q: Do you have a hobby that you do every day?
   A: Yes, I read every night for 20 minutes before I go to sleep.

4 Your local area
   Q: Is there much open space near where you live?
   A: There are a couple of parks but they're not big ones.
   Q: Describe the street where you live.
   A: Well, it's a long street with many tall apartment blocks. The street is wide and usually busy with cars, bikes and other traffic.

5 Learning English or other languages
   Q: What is the most difficult thing about learning English?
   A: The large vocabulary is difficult to learn – also articles and prepositions are impossible!
   Q: What other languages would you like to learn and why?
   A: I'd like to learn Spanish. I think it's supposed to be the world's third or fourth most popular language.

6 Food and drink
   Q: What do you usually eat for breakfast?
   A: I usually grab a bowl of cereal and toast.
   Q: How much water do you drink every day?
   A: Not enough really. Probably about three glasses.

7 Your country and culture
   Q: What country do most visitors to your country come from?
   A: They come from all around the world, but I think Europeans would have to be the most common visitors.
   Q: Are there any places in your country that you wouldn't recommend a visitor to your country to go? Why?
   A: I wouldn't recommend the north-west of my country. It's heavily industrialised and the environment has been terribly degraded.

Exercise 3

2 Subject area: Study
   Exact question: And why did you choose this particular course?
   Clear and related: Yes

3 Subject area: Study
   Exact question: And what are the most challenging or difficult things about your course of study?
   Clear and related: No (The question asks about her course but she appears to focus on difficulties in the workplace.)

4 Subject area: Study
   Exact question: And what do you think you'll do when your course finishes?
   Clear and related: Yes

5 Subject area: Learning languages
   Exact question: Would you say you are good at speaking other languages?

Clear and related: No (She talks a little off-topic – her response is about learning languages in general, whereas the question asks her about her personal experience.)

6 Subject area: Learning languages
Exact question: Why do you think some people are better at learning languages than other people?
Clear and related: Yes

7 Subject area: Learning languages
Exact question: And do you think some second languages are easier to learn than other second languages?
Clear and related: Yes

8 Subject area: Learning languages
Exact question: What do you think is the most effective way to learn a language?
Clear and related: Yes

9 Subject area: Visiting her country (China)
Exact question: Let's talk a little about your country. Have you travelled around it much?
Clear and related: Yes

10 Subject area: Visiting her country (China)
Exact question: What's the most popular region in your country for overseas tourists?
Clear and related: No (Her difficulties with this question appear to be related to vocabulary.)

11 Subject area: Visiting her country
Exact question: Is there a particular city that's popular for tourists?
Clear and related: Yes

Exercise 4
Students' own answers.

Exercise 5
1 (circled) and, but, so, because
Comments: The candidate overuses the conjunction *because*. A wider variety of linking words could have been used in this presentation but these few words perform adequately in expanding the candidates' ideas.
2 because, and, however, but, since
Comments: The candidate uses a variety of linking words.

Exercise 6 (sample answer)
The city I would to visit is Rome, the capital of Italy. It's a city that has always attracted me <u>because</u> of its culture. I'm particularly interested in its architecture <u>since</u> it has examples from all major European styles of building. <u>Besides</u>, it was the capital of the Roman Empire, <u>so</u> it has a wonderful collection of public buildings from that time. What I think is great about Rome is that many of the beautiful and historic buildings are still in use – as galleries, public offices and even houses. They are not all locked up as museums <u>so</u> it's really living history there. <u>Even though</u> it's an expensive city to stay, I'd like to go there for at least a month, <u>as</u> there's so much to see and do. During my time there, I'd have to be careful that I didn't spend too much on Roman food! I'd find a cheap *pensione* – sort of a low budget hotel. It would probably be in the *centro storico*, the old centre of the city, probably within walking distance of the River Tevere. Most visitors to Rome would agree that it is a very special place <u>but</u> for me, it's Europe's most historic and romantic city. <u>While</u> cities like Paris, Vienna and Madrid are lovely too, I think Rome beats them all.

Exercise 7
2 C   3 G   4 A   5 B
6 E   7 D   8 F

Exercise 8 (sample answers)
2 No, changes in food production methods can also have negative effects. As an example, mass-produced food in this country generally doesn't taste as good as naturally grown food. I also worry about the increased amount of chemicals farmers have to use to make sure their soil produces bumper crops. I often wonder if we are eating these chemicals, too.
3 Well, 50 or 60 years ago, my grandparents' generation had a much more limited diet. They ate what was grown locally, what was in season and little else. In addition, most things they ate were fresh as they didn't have very effective refrigeration techniques.

Nowadays, we have a huge variety of food to choose from and we can keep it for as long as we like because of the invention of freezing technology.
4 Actually, patterns of food shopping are changing now. A lot of people are starting to buy food over the Internet because it saves time and energy. Also, gigantic supermarkets – called hypermarkets – are springing up on the edges of large cities. Buying food at these places is cheaper, as they buy in bulk and pass savings on to their customers, so they are becoming very popular.

Exercise 9
Students' own answers.

Exercise 10
1 2
2 Candidate 1 does not speak fluently. She hesitates a lot and uses 'um' and 'ah' too frequently. She also repeats words quite often (for example, 'Um, we are all, we all say, ah, Cantonese' and 'I, I can, I can eat, I can eat cheaply and I can, ah, bought many things ...'). Overall, her delivery is very jerky (stop–start) rather than smooth.
Candidate 2 is somewhat more fluent. Although there are repetitions ('I, when I arrived Australian I, I rent ...') and some hesitations ('Ah, it's a bed, it has two bedrooms ...'), overall these do not interfere with listening as seriously as for the first candidate.

Exercise 11

Candidate 1

Fillers used
Recent development?
But, ah ...
So ah ...
Yes, maybe, ah.
Cities?
And, mm.
Less planned?
Ah, it's ...
Mm, ...

Was he successful?
In general, this candidate is not very successful in this area. He uses fillers, but they are limited to repeating parts of the questions he has been asked ('Recent development?', 'Less planned?') or simple words or sounds ('maybe', 'ah'). His choice of fillers also makes him seem unsure of how to proceed with his response rather than just filling in silent periods.

Candidate 2

Fillers used
Ah, OK. This one is a little bit difficult. I will try, if I can put it this way.
Um, so, …
And, ah, …
I think …

Was she successful?
Candidate 2 is a confident and effective speaker who successfully uses fillers when she needs to. She uses a handy filler when answering the first question by directly addressing the difficulty of the question ('This one is a little bit difficult. I will try, if I can put it this way.'). This gives her enough time to think of a satisfactory extended answer. She uses a limited variety of sound fillers probably due to her high level of fluency.

Exercise 12
Students' own answers.

Exercise 13
Indicate order of importance: most importantly
Indicate a time sequence: after that
Give examples: for example, for instance
Give extra information: also, besides
Give a cause or reason: as a result of, due to
Give an effect or result: as a result, therefore
Introduce an opposite idea: in contrast, nevertheless
Compare: also, similarly
Contrast: however, instead
Note: This is not a complete list of discourse markers that can be used for each function.

Exercise 14 (sample answers)

2 It's generally dry and hot, though there's a short rainy season.
3 Yes, I do, I read it every day.
4 I use it to play sports.
5 No, I haven't. I've never been there.
6 No, we don't. We don't have any trams.
7 Yes, there are a lot of them.
8 Yes, there is. There's quite a lot of crime.

Exercise 15

Candidate: Yes. Ah, the place that I, ah, I have enjoyed living is, um, Kyoto City. I grew up and, ah, I, so, ah. I went to the university in Kyoto and (it) was very fine. Ah, Kyoto is a very popular city for foreigners but I think Kyoto is a, has another as... aspect, so it is a city of students. Kyoto has many school, high school and especially universities, so I was attending (one of these universities). And Kyoto has a lot of, um, entertaining place and the cheap restaurants, as well as the very traditional temples or shrines. So I didn't go to any, (any of these) temples or shrines though, but I enjoyed living (there).

Examiner: Do you think it's, um, still much the same place now or has it changed?

Candidate: Mm, I, I don't think, ah, (it's) changed. It's always a city for stu... many students.

Comments

This extract from Part 2 is reasonably coherent. The listener can follow the description of Kyoto's attractions easily enough throughout. Kyoto is referred to as 'it' twice and once as 'there'. The candidate also refers to his university as 'one of these universities' (referring back to his previous mention of universities). He also refers back to temples and shrines when he adds that he didn't go to any 'of these'. When the examiner asks 'Do you think *it's* still much the same place now or has it changed?', the candidate coherently answers 'Mm, I, I don't think, ah, it's changed.'

Exercise 16 (sample answers)

2 Yes, there are.
   Yes, I think one of the main benefits is that we have better products at cheaper prices.
3 No, there isn't.
   No, I think they're completely harmless.
4 Yes, it does.
   Yes, I feel it does very directly. Students always suffer by having bad teachers.
5 Yes, I do.
   I think they should. It's essential we have educated people running the government.
6 I doubt it.
   It's hard to believe this would ever be the case.
7 No, I don't.
   I don't think they should. It's just not necessary.
8 No, I don't think so.
   I don't think they will. People will still want real animals.

Exercise 17 (sample answers)

3 It's very widespread. I think the majority of people use it at least once a day.
4 I think it should be reasonably difficult. They shouldn't just hand them out to anyone who wants one.
5 It plays a huge role. I don't think people could do without it in their lives.
6 It's extremely important. I don't think children know enough about environmental problems.
7 It's really important. In fact, in my culture, it's probably one of the most important things in life.
8 To a limited extent, I think. Some degree of censorship is justified if it is in the interest of national security.

Exercise 18

Students' own assessment of their performance.

Exercise 19
2 successive (adjective)
3 theme (noun)
4 significance (noun)
5 coincidence (noun)
6 originally (adverb)
7 establishment (noun)
8 influential (adjective)

Exercise 20 (sample answers)
2 Yes, I (most) certainly do.
Yes, I'm definitely in favour of that.
3 Yes, we have a huge amount of crime.
Yes, our crime rate is shocking/terrible/appalling.
4 It's enormous and extremely stylish.
It's really spacious and very attractive.
5 I believe it should be illegal/forbidden.
It shouldn't be allowed, in my opinion.

Exercise 21
2 for
3 on
4 into / to
5 of
6 from
7 as
8 in
9 from / to
10 to
11 between

Exercise 22 (sample answers)
3 There are so many. In fact, my home town is famous for its restaurants.
4 No, I don't think so. We'll always need teachers no matter what.
I doubt it. I imagine that children will continue to go to school.
5 Yes, definitely. I think it's much harder. The subjects are more difficult and you have a lot more individual responsibility.
Yes, it is, actually. Although you have greater responsibility, you also have more freedom.
6 No, I don't think so. In my experience children learn languages far more quickly.
No, not really. As far as I can see, men and women are about equal.
7 Well, it's rather cold but it's extremely beautiful, and the people are very friendly. The northern part of the country is hot and dry, and maybe it's not as attractive as the south, but the food is wonderful.
8 Yes, I most certainly do. It makes all children equal regardless of their background. Definitely. It's important that they feel equal, and I think it's also good for discipline.

Exercise 23 (sample answers)
2 A few years ago my father reached the age when people stop working.
3 I do unpaid work to help people in my free time.
4 This dish is really good for your health.
5 I have a driver's licence but it is not accepted here in Canada.
6 She handed in her assignment on time.
7 He couldn't finish his assignment in time so he asked if he could hand it in late.
8 People who have a strong desire to do something are generally more successful.
9 There are many good reasons to teach your children foreign languages.
10 Many people argue that television has a negative effect on children, but the evidence does not clearly prove or disprove this argument.
11 I think you can trust newspaper reports more than news reports on television.
12 Many people have strongly criticised the government's decision to change the law without discussing it with the public.

Exercise 24
2 So ... ah, you mean that, ah, what do I think about ...
3 Mm, ah, it's ... it's very challenging question but I'm not so sure the word that, that you ask me.
4 Ah, the 'gated community' is that mean the, um, private property?
5 Ah ha, yes. Um, you ask me whether this is good for people to live there or what?

Evaluation

In the example (1), the candidate puts two parts of the question together and makes a more specific question to ask back to the examiner ('Are you asking me about a city planning?') This skill of simplifying the question in your own words is a useful and much used technique in all types of interview situations. She then forces the interviewer to ask the question again, but in a slightly different way ('So ah, you mean that what do I think about ...?')

In the second example, she again checks her understanding of the main topic by asking a specific question about gated communities ('is [does] that mean the, um, private property?'). She then seeks clarification about what aspect of the topic she is being asked about ('Um, you ask me whether this is good for people to live there or what?')

The candidate seeks clarification about questions she is unsure of in a highly appropriate way.

Exercise 25

Students' own assessment of their performance.

Exercise 26

2	B and E	3	E and F	4	B
5	G	6	A	7	E and F
8	F and G	9	B	10	C
11	A	12	C	13	D and F
14	A, E and F				

Exercise 27 (comments and sample answers)

1 **Comment:** Your answer should contain verbs in the past tense. It may contain the form 'used to + infinitive' to describe regular past activity. After verbs such as *like* and *enjoy*, the gerund (*-ing* form) should be used.
Sample answer: I used to play tennis every weekend, and sometimes I used to go hiking. And I always enjoyed watching television and listening to music.

2 **Comment:** The verbs in your answer should be in the past tense. Your answer should include an accurate comparative form. To give an extended answer you should include a reason (explanation).
Sample answer: I found secondary school far more enjoyable than primary school because we had more sport.

3 **Comment:** You need to get the comparative form correct and make sure that you are talking about men and women (plural).
Sample answer: I think women are better drivers than men because they concentrate more.

4 **Comment:** The verbs need to be in simple past tense. You need to know the irregular past tense forms of verbs such as *to feel*.
Sample answer: I had mixed feelings. I was happy to finish, of course, but at the same time I felt sad saying goodbye to all my classmates.

5 **Comment:** The answer requires a conditional expression.
Sample answer: If I won the lottery, I would give some money to my parents and to charity, and I'd keep the rest in the bank for myself. And I would definitely give up working!

6 **Comment:** The answer will probably use simple present tense (although other tenses are also possible). Be careful to use the *-s* ending on present tense verbs. It is also essential to get basic pronoun forms correct (*he/his/him* or *she/her/her*).
Sample answer: My best friend's name is Max. He's about the same age as me, but he's already married, and has three children! He's a social worker and he really loves his job. We met at high school, so we've known each other for about ten years now. He's a great guy.

7 **Comment:** The answer should contain accurate comparative forms.
Sample answer: I've always found British English a bit easier than American English. I suppose that's because all of the foreign teachers at our school came from Britain, and I'm more familiar with British pronunciation and idioms.

8 **Comment:** The answer should contain the '*would* + infinitive' conditional form. If you

use the short form *I'd*, make certain that you distinguish the pronunciation from *I*.
Sample answer: I'd tell her to save her money, study hard, and have a plan. And I'd also advise her to invite her old friends to visit her overseas!

9 **Comment:** The answer should echo the (present perfect continuous) tense of the question. Make sure that you use the plural *years*.
Sample answer: I've been studying English for about ten years now. I started in high school.

10 **Comment:** The answer typically requires a simple present tense verb to describe regular behaviour. Make certain that you use the plural *hours*.
Sample answer: I usually sleep about eight hours a day, but lately I've been sleeping only about five or six hours per day because I've been so busy.

11 **Comment:** The description will contain simple present tense verbs but also past tense or present perfect if talking about the history of the building. Passive forms of the verbs may be necessary to describe the building. If you use the structure *one of the ...*, remember that it is used with a plural form of the noun.
Sample answer: One of the most famous buildings in my country is the Su Temple. It's a huge building and it's completely covered in gold leaf, so it really shines beautifully in the sunlight. I think it was built about 500 years ago – it's certainly very old. I'm not quite sure who built it, to be honest.

12 **Comment:** The full answer should contain the verb *is* and the preposition *on*. You should use one of the standard ways of describing dates. The description of what you do will probably contain simple present tense verbs.
Sample answer: My birthday is on the 29th of June. I usually just go out with a few friends and have a nice meal.

13 **Comment:** To speculate about the future, the future tense will probably be necessary. Modal auxiliary verbs such as *might* are often used to speculate.
Sample answer: I think so. I think cash will probably disappear completely. We might all just use plastic cards instead.

14 **Comment:** The answer must contain suggestions: the easiest structure to control is *I think they should go ...* but other forms (using *advise*, *suggest* or *recommend*) are possible. It is likely that the answer will need to contain superlative forms, for example *the most beautiful*.
Sample answer: I think all visitors should see the north-eastern region of the country. In my opinion it's the most beautiful part of the country and the most interesting in terms of culture. I would advise people to spend at least a week there.

Exercise 28
Part A (sample answers)

2 He was raised by his grandmother because he was (had been) abandoned by his parents.
3 He doesn't have (any) siblings. (He doesn't have any. He has no siblings. He has none. He hasn't got any. He's got no siblings. He's got none.)
4 He worked part time after school because he was poor (because he and his grandmother were poor).
5 He was 16 when he left school. (He left school at [the age of] 16.)
6 He has published two (2) novels.
7 Yes, he has. (He has published some short stories).
8 He earnt it by selling the film rights to his novel *Eternity*.
9 He won it in 2002.
10 He married Elizabeth Charles.
11 He was 27 when he got married. (He got married at [the age of] 27.)
12 He has (got) two daughters.

Part B (sample answer)

Francis James Hatton was born in Newcastle in 1973 and had no brothers or sisters. His parents abandoned him when he was very young and he was raised by his grandmother. She was extremely poor so Hatton had to work part time after school. When he was 16 he left school and went to work in a department store. He left the store in 1992, the same year that his short story 'Black Morning' was published. In the following year he had three more short stories published. In 1995 his novel *This Man* was published and two years later he published another novel, *Eternity*. In 1999 he sold the film rights to *Eternity* for 2.5 million dollars and in 2002 he won an Academy Award for Best Screenplay for *This Man*. In 2000 he married Elizabeth Charles. They have three children, a daughter Clara who was born in 2004, a son Andrew born in 2006, and a daughter May born in 2009.

Part C

Students' own answers.

Exercise 29

Things she has managed well: The past tense is managed successfully ('I went', 'I had' and 'Province was').

Problem areas: There are errors in the use of verb tenses, for example, 'many places that I have been visited' and 'that I have, um, enjoy living in over there'. A major problem is the incorrect use of singular and plural noun forms, for example, 'one of the place', 'first, ah, first reasons', 'for foreigner' and 'a lot of good experience'. Complex grammatical structures are also rarely achieved successfully.

Exercise 30 (sample answer)

Um. Where is the place that I have enjoyed living? Um, there are many places that I have visited and Sukhothai Province is one of the places that I have, um, enjoyed living in. Ah, there are many reasons why I liked living (*or* I like living) there. The first, ah, first reason is its environment and its surroundings. The second reason is that the people there are really nice and friendly. Thirdly, Sukhothai Province is located not far from Bangkok where I live. It is ... it is about 500 kilometres from Bangkok and it is located, ah, in the northern part of Thailand. Ah, Sukhothai Province, um, was the (location of the) first um, dynasty, ah, of Thailand. So there are many, many historical sites there, so that (*or* with the result that) Sukhothai is a very popular place for (*or* with) foreigners. Secondly, ah, I liked Sukhothai because, um, I met many friendly people there. For example, I went to Sukhothai five years ago (for five years) to do some research (*or* to do some of my research), to collect the data (connected) with religious (matters) in, in a village in Sukhothai. Over that period of time (*or* during that time) I had a lot of good experiences with the, with people there.

Exercise 31 (sample answers)

2   ... and encourage people to use public transport.
    ... because the pollution is damaging our children's health.
    ... which are steadily being suffocated by the pollution from vehicle emissions.
    ... although I realise it will not be easy to do.
3   ... and I have no desire to move to a big city.
    ... because there is less pollution and crime.
    ... which is famous throughout my country for its beautiful gardens.
    ... even though it is more difficult to find work here.
4   ... even if we're coming into a busy time at work.
    ... as I've been working hard all year.
    ... that is longer than a week.
    ... though I don't have much money to spend on air-fares.
5   ... yet she doesn't seem interested in being promoted.
    ... since she has been working here so long.
    ... which is a great job to aspire to.
    ... while Anne is on maternity leave.
6   ... so that we can protect their morals.

… because otherwise they will see some shocking images.

… before they are corrupted.

… even if it is almost impossible to do it thoroughly.

Exercise 32 (sample answers)

1   I've been studying English since I started secondary school about ten years ago.
2   I'd like to study at a foreign university so that I can get a better job here at home.
3   It's quite small but it's very comfortable and extremely convenient.
4   I really love speaking English though sometimes it's rather tiring and difficult.
5   I like people who don't take life too seriously.
6   I feel very strongly that people should be able to access a university education without paying.
7   As far as I know, most men usually get married when they're in their late twenties.
8   They learn English because it's the international language and they can get a better job.
9   I try to read the newspaper every day but sometimes I just don't have enough time.
10 I would like to be working in the mining sector as it's well-paid with very generous holidays.
11 It's hard to know which friend I would choose as my best friend, but I suppose it would be Lee. He comes from the same town as me. I've known him for about 20 years, since we studied together in primary school. In fact, we sat side by side throughout primary school and we used to help each other with our schoolwork. Although he went to a different high school and university, we still stayed in touch and remained good friends. When we were teenagers, we were in the same local football club. We're even closer nowadays because our wives have become really good friends. The four of us often go out together. Lee is a wonderful person. He's kind, considerate and generous, and he's got a great sense of humour. I really like people who make me laugh. That's probably the main reason he's my best friend.
12 One film I really enjoyed watching was *Gandhi*. I guess it came out about 30 years ago and I remember that I went to see it about five times. It's about Mahatma Gandhi who of course was one of the leaders of India back in the 1930s, I think it was. It shows the period in India before it became independent. It's quite a long film with a lot of detail and different characters but I never got bored watching it. I suppose I liked it because it was so interesting and because the actor who played Gandhi was so good. Also, it really showed me that you can achieve things peacefully. I always enjoy films that make me think.

Exercise 33

Students' own assessment of their performance.

Exercise 34

Students' own personalised sound list and practice.

Exercise 35

Comments

This candidate has trouble with producing word endings – many words are chopped off – as well as problems with some sounds. Specifically, problems occur in 'ab*out*' (mispronunciation of diphthong /aʊ/), '*car*' (missing word ending), 'a*sked*' (mispronunciation of consonant cluster), 'de*sign*' (missing word ending), 'alway*s*', (missing -*s* ending) 'copyri*ght*' (mispronunciation of consonant cluster).

Exercise 36

2	sing	3	mole	4	lives
5	past	6	type	7	seventh
8	brings	9	expect	10	when
11	fault				

Exercise 37

Two-syllable words: in/spire, mar/riage, eigh/teen

Three-syllable words: so/cia/lise, ar/range/ment, in/ter/fere, pro/ba/ble

Four-syllable words: com/bin/a/tion, ac/a/de/mic, un/em/ploy/ment

Five-syllable words: veg/e/tar/i/an, ca/pi/tal/is/m, pro/ba/bil/i/ty

Exercise 38

2 carrier
3 customer
4 automation
5 passengers
6 announcement
7 unions
8 proposed
9 frequent
10 embedded
11 luggage
12 kiosk
13 conveyor
14 departure

Exercise 39

2 <u>me</u>: The speaker wants to focus on himself as the person needing help.
3 <u>IELTS</u>: The speaker wants to focus on the IELTS exam as the particular exam he needs help with.
4 <u>preparation</u>: The speaker wants to focus on preparation for the IELTS exam as the particular type of help needed.
5 <u>exam</u>: The speaker wants to focus on a particular aspect of IELTS (the exam) for which help is needed.

Exercise 40

I am <u>delighted</u> to introduce <u>ComfortAir's</u> <u>vision</u> for the <u>check-in</u> <u>of</u> <u>the</u> <u>future</u>.

At the moment, check-in is a <u>painful</u> <u>experience</u> for too many of our valued <u>frequent</u> <u>flyer</u> <u>members</u>. It <u>takes</u> <u>too</u> <u>long</u>. It <u>causes</u> <u>stress</u>. Our own research points to what our <u>customers</u> <u>want</u>, and that is <u>speed</u> and <u>ease</u> at check-in.

To ensure this happens, we have commenced a <u>bold</u> <u>new</u> <u>initiative</u>.

Our frequent flyers will soon be able to use their <u>existing</u> <u>card</u>, <u>embedded</u> with a <u>smart</u> <u>microchip</u>. They'll be able to <u>whiz</u> <u>through</u> check-in, <u>simply</u> <u>swiping</u> their <u>card</u> through a <u>reader</u>. <u>Next</u> <u>stop</u> will be a <u>simple</u> <u>bag</u> <u>drop</u> before a <u>final</u> <u>smooth</u> <u>walk</u> through <u>security</u> to their <u>flight</u> <u>gate</u>. Instead of <u>queues</u> and <u>stickers</u> at the desk, the <u>check-in</u> <u>of</u> <u>the</u> <u>future</u> is all about <u>convenience</u> and <u>speed</u>.

With your <u>personal</u> <u>boarding</u> <u>pass</u> and <u>permanent</u> <u>bag</u> <u>tag</u>, <u>checking</u> your <u>baggage</u> will no longer be a <u>tedious</u> <u>chore</u>. Our <u>plan</u> is to <u>halve</u> <u>check-in</u> <u>time</u> – or better.

It's going to be a <u>revolution</u> at airport <u>check-ins</u>, with our <u>staff</u> <u>freed</u> to <u>focus</u> on <u>customer</u> <u>care</u>. And it's a <u>revolution</u> coming <u>your</u> way by <u>year's</u> <u>end</u>.

Comment
The speaker makes prominent those words that stress the problems of the current system of check-in and contrasts this with the benefits of the new check-in system. All the stressed words are content words (that is, mostly nouns, verbs and adjectives).

Exercise 41 (sample answers)

2 (I'm) I'm so happy it's Friday today.
3 (I'll) It's raining, so I'll bring the car to the front door.
4 (You'd) You'd better close the curtains to keep the house warm.
5 (He's) This is Jim. He's got a few orders for you.
6 (She'd) She'd better be home when I get there.
7 (It'll) It'll be cool and cloudy for the remainder of the week.
8 (They're) Can you move over? They're coming to sit here.
9 (They'd) They'd probably want to stay about a week if they came.
10 (Can't) Sorry – I can't help you with that.
11 (Won't) No, I won't do that.
12 (Oughtn't) I really oughtn't be here with you.
13 (Shan't) That's right, she shan't be arriving until midnight.

Answer key Unit 2: Speaking

Exercise 42

Candidate 1 has better English rhythm.

Candidate 1
This candidate has a reasonable English rhythm which he has probably transferred from his first language (Spanish). He stresses words differently depending on their importance to the meaning he wants to convey and uses pausing appropriately.

Candidate 2
This candidate has difficulty in developing an effective rhythm. He speaks slowly, with little evidence of sentence stress and linking. He does use some contractions (*I'm, I've, it's*) but there are many long pauses in his speech, which could make the listener feel uncomfortable.

Exercise 43 (suggested answers)

Examiner: OK, and do you generally like sweet or savoury food?
Candidate: <u>Sweet</u> <u>food</u>.
Examiner: Why?
Candidate: Oh, I like <u>cakes</u>, / I like, ah, <u>everything</u> <u>sweet</u>, / like <u>fruits</u> and yes.
Examiner: When do you generally eat more – during the day or at night?
Candidate: At <u>night</u>.
Examiner: And why?
Candidate: Ah, like in <u>my</u> <u>culture</u>, / ah, we <u>eat</u>, ah, <u>rice</u> <u>every</u> <u>day</u>, / so we <u>eat</u> <u>rice</u> <u>every</u> <u>night</u>, / like a <u>big</u> <u>amount</u> of <u>rice</u> during at <u>night</u>.
Examiner: Does the weather generally change how much food you eat?
Candidate: Yes, <u>of</u> <u>course</u>, / ah, in <u>winter</u> I, I <u>eat</u> <u>more</u> than in <u>summer</u>, yeah.

Exercise 44
2 C   3 B   4 E   5 A

Exercise 45

1 Examiner: Mm hm, what are the most challenging or difficult things about your course?

Candidate: Well ... I think the most difficult part, um, is the reading part, because, um, quite a lot of a new concepts involved in, and, ah, that the things I didn't know before. So I think that's the most difficult part for me.

Intonation used
The candidate shows uncertainty at the beginning of the sentence by an extended fall–rise on the word 'well'. Other intonation in the sentence follows a standard falling tone for the delivery of statements.

Other features
The candidate uses sentence stress on 'most', 'reading' and 'new'. The last sentence is shared (repeated) information, so it is said quickly without stressing.

2 Examiner: And what will you do when your course finishes?

Candidate: Um, teaching, I guess. I would go back and I'm still, I'm doing teaching and I will ... I would prefer actually, prefer to use the, the knowledge I learnt here, so back to teaching again.

Intonation used
The candidate shows she is unsure of her future expectations by use of a fall–rise tone at the beginning. She shows her strong attitude towards the subject by the use of a rise–fall tone in the middle of her answer, and a falling tone with her repeated statement at the end.

Other features

The candidate highlights 'still', 'teaching', 'prefer' and 'knowledge' and uses pausing effectively to display some conflict between her goals.

Exercise 46

Comments

This candidate occasionally answers questions with non-standard intonation. In her first response ('Yes, I think so.'), the candidate uses a falling tone that indicates a statement; however, she sounds unsure of her answer. Probably a fall–rise tone would be better to show uncertainty.

In her second response, the candidate should use sentences with falling intonation to indicate statements. However, her intonation rises on some word groups (for example, on 'newspapers and magazines'), which may confuse her listeners.

The candidate continues to use fall–rise intonation inappropriately on single words (for example, on the first 'quick' and 'Internet') in her final response. Again, this may confuse her listeners as to her attitude and meaning.

Exercise 47

Students' own assessment of their performance.

Practice IELTS Speaking Tests (Exercise 48)

Practice Test 1 (Jade)

Suggested assessment

Speaking fluently	3
Speaking coherently	2
Speaking with effective vocabulary	3
Speaking with effective grammar	2
Speaking clearly	3

Comments

She speaks quite fluently.
Jade speaks at a reasonable pace and usually delivers her ideas quite smoothly. She sounds confident and natural for most of the test. There are more pauses in Part 3 but fillers such as 'um' and 'mmm' fill these gaps and quickly cover any silences. She uses one phrase to give herself thinking time in Part 3 ('Um, its hard question').

She does not always speak coherently.
Jade has occasional problems with coherence in her speech. This is particularly noticeable in Part 2 when it is unclear exactly what topic she is talking about ('And it was some Internet news website and it was about how refugee affect Australia and, um, what I, I'm sorry, economies … And then I was pretty much surprised cause, um, the fact they describe was a kind of twisted fact so I was pretty disappointed by the fact they twisted.') The connection between her topic (refugees) and the fact(s) reported about them on the website is confused. Her Part 2 is little more than a minute, so she could have spent more time on making her presentation more coherent to the listener.

In Parts 1 and 3, it is also sometimes unclear exactly who or what she is referring to. For example, in Part 3 when she is asked if people should believe and trust what they read, her answer is confusing: 'Um, they should accept that is some their information, however believe and trust that information, no I don't think that's a good idea.' Jade could repeat or rephrase the examiner's questions more frequently to ensure she has the correct subject before she extends her ideas.

Her vocabulary is reasonably effective.
Jade uses quite accurate and appropriate vocabulary throughout the interview. In Part 1, she speaks with quite precise vocabulary about her job, bushwalking and sports. Sentences such as 'It was so interesting when I came to Australia I saw cricket and footy's a really big deal in Australia but I never heard about it in my country' display a good grasp of vocabulary, with the idiomatic phrase 'really big deal' used well and naturally. 'Hot potato' is another colourful idiom used when talking about media issues in Part 3. Jade occasionally uses the incorrect form of a word, such as 'objective thing' instead of *objectivity* and 'old generation' instead of *older generation* in Part 3. There are also occasional inaccuracies with collocation. For instance, in Part 3 she uses 'trust on' instead of *trust in*.

Her grammatical accuracy and range is limited.
Jade's grammar is not always accurate. She has some problems with use of articles. For example, she adds an unnecessary article in the sentence 'And young people focus on searching *the* information by themselves' and occasionally her subject–verb agreement is incorrect (for example, 'parents wants'). Her tense usage is also sometimes problematic. For example: 'I (have) always (been) interested in helping other people; I (would) love to work.'

However, Jade's greatest grammatical challenge is her *lack of range* in the area of sentence construction. She relies on simple connectors – particularly 'and', 'cause' and 'so' – to join her ideas. This results in blocks of compound sentences, instead of a mix of compound and complex sentences. This structural issue is most noticeable in Part 2: '*And* it was some Internet news website *and* it was about how refugee affect Australia and, um, what I, I'm sorry, economies … *And* then I was pretty much surprised *cause*, um, the fact they describe was a kind of twisted fact *so* I was pretty disappointed by the fact they twisted. *Cause* I always believe the newspaper or news on the media they should be very, um, objective not focus on twist the fact *so*, yeah, that's about it.' This makes her presentation sound simplistic and repetitious.

She speaks quite clearly.
Jade speaks loudly enough but has a number of other pronunciation issues.

Her production of individual sounds is reasonably accurate. She occasionally has trouble with long vowel sounds (for example, she substitutes the short /ɪ/ for the longer /i/ sound in *peaceful*) and sometimes exaggerates final consonant sounds (for example: 'bus*h*', 'ru*n*').

Jade's identification of word stress is generally correct. She has a tendency to exaggerate word stress at times, but she often does this to emphasise which points she thinks are important, which is appropriate. She could work more on her sentence stress – currently, most words receive equal stress and this sometimes makes her speech sound very emphatic. For example, she stresses the auxiliary verbs *do* and *will* unnecessarily throughout the interview.

Jade's rhythm becomes less assured as the interview progresses. Examples of linking and contractions are rare, and pauses become more frequent in Part 3. However, overall, her speed of delivery is generally acceptable. Jade uses rising intonation in some sections of the interview, which has the effect of making statements sound more like questions. For example, in Part 1 when she talks about cricket she uses this intonation pattern at the ends of sentences: 'I never heard about it *in my country*.' 'It's based on their culture … and I do understand, um, cricket comes from UK so, yeah, depends *on culture*.'

Overall, she is a reasonable speaker.
Jade is a fluent and mostly effective communicator. She has a good vocabulary and is mostly able to communicate successfully on a range of topics. However, she would benefit from making her speech more coherent and working to extend her accuracy and grammatical range. She particularly needs to work on joining her ideas by using more complex structures. She could do this by using more precise subject referencing and introducing more sophisticated discourse markers into her speech. Her speech is mostly clear, although she could work on improving her sentence stress and rhythm.

Practice Test 2 (Jimmy)
Suggested assessment

Speaking fluently	3
Speaking coherently	2
Speaking with effective vocabulary	3
Speaking with effective grammar	2
Speaking clearly	2

Comments

He speaks reasonably fluently.
Jimmy is a fluent speaker who manages to keep the flow of speech going throughout the interview. However, in an effort to avoid silence, he delivers his ideas on each topic rapidly with very few pauses. He uses the informal word *yeah* to give himself some thinking time, particularly

in Part 3. However, a simple *yes* may be a better alternative for the formal conditions of the IELTS interview.

His speech is not always coherent.

Jimmy has some problems with the omission or overuse of cohesive devices. He unnecessarily repeats certain key nouns in some sections of his talk. For example, from Part 1: 'It's very close to city and I'm working in city. My my college is in the city. That's why I choose to live in North Melbourne. Very close to city that's it.' Jimmy could substitute *it* or *there* for the often repeated 'city'. Overuse is also a problem in Part 3, with 'you'/'your' and the absence of the reflexive pronoun *yourself* (for example, 'But when you grow like you be 22 or 24 you have to be more responsible. You have to choose a good career for you. You have to think about your life. You have to find a partner for you, good partner for you because if you do mistake in your, in your you know young age you can't get a good life').

Jimmy's rapid delivery also causes problems for coherence. There are some points in Parts 2 and 3 of the interview where he almost becomes incoherent due to a combination of quick speech and confusion about the subject of his talk. However, he does occasionally deliver a very coherent answer. For example, when he is asked 'What are some of the major differences between those two stages of your life?' he answers very coherently with 'The major difference is responsibilities'.

His vocabulary is reasonably effective.

Jimmy has a good range of vocabulary but this is not matched by his degree of accuracy. He has no trouble handling the concepts he is presented with and comes up with some advanced vocabulary, especially in Part 3 (for example, 'good life partner' and 'responsibilities'). He also demonstrates his familiarity with idioms (for example, 'veggie' and 'plenty of knowledge'). Unfortunately, he is rather inaccurate with some collocated words (for example, he uses 'do' instead of *make* a mistake and 'a four-year child' instead of *a four-year-old child*.

He displays limited grammatical accuracy and range.

Jimmy's grammar is sometimes inaccurate and he displays a limited range. In Part 2, he occasionally slips into present tense when he is talking about a birthday in the past. He also omits the auxiliary verb *do* and makes an error with *be* in the following section of Part 3: 'Yeah, because a teenager is a young stage of your life you no need to worry about what you have to do ... But when you grow like you be 22 or 24.' However, it is possible these problems could be caused more by carelessness due to his rapid delivery rather than deeply embedded grammar issues.

He does use a mixture of sentence types but sentence connectors are confined to a limited range such as *so*, *but* and *because*. Often his ideas are connected by repeating a word or phrase from the previous sentence or adding a linking phrase such as 'I mean to say' or 'in my opinion' that don't blend well into the sentence.

He doesn't speak very clearly.

Jimmy's main problem is his rapid delivery, which affects many other aspects of his pronunciation. In particular, he speaks far too quickly in Part 2.

His voice is generally loud enough and most of his sounds are well-managed. However, he does have a problem with the sound /θ/ (the 'th' sound) and leaves it out in words such as 'birthday' and 'things'. His word stress is good, with a few exceptions: 'event' should be pronounced e<u>vent</u> and 'yourself' needs to be your<u>self</u>. Sentence stress is generally adequate, except it sounds too rushed in some sections – he needs to slow down and emphasise important words.

Jimmy's rhythm is also affected by his rapid speech. He does use linking (for example, 'gonna' for *going to*) and some contractions, but his overall rhythm sounds rushed and may have the affect of stressing his listener.

Overall, he is a reasonable speaker.

Jimmy speaks with good fluency and a wide vocabulary. However, possibly because of nervous excitement he spoke very rapidly and not very accurately in this practice test. He should slow down and deliver his ideas in a more thoughtful way. To aid coherence, he also needs to add discourse markers and other cohesive devices to what he says. Jimmy should work on expanding his range of tenses and concentrating on his grammar at sentence level. Even though he produced a lot of language, Jimmy can be quite difficult to understand. In particular, he needs to improve his overall rhythm when he speaks English.

Practice Test 3 (Madeleine)
Suggested assessment

Speaking fluently	4
Speaking coherently	4
Speaking with effective vocabulary	3
Speaking with effective grammar	3
Speaking clearly	4

Comments
She speaks fluently.
She speaks at a reasonable pace and in a smooth manner. For example, when she says 'If you don't mind, you can call me Madeleine, that's my English name', her words flow together smoothly and rapidly. Her Part 2 presentation is also fluent: the pace is appropriate, and there are no significant hesitations or breakdowns. She sometimes pauses when she speaks, but she generally manages to keep these pauses very brief and fills the silence with *um* and *ah*. For example: 'Um, because, ah, when I was teaching and I thought I should learn something more about the linguistics, and that's why I, I chose this, um, area to study.'

Madeleine uses fillers quite well throughout. In one instance, she gains thinking time by using *well* and then echoing (or slightly rephrasing) the question. (Examiner: 'What are the most challenging or difficult things about your course?' Madeleine: 'Well, I think the most difficult part is ...') In another example, she gains time by making a comment about the question. (Examiner: 'To what extent was this development a result of planning?' Madeleine: 'Ah, OK. This one is a little bit difficult. I will try, if I can put it this way.') Throughout the test she gives the impression that she is thinking about what to say next, not that she is stuck and doesn't know what to say next.

She speaks very coherently.
Her answers in parts 1 and 3 are always relevant to the examiner's questions. Her answers usually show that she has understood the questions by echoing or rephrasing them. (Examiner: 'And do you think large cities will become more or less planned in the future?' Madeleine: 'I think they will become more planned and actually ...')

There are instances when her answers relate very coherently because she consistently uses pronouns to refer back to nouns in the questions. (Examiner: 'What do you think is the most effective way to learn a language?' Madeleine: 'To practise, to use it, to – yep, just to use it, um, with the people from that language, from that culture.')

Madeleine generally presents her points in a very clear and logical manner. In the Part 2 presentation, for example, she first clearly presents her topic (Armidale), then describes its location, and then starts to talk about why she enjoyed living there (thus answering the question), giving examples to illustrate her points. This sequencing of information is easy for the listener to follow.

She uses vocabulary effectively.
Her vocabulary throughout is accurate and appropriate. There appear to be no instances where she has used incorrect words to express her meaning.

She has a reasonable range of vocabulary. For example, in her answer about Taipei she uses words such as *government*, *build*, *international*, *public transportation*, *knocking down*, *buildings*, *parks* and *shopping centres*. She demonstrates a wide knowledge of qualifiers (indicating the extent of something): for example, '*very* difficult', '*quite* a long time', '*some* cities', '*a little bit* difficult', '*quite a lot* of mountains', '*quite* natural', 'developed *too much*', '*more and more* people', '*not that* much'. However, at other times, her range of vocabulary is a little limited: for example, in Part 3 where she tends to limit herself to 'I think' when expressing her opinions.

The words Madeleine uses are appropriate for an examination or interview. For example, at the end of the test, she uses the appropriate 'All right, thank you'. When confronted with an unfamiliar term, she successfully clarifies the meaning by paraphrasing: 'Um, gated community. Ah, just let me check if I got the idea right. Does that mean …'

She uses grammar effectively.
Her grammar is largely accurate. For example, she uses the plural form consistently (in her presentation, she speaks of 'eight hours', 'those trees'). However, in Part 3 there are a few errors (for example, 'each individual areas' and 'a different functions'). Her use of articles is generally quite accurate; for example, in her question confirming the meaning of 'gated community' all four articles are used correctly. Similarly, she uses comparative and superlative forms of adjectives accurately (for example, 'it's easier than French' and 'the most difficult part'), as well as relative clauses (for example, 'I would … prefer to use the knowledge I learnt here'). She also forms tenses accurately (for example, 'I have been to, um, some cities and I have tried to learn French'). She controls adverbs correctly (for example, 'they probably just put a commercial'), and adverbial clauses (for example, 'I don't think that's a very good place for doing business').

There are grammatical errors, such as 'the government has, ah, planning to build the city of Taipei as one of the international city' and 'the most people live there are students from other countries' but these do not cause any significant difficulty for the listener in following her meaning. She uses a range of sentence structures, mixing simple sentences (for example, 'That won't be a good idea') with compound and complex sentences (for example, 'It is actually about eight hours away from Sydney and, um, it's a very small town'; 'One is a city called Taitung which is located in the eastern part of Taiwan').

She speaks clearly.
She speaks loudly enough. Her production of individual sounds is generally quite accurate and presents no significant difficulties for the listener. There are occasional problems: for example, she sometimes has difficulty in distinguishing /l/, and /r/, so that the /r/ sounds in *probably* and *security* are pronounced as /l/. There are a few other relatively minor problems: for example, the first vowel in *natural* ('it's still quite natural') is not accurate.

Her use of word stress is consistently accurate. For example, 'com<u>mu</u>nity', 'an<u>noun</u>cement', 'be<u>fore</u>', 'moti<u>va</u>tion', 'de<u>vel</u>oped', and '<u>gov</u>ernment' are all correct. Her use of sentence stress is generally successful. For example, in 'I don't think that's a very good place for doing business and the most people live there are students from other countries and also from other cities from Australia', she stresses *business* and, *students*, which is appropriate, whereas stress on *cities* is not. Her use of focus stress can be very effective: for example, in her answer to the examiner's question 'And do you think large cities will become more or less planned in the future?' she places a focus stress on *more* and thus responds in a very clear manner to the question.

Madeleine links words effectively when she speaks. There are many examples of appropriate linking, such as in Part 2 when she says that the town is 'not as hot as Sydney'. Because she uses linking and word and sentence stress appropriately, she achieves an overall rhythm that is reasonably similar to the rhythm of native speakers of English.

She uses intonation appropriately to support her communication. For example, when she says 'Rich people?' she uses intonation to present this as a suggestion to be confirmed, and when she says 'I think there are two spots', she uses a low-rise tone to indicate incomplete information.

Overall, she speaks very effectively.
It is clear that she knows how to participate in a formal interview and displays a calm and focused demeanour overall. She is particularly adept at using clarification strategies, fillers

and paraphrasing, which help her maintain her fluency throughout the interview. Her communication is also very coherent and she presents her points in a clear and logical manner. Her grammar and vocabulary show a reasonable degree of accuracy and range. Throughout, she speaks at a good pace and at an appropriate volume. Her pronunciation is clear. To further enhance her score she would be advised to work on reducing the number of grammatical errors she makes and to keep broadening her range of vocabulary.